Interprofessional Working in Practice

Learning and working together for children and families

Edited by Lyn Trodd and Leo Chivers

Open University Press

Open University Press
McGraw-Hill Education
McGraw-Hill House
Shoppenhangers Road
Maidenhead
Berkshire
England
SL6 2QL

email: enquiries@openup.co.uk
world wide web: www.openup.co.uk

and Two Penn Plaza, New York, NY 10121-2289, USA

First published 2011

A catalogue record of this book is available from the British Library

ISBN-13: 978-0-33-524447-8 (pb)
ISBN-10: 0-33-524447-5 (pb)
eISBN: 978-0-33-524448-5

Library of Congress Cataloging-in-Publication Data
CIP data applied for

Typesetting and e-book compilations by
RefineCatch Limited, Bungay, Suffolk
Printed and bound by CPI Group (UK) Ltd, Croydon, CR0 4YY

Fictitious names of companies, products, people, characters and/or data that may be used herein (in case studies or in examples) are not intended to represent any real individual, company, product or event.

The *McGraw·Hill* Companies

Contents

List of figures and tables

Notes on contributors

Lyn Trodd has a background in Early Years teaching, childcare, adult education and inspection. She is currently Head of Partnerships and Ventures in the School of Education at the University of Hertfordshire. Lyn was a member of the DfES Reference Group that conceptualised Early Years Professional Status and Chair of a Task and Finish Group that designed a new national sector-endorsement process for Foundation Degrees. She is currently Chair of the national network of providers of the Sector-Endorsed Foundation Degree in Early Years - SEFDEY. Her research and publishing interests are in the fields of professional identity, learning and leadership and also efficacy development in both children and practitioners.

Leo Chivers is a senior lecturer in Early Years and Professional Learning in the School of Education at the University of Hertfordshire where he leads on postgraduate leadership programmes for children's services. He is also a facilitator on the East of England NPQICL. Leo was a member of the pilot group at Pen Green when the NPQICL programme was rolled out. In the past he has worked in the health service and with adults with learning difficulties. More recently Leo was the manager of the St Albans Children's Centre in Hertfordshire and then the programme manager of the NPQICL at the Eastern Leadership Centre in Cambridge. His doctoral research is into interprofessionalism.

Karen John is a developmental psychologist, academic, author, psychotherapist, counsellor and supervisor of therapeutic and work-based practice. Karen offers training, research and consultancy services to helping organisations, individuals and families to overcome internal and external obstacles that hamper their healthy functioning and development. In addition she helped develop and roll-out the NPQICL at Pen Green and currently tutors on the Pen Green-U Leicester integrated provision and leadership MA and PhD programmmes and works with Children's Centres and Child and Adolescent Mental Health Services.

Sue Webster is a lecturer at University of Warwick and an independent consultant. She worked in the voluntary sector before achieving a leading role in an Early Excellence Centre in Chipping Norton with responsible for outreach and training.

Later leading the development of a Sure Start Local Programme in Coventry, Sue has undertaken a variety of consultancy and evaluation roles with a focus on leadership development and integrated working. Sue has extensive experience developing and writing leadership development materials including contributing to the National Professional Qualification in Integrated Centre Leadership (NPQICL). She has also developed and delivered training for NPQICL facilitators and mentors, facilitates an NPQICL learning community and has coordinated the national Children's Centre Leaders' Network (CCLN). Published work includes research in the EECERA journal and contributions to books with a leadership focus. She teaches on the Early Childhood degree at the University of Warwick and in Singapore. Sue has an MA in Early Childhood Education and is currently undertaking doctoral study to investigate the experience of early childhood in a military family.

Annie Clouston is an independent consultant and a tutor for the Eastern Leadership Centre, Cambridge, which delivers the National Professional Qualification in Integrated Centre Leadership (NPQICL) in partnership with the University of Hertfordshire to children's centre leaders. Having qualified as a social worker she has worked in a number of roles, including as a Probation Officer, a Court Welfare Officer, a family centre manager, and an independent Child Protection Conference Chair and consultant. In 2001, she decided to change focus to prevention and early intervention and became a Sure Start Local Programme manager, before becoming a consultant to the emerging NPQICL programme in 2005. This involved many different roles including researching the impact of the programme, supporting the delivery teams around the country and writing leadership development materials. In 2008, along with Sue Webster, she coordinated the national Children's Centre Leadership Network (CCLN). Annie has a Postgraduate Diploma in Child Protection Studies and an MA in Women's Studies. She remains involved in children's services, and is the chair of the Advisory Board of her local children's centre. She is committed to supporting early intervention that can redress the inequalities of early childhood experience.

Ian Duckmanton is a Children's Centre Leader and independent consultant. He currently leads Action For Children's Poppyland SureStart Children's Centres in Cromer, Mundesley, North Walsham and Stalham in North Norfolk. He completed the NPQICL in 2006 and researched inter-professional communities of practice for his Masters in Education in 2010. He works as a mentor and facilitator for the East of England NPQICL delivery team.

Anne Rawlings is an Early Years Fellow at Kingston University. Anne began her career as a nurse and then trained to be a teacher as a mature student. Anne has published widely in Early Years field and has recently opened a much praised 'Institute for Child Centred Interprofessional Practice' (ICCIP) at Kingston University. Anne is Vice Chair of the national SEFDEY network. Anne's recent publications include a widely used text on work-based learning.

Daryl Maisey is Director of Studies in Early Years at Kingston University and has a special interest in child safeguarding in an interprofessional world. Daryl originally qualified as a teacher in 1987. Since then she has been fortunate to have gained experience of working across different key stages. Her passion for Early Years stemmed from an initial interest of working with children with special educational needs. She is currently a Principal Lecturer at Kingston University working across different programmes from Early Years Education to Primary Teaching and is actively involved in working towards future programmes to promote multi-professional working.

Paty (Panagiota) Paliokosta is a Senior Lecturer in Inclusive Education at Kingston University. She has taught in Primary Education and was an Inclusion Manager for a number of years, before becoming a Local Authority Advisor for Inclusion (SEN/LDD) for Camden Children, Schools and Families. In the context of these positions, she was involved in several projects in collaboration with the School Improvement team, the Education Psychology team and Extended Services (i.e. Inclusion SEF, Transition Guide, Drama for feelings). She also had a leading role in the organisation of the Local Authority SENCO Forum and related conferences (i.e. Parental Involvement and Achievement for All). Currently, she is the programme leader for the BA (Hons) in 'Special Needs and Inclusive Education' and offers teaching contributions across a wide range of post-graduate programmes, including the MA in Professional Studies in Education and the Doctor of Education (EdD) programme with a focus on Professionalism in Education. She has taught and tutored EYPS candidates, has been an internal EYPS moderator and currently leads research seminars for the PGCert in Eary Years. After been awarded her PhD by Canterbury Christ Church University in 2008, her research interests have mainly focused on barriers to inclusive education, social construction and social justice, teachers' and practitioners' professionalism and different types of transitions. In September 2010, Paty set up a local Special Interest Group on 'Inclusion and Social Justice' at Kingston's School of Education. She has been carrying out research on 'reasonable adjustments and multi-professionalism' under the umbrella of the Institute for Child Centred Inter-professional Practice (ICCIP) and presently participates in a project on immigrant social workers' professional identities, led by the Faculty of Health and Social Care. Paty is actively involved in the dissemination of her work in peer-reviewed journals and book chapters.

Sharif Al-Rousi works to promote collaborative arrangements within local strategic partnerships. He has undertaken a number of project roles within local government across a range of multi-agency initiatives, and worked with children's trusts. Sharif has conducted research into how organisations collaborate to promote service redesign, and problem solving in multi-agency settings. A former school teacher, Sharif spent several years working within local Sure Start programmes, and managed a number of children's centres and extended school services. He is a graduate of the NPQICL programme, and mentors and assesses participants within the East of England.

Ute Ward has been involved in the Early Years sector for the past 19 years as a parent, volunteer, play group assistant and play group leader. She has worked with adults as a development officer and tutor for the Pre-School Learning Alliance. In November 2007 Ute became manager of a phase 2 Children's Centre and then developed a phase 3 Children's Centre. She is a graduate of the NPQICL. Until recently Ute mentored NPQICL participants in the East of England. Her current post is as a senior lecturer in Early Years in the School of Education at the University of Hertfordshire. Ute has written a book called Working with Parents in Early Years Settings.

Sajni Sharma is the Head of Newstead Children's Centre in Barnet. Sajni has been an Early Years Manager for the last 20 years. She is a graduate of the NPQICL and now mentors NPQICL participants in the East of England.

Maureen Longley is the NPQICL Programme Manager for the East of England. Maureen is a graduate of the NPQICL herself and was also a Children Centre Manager in Essex before joining the Eastern Leadership Centre in Cambridge to run the NPQICL.

Sally Graham is Director of the Centre for Coaching and Mentoring at the University of Hertfordshire. She works with internal and external colleagues to develop approaches to enquiry into their own practice. Sally has a wide range of experience in Early Years settings, schools and other organisations. She presently leads postgraduate courses in Early Years leadership and practice. Her main focus is facilitating collaborative practitioner enquiry.

Joy Jarvis is currently Faculty Associate Dean (Learning and Teaching) at the University of Hertfordshire. She works with colleagues from a range of disciplines to develop high quality practice. As a teacher she has worked in education and community settings with children, families and professionals in relation to deafness and complex language needs. She is interested in using narrative and arts-informed enquiry processes to facilitate interprofessional working.

LYN TRODD AND LEO CHIVERS
Introduction

On writing a book on 'interprofessionalism' it may be best to begin with a definition of the term as we view it. This term is to denote the myriad ways in which (children's services) professionals collaborate (or attempt to collaborate) at many levels from the strategic to local practice – between both statutory and independent disciplines. The literature in the field uses many different terms (sometimes interchangeably) to denote this process in practice and strategy. These include terms such as *multi/ interprofessional/agency/disciplinary collaboration/partnership for joined-up/integrated working*. The term 'interprofessionalism' is intended to avoid the more directive terms above while indicating a 'mindset' that looks for ways to work together.

The contributors to this book came together with the aim of writing a book that helps to turn the rhetoric of interprofessionalism into reality for readers. Our motivation is that only by using interprofessional understanding and awareness when engaging with practice issues and teaching will we develop the safety and quality essential for working together for children and families. Fundamentally, we recognize that interprofessional working, learning and leading are complex, raising many difficulties and challenges for all involved. Therefore we decided our intent was not to produce simplified, over-arching solutions or models but to offer some personalized insights into what it is like to think, work and learn interprofessionally.

These insights are framed by a shared understanding that perhaps interprofessionalism is a way of thinking that cannot be simply taught didactically or transmitted to practitioners in the field. Rather it is developed experientially through interactions with children, families and colleagues. This interaction provides a set of internalized values or principles that are gathered within the developing 'interprofessional' as self-awareness develops through experiences.

With this in mind we have written the chapters that follow intending that the reader can consider his or her personal response to their themes by approaching them from an intrapersonal →interpersonal→ interprofessional perspective. Our approach to interprofessionalism is that professionals acquire a lens or world view which filters their attention to selected features of the interprofessional world and makes them think about it in particular ways. Its influence leads us to notice and narrate particular problems and to use particular methods for solving them so that our observable professional behaviour is guided and shaped by our individual internal view of the world (Törnebohm 1986).

Our interprofessional lens influences how we use our knowledge of theory and practice and calibrates our evaluations of what is good and bad practice. This 'cognitive apprenticeship' approach (Collins et al. 1987) involves changes to our subjective self-conceptualization associated with the professional role or professional identity. Subjective self-conceptualization associated with the role and professional reflexivity requires individuals to be aware of their situated, relative and relational positions in professional communities.

As editors we believe that interprofessionalism is an *ontological* position, a way of being in the world. It exists as an emerging phenomenon in the world of being a professional in children's services and our contention is that we need to pay close attention to its developing features. By this it is meant that generally we have spent much time and effort complying with directives to work collaboratively and to fit joined-up practice into frameworks or schema that were designed to conceptualize it. What now needs to be done is to undertake an exploration of our actual experiences in working with each other so that we can interrogate authentic accounts that chart the growth of interprofessional identity and confidence.

In many ways the chapters that follow are dialogues with notions and theories of interprofessional working and identity. The formation of personal identity is seen as a dialogic process between a person's self-identification and their interactions with others. The way individuals are perceived by others plays a part in informing their conceptions of their own ways of being (Gee 2004). Sfard and Prusak differentiate between actual (the current) and designated (the aspirational or hoped for) identities. They explain how interacting develops identities so that 'the people to whom our stories are told, as well as those who tell stories about us, may be tacit co-authors of our own designated identities' (2005: 18). This is because people tend to convert the stories of other speakers about themselves and what they do into the first person, particularly if the other speakers are what Sfard and Prusak call: '*Significant narrators,* the owners of the most influential voices . . . carriers of those cultural messages that will have the greatest impact on one's actions' (2005: 18).

Defining identities in this way, as co-constructed narratives, emphasizes the agency and the dynamic quality of identity. A person's control of his or her own story, the degree to which he or she takes responsibility for it and owns it, affect his or her sense of agency and autonomy (Holland et al. 1998). Similarly, a potential motive for storying one's interprofessional identity is to gain professional autonomy, defined in Chapter 3 as choosing the values and principles by which decisions and actions as a professional are taken. An interprofessional identity narrative can also entail telling oneself a story about oneself or in other words, reflective thinking (Sfard and Prusak 2005). While Drake et al. (2001: 2) argue that identities can be: 'understood *as* and *through* stories' (emphasis added), Sfard and Prusak go further. In their view, stories about persons *are* identities, not separate entities described *by* stories.

The themes of interprofessional identity in this book are organized in a structure of context, learning, working and future challenges. Multiple professional heritages are represented in the writing team: hospital management, children centre leadership, community work, nursing, social work, teaching, childcare, lecturing and speech therapy to name but a few. While we are united by our aims for this book, each author has used a different professional voice to improvise their chapter or contribution to a chapter and we have developed our arguments with theories, research and case study materials that are grounded and exemplified in practice dilemmas we have experienced. Each chapter is highly individual and readers will find that the voice and approach in each can differ or contrast as the reader progresses through the book. Although possibly disorientating, this effect is intentional. In the spirit of interprofessional working, we have sought to embrace the diversity within the texts, realizing the strengths that are conveyed through celebrating the different approaches of the authors. Therefore some may concentrate more closely on the theoretical (or even philosophical) background to their discussion, while others are more interested in exploring tangible examples of practice situations for the reader.

The book begins with three chapters that explore discourses in the current context of interprofessionalism. First Leo Chivers explores the ways the policy context served to set frameworks as a way of conceptualizing what to do. Then Sharif Al-Rousi explains a systemic approach used by local authority strategists. Lyn Trodd traces and problematizes some of the historical influences on concepts of 'profession' and 'professional', arguing that such concepts are backward-facing and not fit for purpose for new ways of working interprofessionally. Instead she proposes a new construct, 'interprofessional', as a replacement.

In the next group of chapters learning interprofessionally is explored. Anne Rawlings and Paty Paliokosta explore the needs of interprofessional learners and identify the challenges that they face. Next Ute Ward uses three mentoring schemes as case studies to identify which features in a mentoring scheme support interprofessional working. Ute suggests a framework for peer mentoring. Drawing on their leadership of the Children's Centre Network, Sue Webster and Annie Clouston offer a powerful case study of the effects of engaging in an interprofessional community of practice. In a group of chapters that explore working interprofessionally, first Daryl Maisey goes to the very heart of the call for interprofessionalism to examine and unravel the implications of interprofessional working for safeguarding practice. Sajni Sharma and Maureen Longley look at the place of listening to children and other service users in their chapter. Sajni and Maureen argue that the skill of 'listening' to the voices of children and families is a core element of interprofessional working. The book continues with two chapters that explore aspects of leadership in the Early Years sector. First of all, in a chapter that explores themes that are closely relevant to current challenges in the Early Years sector, Joy Jarvis and Sally Graham look at the way interprofessional organizations can gain resilience and become more emotionally intelligent even though their leaders are working in uncertainty. Then Karen John explains how values and principles were identified and used in the design of the NPQICL, an interprofessional leadership programme for Children's Centres that has become highly influential. In the penultimate chapter of the book Ian Duckmanton offers an account of interprofessional working driven by creative and thoughtful leadership.

It is intended that the values and principles that can be considered as interprofessional can be surfaced on reading the following chapters and that readers gain some further understanding of the contexts they are working in. The book closes with a chapter offering a summary of the key themes addressed and a discussion of the ways these can be used concluding that interprofessionalism as a concept and a way of being, learning, working and leading is here to stay.

References

Collins, A., Brown, J.S. and Newman, S.E. (1987) *Cognitive Apprenticeship: Teaching the Craft of Reading, Writing and Mathematics* (Technical Report No. 403). Cambridge, MA: Centre for the Study of Reading.

Drake, C., Spillane, J.P. and Hufferd-Ackles, K. (2001) Storied identities: teacher learning and subject-matter context. *Journal of Curriculum Studies*, 33: 1–224.

Gee, J.P. (2004) *Situated Language and Learning: A Critique of Traditional Schooling*. London: Routledge.

Holland, D.C., Lachicotte, W. Jr., Skinner, D. and Cain, C. (1998) *Identity and Agency in Cultural Worlds*. Cambridge, MA: Harvard University Press.

Sfard, A. and Prusak, A. (2005) Telling identities: in search of an analytic tool for investigating learning as a culturally shaped activity. *Educational Researcher*, 34: 14–22.

Törnebohm, H. (1986) *Caring, Knowing and Paradigms, Report 10/12*. Goteborg: University of Goteborg.

PART 1

Context

1

LEO CHIVERS
Frameworks for practice?
Ways of seeing what to do

Introduction

This chapter presents a discussion of the recent background of interprofessionalism in children's services in the UK. It is framed by the understanding that strategic directives for collaboration need to be worked through in interdisciplinary interactions between professionals. It is argued that those involved can find that the nature of interactions is uncertain, intangible and hard to quantify in comparison to the convenient visions offered by policy. It begins by discussing the recent policy context by relating it to theories of interprofessional working and learning. It explores the application of the *Every Child Matters* (DfES 2003) framework for practice and offers some conclusions for practitioners as the government agenda possibly shifts from this approach. It is argued that the recurring catastrophe of child deaths (such as addressed by Laming 2003, 2009), indicates that the intent of a systemic, procedural framework is confounded in the process of professional interactions that the agenda requires. It concludes by calling for deeper investigation into the lived experiences of interactions between professionals, offering suggestions for further reflection on the book's theme of interprofessionalism.

The last decade or so has seen the introduction of challenging, unprecedented but largely welcomed policy initiatives for children, schools and family services in England. Arguably, these drives demanded a fundamental shift in the ways we think about how professionals practise and, most essentially, practise together. While certain aspects of this discussion are rooted in the policy directives of the previous New Labour UK government, the themes that arise offer explication for the ways we currently think about practising together for children and families. This chapter intends to chart these policy and practice initiatives with references to literature on interprofessional working. In doing so, there will be a need not only to present the policy drive and linked theories of working but to also provide some discussion of their usefulness for practitioners at the 'front line' of interprofessional working. The challenges presented by a new coalition government intent on massive spending cuts in public services can be better met by practitioners who have a clear understanding of their own values about collaboration and how these equate with recent policy initiatives.

When the DCSF (Department for Children, Schools and Families) was immediately re-named post-election as the *Department for Education*, it was interpreted as signifying that holistic attention to the needs of children and families are not to be the focus of purely 'educational' provision. Regardless of whether the coalition government continues the push for collaboration or undermines the process, it should be recognized that collaboration happens as a naturally occurring process. It occurred prior to the previous regime and it will continue, as those practising for children and families see the need to collaborate for children and families. Initiatives such as those of Early Years pioneers Owen (1771–1858) and McMillan (1869–1931) (Pugh and Duffy 2006) and the collaboration between the sea captain Thomas Coram, the composer George Friedrich Handel and the artist William Hogarth (Douglas 2009) exemplify interprofessional working for children and families due to shared outrage at the plight of children.

The term 'shared outrage' is a useful way to think about how public recognition of significant issues for society such as child poverty, problematic parenting and child death due to abuse was a key factor in the changing nature of services for children (Baldock et al. 2009). It is this sense of outrage and reaction that has driven policy development for the 'radical reform for all children, young people and families' (DCSF 2010). Policy motivating collaboration was driven by and reacting to public consternation over serious case reviews of child deaths. The DoH (1999) guidelines laid out efforts to maintain an integrated interdisciplinary approach for child protection (MacLeod-Brudenell 2004). However, critical issues raised by the inquiry led by Lord Laming into the death of the child Victoria Climbié in 2002 led to conclusions that efforts made for collaboration so far had been largely ineffectual. Chapter 12 (*Critical Issues*) of the report of the inquiry, outlines a catalogue of errors that demanded improved collaboration. In the report, Laming makes a notable (possibly inadvertent) shift from 'multi-agency' to 'multi-disciplinary': 'I am in no doubt that effective support for children and families cannot be achieved by a single agency acting alone. It depends on a number of agencies working well together. It is a multi-disciplinary task' (Laming 2003: 6).

This rapid shift of the process from *agencies* working together to the actual task of interactions between the *disciplines* involved, disguises the enormity of the challenge. The apparently simple switch of terminology represents a common 'thinking gap' between the rhetoric of national policy (however well intended) and the personal challenges for professionals in enacting the 'multi-disciplinary task'. From the privileged viewpoint of hindsight, it can be seen that it was intended that macro-level strategy would simply drive change at a personal, practitioner level.

In short, the creation of a strategic framework for multi-disciplinary practice was seen as a solution in itself. There were significant professional, structural and procedural barriers to successful partnership but 'few conceptual frameworks or theoretical structures for exploring effective multi-agency work' (Fitzgerald and Kay 2008: 3). Strategies described a vision for services which are shaped by and responsive to children, young people and their families and not designed around professional *boundaries* (DCSF 2008a: 10). Fitzgerald and Kay concur with Frost's (2005: 188) assertion that agencies and professionals had been 'exhorted to initiate multi-agency work with little training or guidance'. It is this gap between the policy directives and the thinking on how interprofessionalism works that needs further exploration.

The recent policy context of interprofessionalism for UK children's services

The directive to collaborate to improve the lives of children was founded on a vision of their needs and rights being inextricably bound up with the needs of parents and families within a community ecology, as will be discussed later. The Children Act 1989 enshrined the premise that the rights of children and parents needed to be more clearly recognized within the legislative process. The election of a New Labour government in 1997 saw a vision for improved and standardized provision, in particular regarding Early Years services (Clark and Waller 2007).

For now, the only over-arching vision in UK policy for professionals working collaboratively is that of the *Every Child Matters* (ECM) (DfES 2003), although the whole theme is under review by the coalition at the time of writing. This agenda addressed governmental concerns regarding the shortfalls in national child protection processes and was also intended to achieve wider political objectives such as a commitment to eradicating child poverty and improving the well-being of children. The subsequent ECM programme instigated a government-backed drive for developing integrated practice in initiatives such as children's centres (for Early Years services) or extended schools. Children's Centres were intended as the hubs for 'a multi-agency focus' and extended schools were to be 'no longer the sole site for, and provider for, learning but instead become a gateway to a network of learning opportunities' (Cheminais 2006: 1). Key stakeholders within the child protection process 'greeted the proposals with cautious enthusiasm' (MacLeod-Brudenell 2004: 342) and many professionals broadly welcomed the multi-agency agenda, appreciating the prospect of taking a more holistic approach to the needs of children (Siraj-Blatchford et al. 2007). The ECM programme has been described as the 'biggest change since the introduction of the NHS' (Edwards 2004), consisting of four broad themes:

- increasing the focus on supporting families and carers – the most critical influence on children's lives;
- ensuring necessary intervention takes place before children reach crisis point and protecting children from falling through the net;
- addressing the underlying problems identified in the report into the death of Victoria Climbié – weak accountability and poor integration;
- ensuring that the people working with children are valued, rewarded and trained.

(DCSF 2008b)

The Children Act 2004 served to provide the legislative backbone of this ambitious agenda set out in the National Framework document, *Every Child Matters: Change for*

Children (DfES 2004), outlining a commitment to develop a shared sense of responsibility across agencies responsible for working for children and families. This was intended to improve life chances of children and families through the achievement of five outcomes designed to empower every child to reach their potential:

- be healthy;
- stay safe;
- enjoy and achieve;
- make a positive contribution;
- achieve economic well-being.

The document and an accompanying array of online guidance encapsulate an ambitious attempt to draw together a whole gamut of services and professionals. The intent was to weave a safer and more supportive network of services and its visual conceptualization indicates a consistent dependence on frameworks and toolkits for practice.

Early Years as the starting point

Early Years provision can be seen as the initial hub of the interprofessional agenda for children's services in the UK. For pre-school provision, health visitor intervention for families with young children inter-links with the developing need for child care and nursery education. This necessitated earlier interprofessional collaboration in comparison with the largely *edu-centric* domain of school-age provision. The advantages to be gained by this natural hybridity have been hard to realize due to the disparate nature of these services. This was due to the inherited philanthropic, private or charitable nature of Early Years provision for young children resulting in divided responsibility between the voluntary and state sectors (Rumbold 1990).

The *Ten Year Childcare Strategy: Choice for Parents – The Best Start for Children* (HMT 2004) followed the publication of the ECM with a call to standardize and professionalize the Early Years field while also developing flexibility and choice for parents. It can be seen that the direction of efforts to address fragmentation vacillated between objectives of preparing children for school or providing child care for working parents (Pugh and Duffy 2006). Furthermore, it can be said that the issue of where responsibility lies for the care and education of young children has never been fully debated and explored (Nurse 2007).

For the first wave of the government-designated *Sure Start* children's centres in 2004, this complex agenda engendered practice settings that could encompass teams for social care, childcare, education, health provision, job centre services, parenting support, family learning and adult education. The range and breadth of the undertaking signify the massive paradigm shift that was being called for – a focus on the children and families rather than on the silos of professional services. For the first few years, the benefits of multi-agency working in children's centres proved hard to verify, due to the complexities in identifying why and how shared outcomes had been achieved (Easen et al. 2000). However, Sure Start guidance cited 'considerable evidence that demonstrates the benefits of multi-agency working for staff, parents and most importantly for children and their outcomes' (DfES 2006: 16) and the National Evaluation of Sure Start report (Melhuish et al. 2008) indicated that children living in a Children's Centre area exhibited greater independence and improved social behaviour.

However, the possible benefits were to come with considerable challenges and the *Common Core of Skills and Knowledge for the Children's Workforce* (DfES 2005c) was intended to initiate some shared sense of the abilities that are required for the new agenda. Multi-agency working recommendations for professionals include having the 'confidence to challenge situations by looking beyond your immediate role and asking considered questions'. Additionally, knowing 'your role within different group situations and how you contribute to the overall group process, understanding the value of sharing how you approach your role with other professionals' is also stipulated (DfES 2005c: 19). Anning's paper 'Knowing who I am and what I know: developing new versions of professional knowledge in integrated service settings' (2001) offered welcome insights on these directives. Nevertheless, the recommendations of the *Common Core* can be seen in hindsight as too little too late as recognized in the 2020 Children and Young People's Workforce Strategy: 'The Common Core is for many professions not on their horizons (the "Uncommon Core") – to be effective it needs extending to every relevant profession, tailored to fit the inner or outer circle of professions. So, as well as gaps in content, there are gaps in reach' (Expert Group Member; DCSF 2008a: 31).

The strategy strongly endorsed the belief that, by working together, professionals 'can make a greater difference for children and young people, particularly for those who are most disadvantaged'. However, the review of the evidence identified a number of problems which indicated that integrated working was not always happening effectively, in the ways that children and young people need it to. These are:

- front-line workers not being clear about what is meant by integrated working, and how it relates to other concepts such as integrated services or early intervention;
- a lack of clear evidence and communication about the circumstances in which integrated working will make the most difference to outcomes, and make the best use of people and resources;
- capacity issues in some parts of the workforce, as well as concerns that professional colleagues in other services or sectors will not play a full role, or do not have the skills or capacity to do so; and
- practical *barriers*, including how teams are co-located and managed, challenges in rolling out common tools and systems and how workforce development is funded.

(DCSF 2008)

While the now-defunct ECM website bristled with toolkits for shaping practice in terms of procedures and forms, there was some advice on working with people. The guidance document *Championing Children: A Shared Set of Skills, Knowledge and Behaviours for Those Leading and Managing Integrated Children's Services* (DfES 2005a) addressed behaviours that were intended to facilitate interprofessional working. These recommendations can seem rather trite or superficial in their lack of specificity, for example 'managing the team in a way that encourages professionals constantly to seek service improvement and to act on good ideas' (p. 11). The reader has to ask what this 'way' actually looks like as the detail is crucial for those working with new colleagues in new teams or networks. Nevertheless, the theme of Section 5, 'Working with People', denotes a crucial aspect of interprofessional working, and for the purposes of this discussion, its heart can be said to be in the right place. It extols behaviours that will produce real 'collaborative advantage from the inter-agency team' such as 'visibly upholding esteem between professions', nurturing development and involvement for all staff. Two crucial points stand out:

- *supporting individuals* who feel they are faced with contradictions between the demands of their parent organization or profession and those of the team;
- *fostering a learning culture* that encourages informal knowledge sharing and joint learning, so that integration adds further value

(DfES 2005a).

Boundaries as guidance? Seeing the individuals within structural diagrams

It is hard to see the processes for supporting individuals and fostering learning cultures within the ECM *Outcomes Framework* (DfES 2005d). Such strategic constructs or schematics were intended to frame and help visualize change. However, without in-depth practical direction or insights, these diagrams became thought of as solutions to very complex interactions between practitioners. Strategic meetings across the country resounded with presentation references to this framework for outcomes. This can be likened to the metaphor of a traveller mistaking the map for the road. Placing practice in a framework provides a convenient structure to represent strategic intent but does it help those practitioners walking the interprofessional road?

Much writing on the field of interprofessionalism in children's services reveals a structural language that discusses boundaries, cores and inner or outer circles; either of teams for practice or as in conceptions of practice (e.g. the *Common Core of Skills and Knowledge*; DfES 2005c). This engenders curiosity as to whether these act as barriers or facilitators for thinking about practice. The original version of the *Children's Workforce Strategy* confirmed that the intention was to 'overcome the restrictive impact of professional and organisational *boundaries*' (DfES 2005b). Anning (2001) noted a lack of research conducted into multi-professional working but the acceleration of the ECM agenda called for an exponential rise in thinking about the nature of interprofessional inquiry. The vision for 'teams' (McCullogh 2007) was to be a crucial focus as the task of working across professional boundaries required new levels of awareness for 'increasingly integrated provision and people from a range of different professional and occupational backgrounds' (DCSF 2008b: 14).

In contrast with the call for training, personal development and guidance to embed the strategic drive in practice, a multiplicity of theory perspectives applicable to different organizational scenarios began to grow (Robinson et al. 2008; Siraj-Blatchford and Siraj-Blatchford 2009). Fitzgerald and Kay (2008) classify several layers of working: *multi-agency, intraprofessional within a professional group, interprofes-*

sional, joined up, interagency, interdisciplinary and practitioners working in partnership. Likewise, Anning et al. (2006: 6) refer to Frost et al. (2005) in suggesting a 'hierarchy of terms to characterise a continuum in partnership working' as ranging from four levels of cooperation, collaboration, coordination and finally integration or merger. Anning et al. proceed to describe team types using Øvretveit's (1993) typology for multi-disciplinary teams. These are described as: 'fully managed', 'coordinated', 'core and extended', 'joint accountability' and the 'network association' (Anning et al. 2006: 27). While this process of naming strata is helpful for those studying this emerging field, professionals struggling to practise within these new confines may need more than a typological approach. Robinson et al. (2008) define their review of integrated services research through criteria of structures, processes and the reach of partnerships. Figure 1.1 shows a model for a children's trust based on DfES (2005a).

The personal dimensions within these layers, systems, structures and processes are difficult to discern. Anning et al. (2006) draw upon Bronfenbrenner's (1979) ecological model of child development. This model presents a hierarchical construct which nests systems at 'micro', 'meso', 'exo' and 'macro' levels. The purpose of this was to indicate the external layers of influence upon a setting at a micro-level which in turn influence the child within the practice-centre. Anning et al. then relate this structure to the NESS (National Evaluation of Sure Start) (Belsky et al. 2007: 125) evaluation model as it reflects 'the importance of acknowledging the interrelated nature of influences on the child and family well being and development'.

The fact that different professionals hold different views on child development is certainly useful when considering their interactions, but it also problematizes the

Figure 1.1 'Onion diagram': model of a children's trust
Source: DfES (2005a).

visualization of the child and family at the centre of nested circles. It was recognized that 'professionals could be expected to construct "their" service users within separate and perhaps, competing discourses' and that these 'become central to the ways professionals work together – or indeed fail to do so' (Anning et al. 2006: 51). Anning (2005: 19) had previously noted that 'policy had shifted to the concept of welfare and attainments of the child being nested within the social context of family and community'. This mode of presentation (the 'nested' centrality of child and family) in interprofessional working appears to have become nationally attractive. While it visually and ideally places the child within a comforting ring of support networks, it is debatable as to whether it is borne out in actual practice.

This issue can be seen in the model for Children's Trusts commonly termed as the inter-agency 'onion' (see Figure 1.1). While this enables a convenient vision of the levels of interaction necessary for children and families, its simplification denies the complexity and bureaucracy of the undertaking. This depiction could be seen as a kind of diagrammatic rhetoric that presented an image of the centrality of child and family in the system to councillors, planners and strategists. Many families (and those that worked with them) would not agree that their needs were at the core of holistic service provision. Similar visual designs can be seen as manifestations of the classic gap between what Argyris and Schön (1976) describe as 'espoused theory' and 'theory in action' as they offer no real exploration of what really needed to be en-acted, in other words, the interaction between professionals practising in the circles.

When discussing the need for managerial support in times of change 'policy changes at the outer, macro level of systems can seem oppressive to those struggling to implement them at the micro-level of their workplaces ... practitioners need support at critical times ... to face up to and manage change' (Anning and Edwards 2006: 164; cited in McCullough 2007: 42). McCullough then quotes Little (2005: 3) who bemoans the approach of some local authorities in this respect: 'Sadly most local authorities will begin with structures and then spend several years trying to fit the children, the evidence about need, the services and the ideas about outcomes into those structures. And in the worst case scenarios thinking it will start and end with structures.'

Worsley (2007: 147) agrees that Lumsden (2005) rightly argues 'that an attractive ideology proposed by policy makers can disguise the underlying restrictive barriers, so that practitioners who have the responsibility of translating policy into practice may do little because they lack understanding'. She then confirms that the 'rhetoric of multi-disciplinary work and joined up thinking ... has re-conceptualised the role of Early Years practitioners' but confirmed 'there needs to be time for the consolidation of new knowledge and skills' (2007: 147). Edwards (2004) sees the task in hand as being one where practitioners need to be working more fluidly and fluently across these barriers, layers or boundaries. Also mentioned is the fact that there are several issues for joining professional cultures that include 'professional multi-lingualism, fluid trusting interprofessional working, the capacity to make their expertise explicit, the negotiation of broad local alliances and the co-construction of provision with service users' (Edwards 2004: 5). She concludes that the necessary learning will take time and for many practitioners it meant learning 'on the job', through interactions.

Learning through interactions

Establishing a shared learning culture between professionals is vital for ensuring practitioners understand each other enough to work collaboratively. Before concluding that governance structures and multi-agency team checklists will move multi-professional practice forward, Anning et al. (2006) make valuable reference to theories about organizational learning and development. Their discussion offers an insightful account of various types of 'multi-professional' teams and how their 'communities of practice' (Lave and Wenger 1991) develop. Lave and Wenger (1991) and Wenger's (1999) 'communities of practice' and Engeström's (1999) 'knotworking' activity theories play essential parts in their theoretical framework.

Lave and Wenger (1991) used the phrase 'community of practice' to define learning through collaboration in everyday life. Wenger went on to define this further for organizational development in 1999. The concept (primarily focused on commercial practice) has resonance with thinking on learning as socially constructed through participation to negotiate and co-construct new forms of knowledge (e.g. Bandura 2001). Wenger's thinking is particularly useful for the interprofessional agenda as it offers the notion that practitioners may be constructing new professional identities in their interactions. Whalley (2001) calls for the fostering of 'learning communities' for the development of Early Years teams and this 'educational' arena can be used as a focal hub for practice development.

Some groups of professionals may not work or see themselves as practising in a community as such. They may only come together or interact intermittently over certain key shared tasks. In contrast to Wenger, Engestrom et al. (1999) focus less on the community continuum where progress is steadily realized through interactions and take a view of interprofessional collaboration that focuses on processes of constant change. This is termed 'knotworking' where the idea of teamwork concentrates on situation-specific, object-orientated, distributed activities (Anning et al. 2006) rather than on the specific professionals involved. 'The unstable knot itself needs to be made focus of the analysis' (Engestrom et al. 1999: 347). Engestrom's more recent work involves experiments carried out in what are described as 'boundary crossing laboratories' that are established in settings to study these knots. His techniques involved getting practitioners to 'bring to the surface contradictions between their previous ways of working and proposed new ways of working within teams'. Anning et al. (2006: 84–5) conclude with several points that include:

- much knowledge in the workplace remains tacit, but professionals working in multi-agency teams are required to make it explicit for their colleagues;
- there are two types of knowledge – codified and personal – and professionals need to be trained to deploy both in the workplace;
- professionals generate theories about their work through daily situated experiences of and reflection on delivering services;
- there may be a tension between the desire to reach consensus (as in a community of practice model) and to confront conflict (as in a knotworking model).

There is a need to surface tacit knowledge because every discipline has its own, distinctive knowledge base (Polanyi and Sen 2009), crucial for negotiation to take place on what new shared knowledge can be constructed. This process could be one of the ways that interprofessionalism develops; its enactment is a way of being inter-professional. The idea of revealing the hidden indicates that practitioners need to reflect on what goes on underneath the immediate veneer of recorded professional interactions. As an alternative visual construct, Schratz and Walker's (1995) use of the Freudian iceberg theory of the human mind is helpful in its indication that much more than meets the eye occurs beneath the visible surface of human interactions.

Thinking about *being* interprofessional

Professionals learn about their practice within the traditional routes of their own particular silos but then need to learn to work together upon qualification. The Venn diagram (Figure 1.2) indicates a version of the traditional tripartite of provision in UK Children's Services, where the overlap areas indicate areas for collaboration. The impor-tance of the voluntary and independent sectors (especially in early years) complicates this picture, as does the realization that each sector contains many separate professional disciplines. Furthermore, there is also the essential need to interact effectively with parents and communities with an understanding of the sensitivities involved. Practitioner guidance and reflection need to be focused within the zones of interaction between all these groups, professions or disciplines. Concern for how learning from interaction develops can be said to be the lynchpin for developing interprofessional work.

While Figure 1.2 presents an initially useful visualization, reflection needs to move away from an approach based on diagrams and structure-based constructs to explain the complex lived experience of interactions. Simplifying and categorizing practice can serve as a help and a hindrance to those struggling to work out what is really going on when professional relationships do not work well. Perhaps thinking on interprofessionalism needs to examine small details of the world as it actually *is* rather than referring to overviews or typologies that impose restrictive strategic visions.

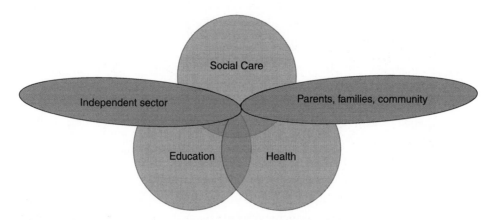

Figure 1.2 Some possible zones of interaction: an over-simplified version of the task

Ways of *seeing* the interprofessional arena may not directly relate to ways of *being* interprofessional.

A focus on what it is like *being* interprofessional offers an alternative viewpoint on practice. This is the approach of *ontological* inquiry that explores experiences of those involved with a phenomenon (e.g. interprofessionalism). Heidegger (1927) described ontological inquiry as exploration of *being* itself. He saw this as opposite to an external approach concerned with '*ontic*' knowledge which he defined as ways of quantifying, measuring and categorizing such as is presented by a framework for practice approach. An ontological approach could enable deeper insight into what it is like to '*be*' a professional striving to work with other professionals, uncovering authentic accounts of interprofessional interaction.

An inquiry into being interprofessional will address how we come to think of ourselves or our professional identities as *interprofessional*. Anning et al. (2006: 11) assert that Wenger's work can be 'utilised to make the point that experienced professionals in multi-agency teams will have undergone different historic processes of both self-determination and social determination of their professional identity'. Ibarra (1999) discusses 'provisional selves' as being created during the adaptive techniques that professionals employ during transition to new roles. This discourse of identity links to an ontological approach in attempting to explore what it is like to '*be*' a professional working with other professionals. If we are to accept the convenient visualization of the interprofessional agenda as an onion, its layers need to be more radically peeled to reveal what lies beneath – within the core. Heidegger's view of 'ontic' categorizing and quantifying resonates with Wenger's view of attempts to design learning or impose a framework on it:

> Learning cannot be designed. Ultimately, it belongs to the realm of experience and practice. It follows the negotiation of meaning; it moves on its own terms. It slips through the cracks; it creates its own cracks. Learning happens, design or no design . . . By 'design' I mean a systematic, planned, and reflexive colonization of time and space in the service of an undertaking.
>
> (Wenger 1999: 225–6)

So the drive to design, impose systems upon and quantify processes can lead to restrictive views of practice. It could even lead to painfully inhuman containers for those practising within so that professionals feel unnecessarily bounded by the overarching frameworks and standardization. As politicians and policymakers framed the process of collaboration to serve the political agenda, there was a drive to evaluate, categorize and benchmark real improvements for children and families. This way of rationalizing the world of practice extended to the drive for *outcomes* (DfES 2005d) for children and families. The evaluation of the Sure Start programme (Melhuish et al. 2008) rightly sought to define quantifiable 'outcomes' – real improvements in the lives of children and families. However, those working within this regulatory 'gaze' (Osgood 2006) or 'framework' (Miller 2008) found themselves driven in new directions: to share 'outcomes' with other professional disciplines in an increasingly complex environment that was fraught with uncertainty (Urban 2008). This approach led to systematizing and recording practice to the extent that activity under each category needed to be formally recorded to prove that it had happened, ironically reducing the time for further activity.

Summary, conclusion and reflection points

Habermas (1981) critiqued what he saw as a biased modernization process led by the powers of economic and administrative rationalization. He highlighted a growing tendency of intervention by formal systems into the everyday sphere and linked this to the growth of the welfare state and corporate capitalism, describing a generalizing logic of efficiency and control. It could be that the ECM inter-agency onion enabled a sense of control while it could well have had little to do with actual practice, offering a false certainty around the undertaking. The way forward could be to ask practitioners to describe their experiences and then link these (in collaboration with the practitioners) to new ways of working towards *being* an interprofessional in very uncertain times.

It is worth considering Evans's (2008: 34) thinking on what needs to be done to reshape the professional identities in services for children and families:

> the best chance initiators have of attaining what they perceive as attitudinal development among professional groups is to recognise and incorporate into their required changes to a specific professionalism consideration of its individual-professionality-determined heterogeneity. This may involve flexibility and a degree of compromise, where expectations of uniformity and standardisation give way to acceptance that a broad working consensus may be the best that may realistically be hoped for.

Jarvis and Trodd (2008) stress the importance of exploring professional identity in learning for new professional teams. They describe techniques to use imagination as a lens for 'other ways of seeing' either other professionals or children. They cite Andrews' (2007: 489) apt statement on research: 'cross-cultural narrative research is predicated on narrative imagination ... If we wish to access the frameworks of meaning for others, we must be willing and able to imagine a world other than the one we know'. This will involve engagement at a deep level, using research to uncover meaning in everyday experiences of professionals and families. This awareness will enable the growth of resilience in uncertain times, a personal capacity to reflect on the worth of our (collective) actions.

The essential element to provide resilience, in what will continue to be trying times for those working in children's services, is *reflective practice* to develop awareness, such as championed by Schon (1983), Dewey (1933/1997) and Argyris and Schon (1976). In the challenging contemporary climate for public services, interprofessionals need to be encouraged by the collaborations they find themselves undertaking for children and families. Finding out more about how we experience and learn about these interactions will be the crucial focus of further research for interprofessionalism. Engaging more deeply with stories and accounts from practitioners and families could help develop future policy and practice away from mechanistic frameworks. It could help create clearer notions of processes for attitudinal development of professionals and educators in the field, inspiring them to work creatively.

REFLEXIVITY CHECK-IN POINT

Do any of the following affect you personally or professionally?

Potential 'interprofessionals' may care to consider the following issues and themes that will be discussed further in this publication:

- learning cultures and how you develop them (e.g. *learning communities* and *communities of practice*);
- how you and colleagues address competing notions of professional identity;
- how imagination can be utilized to help practitioners envisage each other's roles;
- how you and colleagues work in uncertainty – is there a set of values and attitudes that can help?
- the emergence of interprofessionalism as a field or discipline – of thought and practice?

References

Andrews, M. (2007) Exploring cross-cultural boundaries. In D.J. Clandinin (ed.) *Handbook of Narrative Inquiry: Mapping a Methodology*. London: Sage.

Anning, A. (2001) *Knowing Who I Am and What I Know: Developing New Versions of Professional Knowledge in Integrated Service Settings*. Leeds: British Educational Rsearch Association.

Anning, A. (2005) Investigating the impact of working in multi-agency service delivery settings in the UK on early years practitioners' beliefs and practices. *Journal of Early Childhood Research*, 3: 19.

Anning, A., Cottrell, D., Frost, N., Green, J. and Robinson, M. (2006) *Developing Multi-professional Teamwork for Integrated Children's Services: Research, Policy and Practice*. Maidenhead: Open University Press.

Anning, A. and Edwards, A. (2006) *Promoting Children's Learning from Birth to Five*. Maidenhead: Open University Press.

Argyris, C. and Schön, D.A. (1976) *Theory in Practice: Increasing Professional Effectiveness*. San Francisco, CA: Jossey-Bass.

Baldock, P., Fitzgerald, D. and Kay, J. (2009) *Understanding Early Years Policy*. London: Sage.

Bandura, A. (2001) Social cognitive theory: an agentic perspective. *Annual Review of Psychology*, 52: 1–26.

Belsky, J., Melhuish, E.C. and Barnes, J. (eds) (2007) *The National Evaluation of Sure Start: Does Area-based Early Intervention Work?* London: Policy Press.

Bronfenbrenner, U. (1979) *The Ecology of Human Development: Experiments by Nature and Design*. Cambridge, MA: Harvard University Press.

Cheminais, R. (2006) *Effective Multi-agency Partnerships: Putting Every Child Matters into Practice*. London: Sage.

Clark, M.M. and Waller, T. (2007) *Early Childhood Education and Care: Policy and Practice*. London: Sage Publications Ltd.

DCSF (2008a) *2020 Children and Young People's Workforce Strategy*. Nottingham: DCSF Publications.

DCSF (2008b) *The Background to Every Child Matters*. Online document.

Dewey, J. (1933/1997) *How We Think*. New York: Dover.

DfES (2003) *Every Child Matters* (Cm. 5860). London: HMSO.

DfES (2004) *Every Child Matters: Change for Children*. London: HMSO.

DfES (2005a) *Championings children: A Shared Set of Skills, Knowledge and Behaviours for Those Leading and Managing Integrated Children's Services*. London: HMSO.

DfES (2005b) *The Children's Workforce Strategy*. London: HMSO.

DfES (2005c) *Common Core of Skills and Knowledge for the Children's Workforce*. London: HMSO.

DfES (2005d) *The Every Child Matters Outcomes Framework*. London: HMSO.

DfES (2006) *Sure Start Children's Centre Practice Guidance*. London: Sure Start.

DoH (1999) *Working Together to Safeguard Children*. London: HMSO.

Douglas, A. (2009) *Partnership Working*. Abingdon: Routledge.

Easen, P., Atkins, M. and Dyson, A. (2000) Inter-professional collaboration and conceptualisations of practice. *Children and Society*, 14: 355–67.

Edwards, A. (2004) The new multi-agency working: collaborating to prevent the social exclusion of children and families. *Journal of Integrated Care*, 12: 3–9.

Engeström, Y. (1999) Innovative learning in work teams: analyzing cycles of knowledge creation in practice. In Y. Engstrom, R. Miettinen, and R. Punamaki (eds) *Perspectives on Activity Theory*. Cambridge, MA: Harvard University Press.

Evans, L. (2008) Professionalism, professionality and the development of education professionals. *British Journal of Educational Studies*, 56: 20–38.

Fitzgerald, D. and Kay, J. (2008) *Working Together in Children's Services*. London: Routledge.

Frost, N., Robinson, M. and Anning, A. (2005) Social workers in multidisciplinary teams: issues and dilemmas for professional practice. *Child & Family Social Work*. 10: 187–96.

Habermas, J. (1981) *Theory of Communicative Action*. Boston, MA: Beacon Press.

Heidegger, M. (1927) *Being and Time*. New York: SUNY Press.

HMT (2004) *Choice for Parents, the Best Start for Children: A Ten Year Strategy for Childcare*. London: HMSO.

Ibarra, H. (1999) Provisional selves: experimenting with image and identity in professional adaption. *Administrative Science Quarterly*, 44: 764–91.

Jarvis, J. and Trodd, L. (2008) Other ways of seeing; other ways of being: imagination as a tool for developing multiprofessional practice for children with communication needs. *Child Language Teaching & Therapy*, 24: 211.

Laming, H. (2003) *The Victoria Climbié Inquiry Summary Report of an Inquiry*. London: HMSO.

Laming, H. (2009) *The Protection of Children in England: A Progress Report*. London: HMSO.

Lave, J. and Wenger, E. (1991) *Situated Learning: Legitimate Peripheral Participation*. Cambridge: Cambridge University Press.

Little, M. (2005) Building effective prevention strategies in children's services. Keynote Presentation at the National Evaluation of the Children's Fund, available at http//www.ne-cf.org.

Lumsden, E. (2005) Joined up thinking in practice: an exploration of professional collaboration. In T. Waller (ed.) *An Introduction to Early Childhood: A Multi-disciplinary Approach*. London: Paul Chapman.

MacLeod-Brudenell, I. (2004) *Advanced Early Years Care and Education*. Oxford: Heinemann.

McCullogh, M. (2007) Integrating children's services: the case for child protection. In I. Siraj-Blatchford, K. Clarke and M. Needham (eds) *The Team Around the Child*. Stoke on Trent: Trentham Books.

Melhuish, E., Belsky, J. and Leyland, A. (2008) *National Evaluation Report: The Impact of Sure Start Local Programmes on Three Year Olds and their Families*. London: Institute for the Study of Children, Families & Social Issues.

Miller, L. (2008) Developing professionalism within a regulatory framework in England: challenges and possibilities. *European Early Childhood Education Research Journal*, 16: 14.

Nurse, A.D. (2007) *The New Early Years Professional: Dilemmas and Debates*. London: Routledge.

Osgood, J. (2006) Deconstructing professionalism in early childhood education: resisting the regulatory gaze. *Contemporary Issues in Early Childhood*, 7: 5–14.

Øvretveit, J. (1993) *Coordinating Community Care: Multidisciplinary Teams and Care Management*. Buckingham: Open University Press.

Polanyi, M. and Sen, A. (2009) *The Tacit Dimension*. Chicago, IL: University of Chicago Press.

Pugh, G. and Duffy, B. (2006) *Contemporary Issues in the Early Years*. London: Sage.

Robinson, M., Atkinson, M. and Downing, D. (2008) *Supporting Theory Building in Integrated Services Research*. Slough: National Foundation for Educational Research.

Rumbold, A. (1990) *Starting with Quality: The Report of the Committee of Inquiry into the Quality of the Educational Experience Offered to 3-and 4-year Olds*. London: HMSO.

Schön, D.A. (1983) *The Reflective Practitioner: How Professionals Think in Action*. New York: Basic Books.

Schratz, M. and Walker, R. (1995) *Research as a Social Change*. London: Routledge.

Siraj-Blatchford, I., Clarke, K. and Needham, M. (2007) *The Team Around the Child: Multi-agency Working in the Early Years*. Stoke on Trent: Trentham Books.

Siraj-Blatchford, I. and Siraj-Blatchford, J. (2009) *Improving Development Outcomes for Children through Effective Practice in Integrating Early Years Services*. London: Centre for Excellence and Outcomes in Children and Young People's Services (C4EO).

Urban, M. (2008) Dealing with uncertainty: challenges and possibilities for the early childhood profession. *European Early Childhood Education Research Journal*, 16: 18.

Wenger, E. (1999) *Communities of Practice: Learning, Meaning, and Identity*. Cambridge: Cambridge University Press.

Whalley, M. (2001) Working as a team. In G. Pugh (ed.) *Contemporary Issues in the Early Years: Working Collaboratively for Children*. London: Pual Chapman.

Worsley, J. (2007) Early years practitioners in a newly established children's centre. In I. Siraj–Blatchford, K. Clarke and M. Needham (eds), *The Team Around the Child*. Stoke on Trent: Trentham Books.

2

SHARIF AL-ROUSI
Interorganizational dynamics and trends: system-wide thinking

Introduction

This chapter examines an emerging trend in children's services to focus resources on targeted groups of service users through collaborative partnerships. It discusses the implications of these changes on individual practitioners and managers. The chapter begins by examining the nature of collaboration between partner organizations delivering children's services, and then considers how locally based public sector bodies are responding to the new economic and political environment. This is exemplified by changes to the nature of strategic-level collaboration between delivery partners and the trend in reconceptualizing service users. These trends are brought together in the ongoing evolution of collaborative approaches to dealing with 'high-demand' service users, who place the largest burden on public sector budgets. The potential implications for the design of collaborative services based in communities are discussed before drawing out the implications of a continued evolution of these trends for the children's workforce.

Strategic-level collaboration in children's services: an introduction

For those working on the front line in interprofessional settings and teams, it is not uncommon to hear practitioners and managers bemoan the lack of understanding of integrated working issues at a strategic level. This has been attributed to many things; from a lack of experience in those occupying senior positions in public sector bodies that have not 'walked the walk' in integrated working and multi-disciplinary environments, to an organizational preoccupation with service-specific targets and measurements. Thankfully, this has changed over time. Many practice frontline projects such as Sure Start Local Programmes which started at the periphery of organizations, have been 'mainstreamed' over time. With that change, senior managers have begun to understand the context and interrelationships of these services in their own portfolios.

Despite this evolution in awareness, however, traditional service structures and practices have persisted alongside the increase in interprofessional working patterns within children's services. Looking to the future, the delivery of public services looks very different. In a tight fiscal environment publicly funded organizations are responding to the financial challenge by considering radical alternatives to traditional styles of service delivery. Interagency collaboration is suddenly very big on the strategic-level agenda, but perhaps not in the way those on the front line had hoped for.

A collaborative environment?

In such a financial environment the pressure for many potential business partners to collaborate strategically has never been greater. This is particularly the case as the public sector has been forced to adjust to straightened economic conditions in 2010–11. In the previous decade concerted efforts to encourage collaborative working between agencies responsible for children's outcomes had largely been driven by policy:

> Multi-agency working is about different services, agencies and teams of professionals and other staff working together to provide the services that fully meet the needs of children, young people and their parents or carers. To work successfully on a multi-agency basis you need to be clear about your own role and aware of the roles of other professionals; you need to be confident about your own standards and targets and respectful of those that apply to other services, actively seeking and respecting the knowledge and input others can make to delivering best outcomes for children and young people.
>
> (DfES 2004: 18)

To support policy initiatives, funding was allocated to projects such as Sure Start Local Programmes and Children's Centres, and Extended Schools. The aspiration for these collaborative projects was that coordinated service delivery would lead to improved outcomes for children and young people.

However, in the current climate there is a significant drive for collaborative working at a strategic level, with a strong focus on efficiency. Professionals and policy makers have been aware of duplication of services and uncoordinated service delivery for a long time. Now, however, that situation is untenable. Collaboration between public sector bodies has been recognized as one way to achieve the required efficiencies in this new environment, such as combining back office functions across organizations, reducing duplication of services to the same populations or by working in new and innovative ways. Despite these perceived benefits, the nature of collaboration is rather more difficult to specify. 'In its overuse, the term "collaboration" has become a catchall to signify just about any type of inter-organisational or inter-personal relationship, making it difficult for those seeking to collaborate to put into practice or evaluate with certainty' (Gajda 2004: 66).

In their literature review of collaboration and integration in children's services, Horwath and Morrison (2007) show that current research has no common language to describe collaboration. What there is focuses on front-line activity rather than systems management at an organizational level. Looking beyond children's services and drawing, from the literature focused at the organizational level, a number of researchers put forward the view that collaboration can be seen as a continuum, from degrees of goal alignment and organizational autonomy (Peterson 1991), dimensions of formality and the extent to which collaboration permeates an organization (Horwarth and Morrison 2007), to intensity of relationships, activities and planning (Gajda 2004). More specific to children's services, Anning et al. (2006), drawing on work by Frost (2005), describe a continuum of partnership working where planning becomes increasingly formalized, and in its ultimate form results in different organizations merging for the purpose of enhanced service delivery.

Whatever the degree of collaboration sought by organizational partners, achieving interorganizational collaboration in the current economic environment presents its own challenges. Not least are the apparent efficiencies available:

> Collaboration is often assumed as one way to efficiently allocate scarce resources while building community by strengthening interorganizational ties. Case research suggests, however, that practitioners in this environment face significant collective action problems that undermine their potential for building collaborative relationships. Different accountability standards across organisations have the ironic effect of straining already tenuous collaborative efforts.
>
> (Thomson et al. 2007: 2)

Other threats to the success of inter-agency collaboration at an organization level include the lack of relationship building between senior leaders and the period of initial 'uncertainty' and 'ambiguity' that characterizes the early stages of collaborative activity between organizations (Kelly et al. 2002). The required speed of budget reduction over the next few years would appear to give little time for prolonged efforts by senior leaders to build relationships with external organizations, and at the same time their own accountability structures are necessarily becoming increasingly demanding. However, it has been argued that turbulent business environments can serve to advance collaborative efforts between organizations (Kandemir et al. 2006: 336).

Collaboration at the organizational level

Anning et al. (2006) describe a range of joined-up or integrated working practices in children's services that grew throughout the 2000s. These include distinct programmes or projects such as Sure Start programmes, teams hosted by a main agency such as child and adolescent mental health teams and youth offending teams, and time-limited teams established to work on specific cases such as child protection conferences. However, interagency collaboration has not, in their view, delivered the improvements to services that were their aspiration.

Investigating the causes of under-performance in child protection systems, Horwarth and Morrison (2007) outline a number of organizational issues. They specify inflexible organizational structures, conflicting professional ideologies, lack of budget control and poor understanding of roles and responsibilities among professionals. Much of the literature on interprofessionalism in children's services discusses boundaries, cores and inner or outer circles. Curiously and conspicuously, the important dimension of the working reality for practitioners and managers is largely neglected.

Projects and teams where integration was embedded by the structural integration of different professionals developed leadership characteristics more appropriate to their environments. However, penetration of these 'softer characteristics' into main-stream services was less straightforward. In these 'mainstream' silos of service, workers were subject to the forces of organizational and service-based reporting. Huxham (1996: 5) calls this the 'autonomy–accountability dilemma': 'Unless the individuals representing their various parent organisations are fully empowered by their organisa-tions to make judgements about what they may commit to [in the collaboration] they will constantly have to check in with their parents before action can happen.'

Department for Education research into pathfinder projects focused on rede-signing provision for families with multiple problems finds a similar phenomenon:

> In many areas there is evidence of polarised engagement with approaches to the concept of family focused working and processes. Within the Pathfinder delivery teams, there is strong, bottom-up support and direct engagement with frontline professionals. At the very top, there is commitment from the most senior managers represented on strategic boards. What is often lacking is active support from management in the middle.
>
> (DfE 2010)

As one informant said:

> Frontline staff have been enthusiastic, but have not always been able to have their time freed up to take up the task. There is not enough top-down support to crack local management commitment. Our Chief Executive supports the Pathfinder approach, but most of our service managers don't.
>
> (DfE 2010: 32)

Huxham (1996) concludes that those required to change became prisoners of 'collaborative inertia'. This tendency for organizations and their management to resist change and retain engrained behaviours can be described as their 'dominant logic' (Prahalad and Bettis 1986):

> The dominant logic of the company is, in essence the DNA of the organisation. It reflects how managers are socialised. It manifests itself often, in an implicit theory of competition and value creation. It is embedded in standard operating procedures, shaping not only how the members of the organisation act but also how they think. Because it is the source of the company's past success, it becomes the lens through which managers see all emerging opportunities. This makes it hard for incumbent companies to embrace a broader logic for competition and value creation.
>
> (Prahalad 2004: 172)

The power of the dominant logic needs to be taken into account when trying to effect change in organizational behaviour. (DfES 2005) recommends fostering a learning culture that considers the dominant logic of the organization from the outset. Collaborative ventures in turn should consider the dominant logics of their critical delivery partners.

The top-down view

At the organizational level, partnerships between public sector organizations are not new. Current developments build upon the foundations laid down in Local Area Agreements (LAAs) and Sustainable Community Strategies (SCSs). At this strategic level, Children's Trusts were introduced as the governance component of inter-agency collaboration. This followed the earlier establishment of Local Children's Safeguarding Boards to act as the overarching superstructure to ensure that child protection was a multi-agency responsibility. Legislation that placed a statutory duty on local authorities to establish Children's Trusts in their area was repealed in late 2010 by the new coalition government. However, the early signs are that Local Authorities have no wish to dismantle their infrastructure.

The repeal of the Children's Trust legislation was followed by the removal of the requirement to publish Children and Young People Plans (CYPPs). While some LAs obviously found Children's Trusts and Children and Young People Plans useful vehicles in bringing about significant change, particularly in pooling budgets, others have achieved more modest gains. They were certainly successful in formalizing existing relationships and giving partners (particularly from the voluntary sector) a voice in the shaping of services at a local level. Within the CYPPs the rationale for joint planning was improvement in children's outcomes by acting collaboratively. As noted earlier, the motivation has shifted to an economic imperative.

One recent trend, a response to the learning from Total Place pilots, is that Local Authorities and local partners are increasingly formalizing their collaborative planning processes through the production of Single Delivery Plans (SDPs). These go beyond the scope of collaborating in discrete outcomes areas (such as children's outcomes for CYPPs) and encompass projects and workstreams that represent a range of reasons for collaboration. This includes, for example, realizing efficiencies through sharing back-office systems across partners, coordinated disposal of capital assets, improved market intelligence through information sharing, and integrated frontline delivery of services.

The bottom-up view

Frontline practice can also shape the nature of organizational collaboration. Recent studies of integrated and multi-agency working in children's services offer some promising evidence of 'what works' in delivering enhanced outcomes through integrated working. Atkinson et al.'s (2007) review of the literature identified the 'main beneficial impact on service users of multi-agency working was improved access to services, through speedier and more appropriate referral, and a greater focus on prevention and early intervention'. The Centre for Excellence in Outcomes (C4EO) review conducted by Siraj-Blatchford (2009) demonstrated 'robust evidence that suggests that the adoption of combined approaches to intervention is effective and this may be considered to provide indirect evidence of integration' and that 'lead professional and key worker were exemplars of service coordination'.

A final trend in organizational collaboration, demonstrated at both the strategic and frontline level, is to focus on certain populations. Often, but not always, this is geographically based. Thomson's (1999) study of collaborations in national service identified that a commitment to similar target populations was one of the most important factors holding collaborations together, and gave as a case study organizations continuing to fund collaborative activity jointly through their own budgets after expected external funding did not materialize.

Unification: a systems or systemic approach

While it has been suggested that senior leaders do not have a firm grasp of how to develop organizational alliances and partnerships (Todeva and Knoke 2005), attempts to do so have been undeterred. With the adoption of both top-down and bottom-up strategies to steer collaborative efforts, the foundations are laid for a system-wide approach. In particular, piecing together the collective insights of each partner organization can illuminate patterns of behaviour that have been hitherto hidden to the organizations. For example, before establishing its Family Recovery Project (FRP) aimed at providing intensive support to chaotic families with complex needs, Westminster City Council identified that a collaborative approach was most suited to:

> families in the city that suffer from the consequences of social exclusion and a toxic combination of housing problems, low school attendance, substance misuse, domestic violence, poor parenting skills and an entrenched dependence on benefits.
> (Local Government Leadership and Westminster City Council 2010: 8)

While this was probably apparent to many practitioners working with those families, this was effectively invisible to organizational intelligence gathering and planning systems. The dominant logic of each partner was too strong to risk deviating from their embedded approach. However, the emerging evidence points to the fact that collaboration will be designed around service or care pathway. Thus the functional incentive for collaboration starts with the service user firmly in mind.

Reconceptualization of the service user

This 'reconceptualization' of service users will now be more thoroughly examined as it has profound implications for both professional knowledge creation and learning, shared organizational learning and professional identity. This trend could be seen as a 'scaling-up' of the systemic thinking model that was observed in some children's services teams during the fieldwork for the MATCh (Multiagency Teamwork in Services for Children) project (Anning et al. 2006). Systemic thinking at this level meant teams taking into account the complex 'systems' within which families are located,

> including key social contexts such as schools, housing and peer groups. Family issues for this team thus have to be seen as part of a 'family system' situated in a network of wider systems.
>
> (Anning et al. 2006: 52)

Interestingly, the research also showed that despite the teams recognizing these systemic factors and their impact on the families they worked with, they were often powerless to impact on some of them:

The complexity of real-life problems made it difficult for agencies to target intervention. The use of this systemic approach by a team dedicated to improving children's psychological health led the team to dilemmas of identifying boundaries between agencies. A team member reported: 'A lot of families, I think, locate the difficulties purely within the children and in fact the issues are far more systemic and that generates huge issues for all agencies because there are so many families that could fall between everybody's camp.'

(Anning et al. 2006: 53)

This, perhaps, further points to the need for systemic thinking to be applied at an organizational level.

Reconceptualizing the service user: 'high' and 'low' demand users

Reconceptualization of the service user requires delivery partners to share their intelligence to reconstruct the profile of individuals engaging (or not) with their services. The result of this process is likely to be a change in the way we see service users:

> from addressing parts to addressing wholes, e.g. that an alcoholic may also be unemployed and have family problems. This means more than an expensive and often ineffective multi-disciplinary approach. It means turning on its head the way we think about social support so that the focus is all of an individual's life, not just the presenting issue.

(Taylor and Swann 2009: 22)

The process of reconceptualizing collaboratively is akin to the process of group learning described by Kasl et al. (1993). Drawing on work by Schön (1983), they describe a process whereby initial perceptions of an issue or situation are reframed, a synthesis of diverging viewpoints is reflected upon, and new hypotheses are built. For such work to happen, individual organizations need to collaborate initially in the area of identification of similar sub-categories of service users. Evidence would suggest that some organizations will find this a considerable challenge, and therefore it is an area for future organizational redesign. In its study of early intervention approaches in children's services, C4EO observes: 'Existing data, well used and interrogated, would often highlight needs earlier. And asking the right questions would often lead to more effective forms of intervention.' Evidence suggests that the use of data is a systemic weakness and 'Sufficient analytical capacity within children's services needs to be addressed as a workforce development priority' (C4EO 2010: 8).

The learning from multi-professional and multi-organizational programmes such as the Family Intervention Projects (FIPs) and Family Recovery Projects (FRPs) has shown that services designed with one type of service user in mind can have dramatic impacts on outcomes. Westminster identified that its existing adult and child interventions 'were not tailored to individual needs and many families were being offered too many services that ran concurrently, were poorly phased or were contradictory' and 'assessments of families were being repeatedly conducted by a range of agencies and council departments without any coordination of information or action, resulting in inefficiency and duplication' (Local Government Leadership and Westminster City Council 2010: 9).

Redefining sub-populations of service users

One strategy pursued by LAs is to identify sub-populations for receipt of service packages. This could be seen as a segmentation strategy (Porter 1980) in terms of business and competition, whereby an organization targets different populations with different products or services, tailored to those markets. Porter argues that businesses that focus in such a way will be more successful than those who have a confused strategy or lack of understanding or inability to deliver what is valued by target populations. This is because in order to achieve optimum performance, all organizational architecture should be aligned to delivering value for its target market. The target population/service user, and what constitutes value for them, will determine the dominant logic of that organization. This is of profound importance if we consider the patterns of usage and engagement in public services of different groups of service users: 'The problems experienced by some children and families will respond to a single intervention, others will require longer-term support; some will be complex and may even cross generations' (C4EO 2010: 7).

Currently, LAs and most other large public sector organizations have a dominant logic that is dictated by professionalisms. In the main, they are not sensitive to the needs of the children and families that C4EO is concerned about. As lifestyles have changed, so has what constitutes value in public service delivery for different population groups. However, the constancy of organizational dominant logics has impeded the penetration of initiatives that have been successfully designed around providing value for specific groups.

Through their collaborative efforts, partner organizations can share understandings of different service user groups. For instance, for those families and individuals who are able to engage successfully with single professionals and services, there is arguably no need to work in an integrated way. For families and individuals who consistently fail to have their needs met by single service interventions, integrated delivery should be designed by all organizations in the service user's eco-system. Table 2.1 illustrates the different needs of these two hypothetical groups, and what value-giving service delivery might look like.

When dominant logics of partner organizations have changed to take account of what constitutes value, services for high-demand individuals and families can be designed to work within the users' lifestyle constraints: 'Some interventions, particularly those involving outreach or intensive support, require changes of practice to enable services to be offered out of "normal" hours in order to meet families' needs' (C4EO 2010: 7).

An attractive element of involving all services that 'touch' such families is the ability to get previously remote partners to actively engage in service delivery. An example from Westminster's FRP is that adult mental health services were successfully involved in work with families. Wider service redesign, based on such successes is already happening, not least because of the attractive financial case for doing so: 'It is well understood in the commercial world that 20% of customers probably account for 80% or more business. Demand for many public services is far more

Table 2.1   Characteristics of low-need and high-demand service users and suggested differences required in organizational response

Type 1 – Low need	Type 2 – High need/high demand
Large numbers of service users	Small numbers of service users
Characteristics	**Characteristics**
Families who are resilient, have stable lives with predictable routines, regular income, plus occasional needs, usually limited to one individual	Families who are much less resilient, who have chaotic lifestyles, irregular or inadequate income, with many individuals who have one or more unmet needs requiring service delivery
Inter-family dynamics are supportive or at least non-destructive	Inter-family dynamics in some cases dysfunctional and destructive
What constitutes value	**What constitutes value**
Fast, and efficient access to services (e.g. 'one stop shops')	Flexible delivery negotiated with service user and responsive to rapid change
Reliable delivery	Coordinated planning of multiple interventions by different agencies
Low cost to tax payer	Intensive and sustained support with monitoring of progress
Requirements of organizational dominant logic	**Requirements of organizational dominant logic**
'Quality' determined by service/ professional considerations	Shared understanding and intelligence of service users by all deliver partners
Speed, efficiency and low cost are key to performance measures	'Quality' determined by needs of individual cases on a case by case basis
	Cost avoidance
	Collaborative approach to planning service delivery and interventions
	Labour-intensive work produces the required quality

Source: Modified from work produced at a workshop organized by the Regional Improvement and Efficiency Partnership (RIEP) for the East of England, January 2011.

concentrated. If attention is focused on these high cost users there is an opportunity to break recurring patterns of service demand and dramatically reduce overall expenditure' (Taylor and Swann 2009: 22).

C4EO's (2010) research into early intervention in children's services found targeted approaches to be much more cost effective than universal ones. Cost-avoidance models have demonstrated that for every £1 spent on Family Recovery Projects, between £2.10 and £3 is avoided by the public purse during one year of intervention (Local Government Leadership and Westminster City Council 2010). Service redesign in this way also enables organizations to make the case for committing a higher proportion of their resources to intensive integrated service delivery. Without it the effective work of some organizations can be impeded by mismatched caseloads (Siraj-Blatchford 2009).

Implications of designing services for 'high-demand' users

The case has been made for public and voluntary sector partners to collaborate in the design and delivery of services for high-demand users. This presents those working in children's services with opportunities to tailor service delivery around users with chaotic lifestyles, work intensively to build resilience in families, and tackle the needs of adults within families through integration of adult-centred services into support packages. Indeed, learning from Westminster's FRP shows that a key to developing partnerships with adults in their client families is that they were 'treated as adults and not parents'. Their needs were explicitly diagnosed and treated as equally important to those of children and young people in the household.

However, there are implications at both organizational and practitioner level of delivering services in this way. As previously stated, what constitutes quality in terms of service delivery for this group is likely to be very different from 'low-demand' users. For instance, value in one case might be halting the inter-generational replication of high need in a family, ensuring that children do not replicate the costly behaviours of older relatives. Cost-avoidance models, which look at engagement patterns before and after interventions, have been developed as a tool to compare the cost to the public purse. In realizing changes in behaviour, sustainable resilience needs to be built in families. This requires a change in performance management regimes to allow organizations working with 'high-demand' users to move away from simply measuring numbers of people receiving interventions. It will also allow organizations to recognize and capture the impact of work with 'high-demand' families on the communities in which they live.

The community dimension

Recognizing the significance of community can first be considered from its effect on the recipient of the service. Communities are the context; they are part of the story of the service user's life. As such, they are filled with actors in the story who can serve to constrain an individual's development. What the community expects of people is a powerful factor. Potentially, the community has the power and resources to support rather than constrain an individual's development. However, they need to be involved in that individual's story (and the service delivery). There is something 'real' about individual engagement with those that live around you; something that is often missing from the lives of the most vulnerable, who find themselves isolated within a neighbourhood, rather than part of a community. The case for engaging the local community in providing sustainable and local support has been made by the research: more needs to be done to promote the use of peer support: volunteers from the community (including local parents) who are trained to work alongside professionals, but whose similar life experiences bridge the 'approachability gap' (C4EO 2010: 4). Taylor and Swann (2009: 22) endorse this point:

> The demand for public services is bottomless if people assume that the state rather than their family, friend or neighbour is the first and natural source of support. So we look for better ways to help households and communities become self-confident and self-reliant.

A second argument for involving the community comes from considering the indirect beneficiaries of the work. Community members deserve to know how the services they pay for (through taxation) are being deployed in the area that they live. Setting aside the perennial issues of data protection and confidentiality for one moment, let us consider how transparent the majority of our services for children and families are, particularly those we could call high-demand. If the problems in such families have an impact on the surrounding community, should that community also be party to the services introduced to solve them? This community dimension was explicit and central to the ethos of Sure Start Local Programmes.

This offers a tremendous opportunity to reconnect the public at large, in a political sense, with the services that could transform the quality of life for those living around them. Performance management could reflect the impact work with high-demand families has on those among whom they live. Evidence of this kind of impact was gathered in the Westminster FRP's area where there was a 69 per cent reduction in crime and disorder offences. A survey of neighbours found that two-thirds were either satisfied or very satisfied with the collaborative response of the police and the council (Local Government Leadership and Westminster City Council 2010).

We should recognize the role that the media has in shaping the attitudes of those in communities to some high-demand service users. Negative reporting that focuses on 'slivers' of reality (e.g. specific incidents of substance misuse or problem parenting) is unhelpful. For high-demand families, these 'slivers' are factors in a complex array of issues for the individual, significant others within and around the family, and the community context in which the individual is embedded. A more responsible and responsive approach by the media might have an impact on community opinion and response. The underside of 'problem families' might evoke a more caring community reaction to the mother abused by her teenage children, the victims of domestic violence, young carers, those scapegoated by neighbours, drowning in debt, made ill by inadequate housing. By acknowledging and appreciating the complexity, contextualization and dynamism of these issues they can be reframed: substance misuse as a symptom of unmet mental health needs and an environment devoid of support; problem parenting as the result of an inability to manage the competing demands of financial and relationship pressures, and so on.

The child is not (necessarily) at the centre

A key success in engaging parents in the Westminster approach in its family recovery project was having a key worker focused on the adults in the family being worked with. It has often been difficult for children's practitioners to engage adult practitioners fully when working with families. Here, organizational structures and dominant logics can often represent a barrier. I recall one interchange between a child health practitioner and a manager of a local community safety partnership in early discussions to construct a new team to work with 'high-demand' families. The child health practitioner, almost unconsciously, used the phrase, 'of course, the child is at the centre'. The response to this from another professional was, 'Well, for me, the child is not at the centre, and never will be.' This is extreme, and was said with a level of irony, but it illustrates that there is a tension between those parts of our professional identities that are inextricably linked to our organizations' dominant logic (child focus and adult focus respectively) and the professional identities that we inhabit when working this way. Experience shows that it is difficult for practitioners by themselves to break through such powerful dominant logics. Perhaps organizational redesign can assist in this area. By thinking along the lines of family 'touchpoints', points at which members of the family (adult or child) interact with the services of collaborative partners, opportunities to acquire information, support or intervene multiply.

Another learning point from Westminster, was that the adults in families responded well to being treated as 'adults in their own right' and not as 'parents'. Adults who are parents also have other roles to fulfil, perhaps as parents to other, older children, as workers, as carers to elderly relatives, or more problematically as addicts or patients. What is needed is not only professionals embracing the challenge to become joint problem-solvers with these families, but also for their parent organizations to evolve in a way that will recognize and unlock their capabilities. C4EO's findings about successful early intervention: 'repeatedly demonstrate the importance of engaging parents in a collaborative approach, building on their strengths and taking account of their views and experiences. They highlight the need to recognise the problems that families themselves often face and to develop strategies that build confidence and capacity to enable parents to properly fulfil the crucial role they play' (2010: 5–6). Thus we might conclude that working with adults 'as adults' is a key component of a systemic and collaborative approach organizations must take in working with high-demand families.

Implications for practice and practitioner learning

As organizations delivering children's services begin to evolve along the lines described here, what are the implications for those working on the front line? In his research on managers, Watson (2001) argues they need to learn 'how they should be' and 'how they need to be', with regard to the specific cultural demands of their context or workplace. The implication of this is that organizational dominant logics will have a big impact in shaping workers' self-identity and relational issues. Watson describes a process of 'conflict, compromise and resolution' where the existing sense of self, and behaviours are incompatible with information about the new environment/ situation. This is a process which sometimes is not wholly resolved, but continues to manifest itself as a tension that is resolved in small steps as individual situations arise. It seems reasonable to suggest that as organizations evolve their dominant logics and collaborations in refocusing on targeted groups, that these individual conflicts over self-identity will feature strongly.

Work with high-demand families, involves engaging with many members of the family, adult and child, and perhaps significant individuals in the community who form part of the family's 'ecology'. This requires skill in engaging and negotiating with all these individuals. The professional 'role' of any one practitioner is likely to be redefined in each family, in line with its unique needs and its unique ecology. This has implications for the content and quality of supervision and line management of such workers.

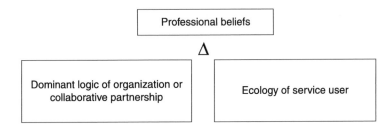

Figure 2.1 The evolution of professional identity

Figure 2.1 depicts a central triangle, representing the evolution of professional identity, and in turn, the evolution of procedural knowledge of working with targeted groups developed through a three-sided relationship between an individual's professional beliefs, the dominant logic of an organization or collaborative partnership and the ecology of the service user.

REFLEXIVITY CHECK-IN POINT

Do any of the following questions affect you personally or professionally?

- How do organizational dominant logics impact on the professional identity of practitioners and managers?
- To what extent will collaborative service design overcome the difficulties that frontline professionals face in working interprofessionally?
- How 'fit for purpose' is the children's workforce to work with adults in high-need families?
- How will community-based work affect practitioner identity and professional learning?

References

Anning, A., Cottrell, D., Frost, N., Green, J. and Robinson, M. (2006) *Developing Multi-professional Teamwork for Integrated Children's Services: Research, Policy and Practice.* Maidenhead: Open University Press.

Atkinson, M., Jones, M. and Lamont, E. (2007) *Multi-agency Working and Its Implications for Practice: Review of Literature.* Reading: CfBT Education Trust.

Barratt, M. (2004) Unveiling enablers and inhibitors of collaborative planning. *The International Journal of Logistics Management,* 15: 73–90.

C4EO (2010) *Grasping the Nettle: Early Intervention for Children, Families and Communities. Executive Summary.* London: C4EO.

DfE (2010) *Redesigning Provision for Families with Multiple Problems: An Assessment of the Early Impact of Different Local Approaches.* London: HMSO.

DfES (2004) *Every Child Matters: Change for Children (Common Core of Skills and Knowledge for the Children's Workforce)*. Nottingham: DfES Publications.

DfES (2005) *Championing Children: A Shared Set of Skills, Knowledge and Behaviours for Those Leading and Managing Children's Services*. London: HMSO.

Frost, N. (2005) *Professionalism, Partnership and Joined Up Thinking*. Dartington: Research in Practice.

Gajda, R. (2004) Utilizing collaboration theory to evaluate strategic alliances. *American Journal of Evaluation*, 25: 65–77.

Horwarth, J. and Morrison, T. (2007) Collaboration, integration and change in children's services: critical issues and key ingredients. *Child Abuse and Neglect*, 31: 55–69.

Huxham, C. (1996) Advantage or inertia? Making collaboration work In R. Paton, G. Clarke, J. Lewis and P. Quantis (eds) *The Managing Care Reader* (pp. 238–54). London: Routledge.

Kasl, E., Dechant, K. and Marsick, V. (1993) Internalizing our model of group learning. In D. Boud, R. Cohen and D. Walker (eds) *Using Experience for Learning*. Buckingham: Society for Research into Higher Education and Open University Press.

Local Government Leadership and Westminster City Council (2010) *Repairing Broken Families and Rescuing Fractured Communities*. London: Local Government House.

Peterson, N.L. (1991) Interagency collaboration under part H: the key to comprehensive, multidisciplinary, coordinated infant/toddler intervention services. *Journal of Early Intervention*, 15: 89–105.

Pisano, G.P. and Verganti, R. (2008) Which kind of collaboration is right for you? *Harvard Business Review, The Magazine*, December.

Porter M.E. (1980) *Competitive Strategy: Techniques for Analysing Industries and Competitors*. New York: The Free Press.

Prahalad, C.K. (2004) The blinders of dominant logic. *Long Range Planning*, 37: 171–9.

Prahalad, C.K. and Bettis, R. (1986) Dominant logic: the elusive linkage between diversification and performance. *Strategic Management Journal*, 7: 485–501.

Schön, D.A. (1983) *The Reflective Practitioner: How Professionals Think in Action*. New York: Basic Books.

Siraj-Blatchford, I. (2009) *Improving Development Outcomes for Children Through Effective Practice in Integrating Early Years Services*. London: C4EO.

Taylor, S. and Swann, P. (2009) Ten key lessons from the Total Place pilots. The online management journal for local authority business (23 November). London: Local Government Association, pp. 22–3.

Thomson, A.M. (1999) *AmeriCorps Organizational Networks: Six Case Studies of Indiana AmeriCorps Programs*. National Service Fellows Program. Report for the Corporation for National Service, Washington, DC: Corporation for National and Community Service.

Thomson, A.M., Perry, J.L. and Miller, T.K. (2007) Conceptualizing and measuring collaboration. *Journal of Public Administration Research and Theory Advance Access*, 19(1): 23–56.

Todeva, E. and Knoke, D. (2005) Strategic alliances and models of collaboration. *Management Decision*, 31: 1–22.

Watson, T.J. (2001) The emergent manager and processes of management pre-learning, *Management Learning*, 32(2): 221–5.

3

LYN TRODD
From a professional to an interprofessional?

Introduction

This chapter serves as a framework for the chapters that follow. It problematizes the notion of professions and a professional. The meanings of the terms 'profession' and 'professional' are significant because they, and terms derived from them, carry expectations that influence professionals, employers, governments and clients. Both constructs are used loosely, frequently and sometimes prescriptively. Although their meaning is usually taken as understood and obvious in everyday life, at the same time the nature of the two constructs continues to be debated in a large, established field of academic discourse. In this chapter recurring dimensions of the constructs are highlighted in order to identify expectations and assumptions that influence professional identities. It also discusses influences on our understanding of 'profession', 'professional' and related terms in order to identify the established discourses framing expectations of professional behaviour. It begins to explore the kind of professionalism and principles and values needed in new evolving roles in the Children's Workforce in the twenty-first century, themes that are exemplified in the chapters that follow. A number of tensions between professionalization and work roles in the Children's Workforce are identified. One of these is 'strategic non-compliance' where members of a values-based profession resist external control exercising professional agency to determine how to work and how to define themselves as professionals. A revised conceptualization of professional autonomy is offered and the recent concepts of 'democratic professional' (Oberhuemer 2005), 'activist professional' (Sachs 2001, 2003b), 'dialogic professional' (Rinaldi 2006) and the 'worker as researcher' (Moss 2006) are considered. Finally, a new construct of an 'interprofessional' is proposed.

Profession?

Although it is one of those terms in common parlance that everyone understands in their own way, it has proved impossible to agree on a definition of a 'profession'

(Squires 2001). There is a 'folk concept' of 'profession' (Becker 1970) which adds confusion to the difficulties of arriving at a precise definition of its meaning. Becker argues that, in his view, a 'profession' is a symbol used in several ways by a range of people and groups, each with different motivations. However, he is willing to acknowledge one consistent characteristic – that a profession is seen as 'honorific'. This perception offers us an explanation for the current widespread use of the words, 'profession' (and 'professional') to convey 'good' in the sense of being consistent or of high quality or trustworthy.

In the past the defining characteristics for the early model of professions were probably based on the medieval guilds, the learned professions of the clergy, doctors and lawyers. One of the key features was that the professions were self-regulating (O'Day 2000) and so set and enforced guidelines for those who could enter the profession and also those who should be disbarred because their work did not meet the required standards (Freidson 1984). Thus acceptance as a member by a professional body was crucial to gaining professional status just as exclusion from it due to 'misconduct' usually barred the ex-member from holding professional status and therefore practising legitimately. In this way the professional bodies tried to preserve the respect, privilege and credibility derived from membership by exerting discipline over their members' behaviour and limiting the general understanding of outsiders about the way their practices and services work (Harding and Taylor 2002). Goode (1957: 199) explains that 'colleague criticism is rarely permitted before laymen, and the professions justify the rule by asserting that such criticism would lower the standing of the profession in the larger society'. By protecting positive expectations of the professions and passing on their exclusive knowledge and values to new members, professional bodies ensured that entrants were guaranteed respect, privilege and credibility.

Early academic studies of the professions identified lists of 'traits' to distinguish them from other occupations. Dingwall (1976: 331) called the lists of 'traits' 'the attributes approach'. The approach was founded on the belief that it was both possible and desirable for a 'profession' to be clearly defined. Clarity would enable strict control over who was and who was not in a profession and thus maintain its exclusivity so that each profession could uphold the high market value of the benefits derived from membership (Atkinson and Delamont 1990).

There are recurrent similarities in lists of the attributes of a profession. Abraham Flexner's view was that six traits set professions apart from other groups of workers.

[They] involve essentially intellectual operations with large individual responsibility; they derive their raw material from science and learning; this material they work up to a practical and definite end; they possess an educationally communicable technique; they tend to self organization; and they are becoming increasingly altruistic in motivation.

(Flexner 1915: 156)

Approximately 50 years later, Millerson (1964) noted a range of 23 traits being used to define the term 'profession' in academic literature. As incidences of these definitive lists of traits proliferated, the use of such a checklist of characteristics was seen as a credible process to evaluate the potential or actual professional status of groups of workers. An example is the following list used by Rice and Duncan (2006) to consider whether ergonomics workers belonged to a profession or not. A profession is an occupation whose members share the following ten common characteristics (Freidson 1970; Argyris and Schön 1974; Rice and Duncan 2006).

1 Prolonged specialized training in a body of abstract knowledge.
2 A service orientation.
3 An ideology based on the original faith professed by members.
4 An ethic that is binding on the practitioners.
5 A body of knowledge unique to the members.
6 A set of skills that forms the technique of the profession.
7 A guild of those entitled to practise the profession.
8 Authority granted by society in the form of licensure or certification.
9 A recognized setting where the profession is practised.
10 A theory of societal benefits derived from the ideology.

An obvious problem with the 'attributes approach' to describing and identifying a profession is that it relies on a backward-looking analysis of the characteristics of established professions which means that, at any one time, it may not fully reflect the current realities of professions, be responsive to change or inclusive of new professions. The earlier examples of the 'attributes approach' are not out of step with wider social values and beliefs. The existence and value of professions as a beneficial part of society have remained largely unquestioned. George Bernard Shaw's famous definition of the professions in Act One of the *Doctor's Dilemma* as 'a conspiracy against laity' (1906: 36) was not the generally respectful and accepting view of the professions that was typical of his era or in the intervening years. In Western culture the words 'profession' (and 'professional') tend to be imbued with respect and exclusivity and 'the concept of "professional" in all societies is not so much a descriptive term as one of value and prestige' (Hughes 1958: 44). Writing about teachers, Popkewitz's (1994) list of accepted characteristics of a profession are: an autonomy of practice, an exclusive knowledge base, occupational control of rewards, a *'noble work ethic'* (emphasis in original). Dent and Whitehead (2002: 1) define the 'trusted' professional in a similar vein: 'The professional was someone trusted and respected, an individual given class, status, autonomy, social elevation, in return for safeguarding our well-being and applying their professional judgement on the basis of a benign moral or cultural code.'

There is a theme to these positive views of professions and they are typical of how professions are conceptualized as mixture of objective traits but also aspirational and subjective qualities such as having a 'noble work ethic', 'safeguarding our well-being' and being 'honorific'. Functionalists accept this kind of valorization of professions and professionals because they view the professions as providing an essential, beneficial function to society that keeps it functioning in equilibrium. The exclusivity of the professions rations success in society and thus plays a part in maintaining its stability. Talcott Parsons (1954: 34), a leading functionalist, writes: 'It seems evident that many of the most important features of our society are to a considerable extent dependent on the smooth functioning of the professions.'

According to Parsons (1939: 460), the defining feature of a profession is what its members know and do: 'A professional man is held to be "an authority" only in his own field' and the authority of the professions is based on 'functionally specific technical competence' (Parsons 1939: 460) and not on social status. In Parsons's view the authority of an individual member of a profession has a mandate because his or her expertise involves knowing the best interests of the client and is applied with 'disinterestedness' (1939: 458) or objectivity. He reflects this view in his own list of the attributes of a profession:

1 Formal technical training, including especially an intellectual component, in an institutional setting that certifies quality and competence.
2 Demonstrable skills in the pragmatic application of this formal training.
3 Institutional mechanisms to ensure that this competence and skill will be used in a socially responsible way.

(Parsons 1968: 541)

It is interesting that, even though Parsons (1954: 48) thinks that 'our received traditions of thought' that differentiate between professionals and non-professionals on the basis of altruistic motivation and egotistic motives involve a false dichotomy that is simplistic, he still finds himself underwriting the construct of a profession with trust, as well as functional knowledge and competence. While arguing that this focus on altruistic and egotistic motives obscures other important elements of the meaning of 'profession', Parsons argues for an alternative version of professional 'trust' based on the qualities of reliability and consistency, rationality (evidence-based thinking), universalism (knowledge and skills applied according to rules or standards that are applied generally) as well as the functional specificity and disinterestedness he sees as distinctive in a profession (Parsons 1939). Both the 'attributes approach' and functionalism illustrate a discourse where qualities of being honorific and trustworthy with a consistent service ethic have become part of the expectations of professional behaviour of professionals and clients alike.

Functionalists like Parsons and his academic peers do not question the power base or rights of the trusted professions but are focused on their role in maintaining society and their position in its structure. As such, Parsons's work is often criticized because it has no sense of resistance to 'mainstream' values or dissent and tends to ignore social conflict and change. In common with the rest of society, functionalists are uncritical when expounding the narratives that described and legitimized the evolution and status of professions. Similarly, they ignore the gap between the rhetoric and ideology of professions about trustworthiness and the service ethic on one hand, and the reality of the ordinary, human self-interestedness of many professionals on the other.

Challenging 'our received traditions of thought' about professions in different way to Parsons, Eraut uses the word 'ideology' to propose that the professions and professionals and their exclusivity and power are not to be taken for granted. He argues that: 'three central features of the *ideology* of professionalism are a specialist knowledge base, autonomy and service' (Eraut 1994: 223, emphasis in original). Eraut's use of the word ideology suggests a system of ideas about professions that corresponds to the needs and aspirations of professionals and professional bodies as well as other parties who have a vested interest in them. At the same time, the term ideology suggests that this system of ideas derives from the political, economic, or social system of which the professions are a part. Although Parsons and Eraut both recognize the concept of profession as embedded in a system of thinking linked to the needs of society, an important difference is that Parsons does not see the need to challenge the place of professions, while for Eraut, viewing a profession as ideological raises questions about whose interests professions serve and their likelihood of being outmoded.

While the 'attributes approach' and functionalist perspective, which have dominated discussions of the professions for many years, remain influential, in recent years there has been evidence of more criticality and suspicion of the professions and the power they hold that would have pleased George Bernard Shaw. 'Benign and "attributional" models of the professions have lost some of their appeal, among both academics and the wider public. Examples of demonstrable corruption or ineptitude on the part of some certified professionals have become more widely publicized' (Geison 1983: 5). Geison explains why there is growing awareness in society of the gap between the valorization of professional ethics and codes of practice and the motivations and fallibilities of the members of professions.

Some members of the public see professions as exercising undue social control over others, being unresponsive to change, guarding their specialized knowledge from those outside the profession, using jargon to mystify their work, putting the interests of the profession above those of the client or user and resisting being held to account. Perhaps this explains why there continues to be a move towards making the professions more accountable. Some professions, however, such as solicitors, have attempted to resist accountability from outside by developing a separate, detailed rule book about the behaviour of members to ensure that the requirement to be honorific and trusted is explicitly expressed, while at the same time trying to establish clearer criteria to be used in judging whether a member of the profession should be 'struck off' (disbarred).

While some professions seek to preserve their identity and standing by codifying their expectations of members, some professional bodies themselves challenge the traditional views of the professions. The Royal College of Physicians, for instance, one of the professional bodies that has fiercely guarded the medical profession in the past, reports: 'The idea that a profession is a bounded group – bounded by a discrete body of knowledge, a monopoly of service, autonomy over conditions of work, and a unique code of ethics – is outdated' (2005: 21). Although the Royal College of Physicians' view demonstrates consciousness that much of the thinking about the professions is out of step with current realities, in one way it aligns its views with Parsons's 'functionally specific technical competence' (1939: 460) as the key to the identity of a profession in the current context. In the view of the Royal College the possession of specific competences and expertise may be the best way to distinguish members of today's professions especially when members are required to work in *interprofessional* partnerships with other professionals.

Geison (1983: 6) also argues that the existing constructs of a 'profession' fail to mirror the diversity and range of what is seen:

> There is, in fact, good reason to suspect that all of the existing models of professions and professionalization are inadequate to some degree and in some respects. Whether they conceive of professionalization as the emergence of benign, apolitical, 'non-economic,' and homogeneous 'communities of the competent,' or whether they see it as a conspiratorial, stratifying, and exploitative process in tune with the needs of capitalism, the existing models are simply unable to account for the richly diverse forms and distribution of professional groups as we meet them in actual historical experience.

In recognition of the disconnection between the traditional models of the professions and current experiences of them, McCulloch et al. (2000) argue against an attempt to capture an agreed definition of a profession. They do not go as far as Hanlon (1998) who represents recent sociological thinking about a profession as whatever people think it is at any particular time, but argue for a 'profession' to be seen as socially constructed, responsive and pliable. McCulloch et al. propose that different conceptualizations should arise in response to changing expectations for professional groups. For these authors the nature of a particular profession 'represents judgements that are specific to times and contexts' (2000: 6).

If it is the case that the term profession does not describe any particular set of commonalities, agreed Weberian ideal type (Weber 1904) or one definitive, generic construct of 'profession', there is room for members of each occupational group to contribute to the construction of their own unique, self-defined and situated, and therefore meaningful and workable construct of profession. This may shift the focus of professionals, academics and professional bodies onto *differences* within and between professions, not uniformity and compliance. A substantial shift of perspective that questions traditional expectations of a profession for groups of workers in the Children's Workforce may be enabled. There is a chance for such groups to construct their own professional identities in relation to, but not in imitation of, other professions and therefore establish new concepts of 'profession' and 'professional' that fit with the current demands for interprofessionalism in work with children and their families.

In this chapter in response to problems arising from traditional expectations of professionalism, the terms 'interprofession' and 'interprofessional' are suggested as a means of describing a new stance in which professions and professionals cross and bridge boundaries rather than create them. An interprofessional pays attention to working with others in order to promote the best possible life chances for children and their families using creativity, self-awareness and empathy to do so. Work on new thinking about professions and professionals is already underway: in the next part of the chapter, recent constructs of democratic, dialogic and active professionalism and workers as researchers are considered as examples of active, questioning and responsive approaches to being a 'professional'.

Professional, professionalism and professionality?

Earlier we noted that there are long-standing issues with constructs of a profession. It tends to be unrealistic and outmoded but virtually unchallenged in wider society and vague in common usage. The construct 'professional' is even more problematic. Defining it has proved so difficult that Watson (2002) suggests substituting the phrase – relating to an 'expert occupation' or 'knowledge-based occupation' – for the term 'professional'.

The word 'professional' holds at least three meanings. Used as a noun it can mean someone who belongs to a profession, but alternatively it can mean someone who is paid for their services, that is, in contrast to an amateur. Used as an adjective it describes behaviour that is appropriate for a member of a profession, implying that all professions share a unifying code of behaviour and ethics which, of course, as we have seen, they do not. A doctor, for example, is bound by the Hippocratic Oath as in 'What I may see or hear in the course of treatment or even outside of the treatment in regard to the life of men, which on no account one must spread abroad, I will keep myself holding such things shameful to be spoken about' (Edelstein 1943). However, a social worker knows that promises of confidentiality to clients are curtailed by his or her code of practice and the constraints of child protection law. Although codes of practice and professional ethics are different among professionals, other types of controls on their behaviour and performance exist that are similar. Freidson (1994, 2001) argued that a unique form of occupational control of work is professionalism and Evetts's (2003: 411) view is that professionalism can be seen as both a 'normative value system' and an 'ideology of control'.

Recognizing views such as these as situated in Western epistemologies, Carlina Rinaldi (2005) problematizes some of the dualities that influence the concept of a 'professional' and recognizes some of the systems of thought shaping it. For example, in arguing for her proposal of a dialogic professional, which we discuss later, she draws attention to perceived dichotomies such as between mind and body; academic and vocational learning; and masculine and feminine discourses that shape more traditional concepts of a professional. Applying these dualities to the professionalism of practitioners working with children draws parallels and connections between audit-based professionalism and the value system of the 'rational male professional' in contrast to the values-based professionalism of the 'caring female non-professional'. It suggests that there is likely to be a tension in the recent process of professionalization (by the state) of practitioners who work with young children who are mainly women. Professionalization by the state may require these new professionals to reject qualities associated with feminine discourses in Western culture such as intuitive responses, informality and expressiveness in order to be perceived as full professionals. Etzioni (1969) gives an example of the strong and enduring gender discourse that describes a powerful view of the teacher as a nurturing, maternal figure which in his view has ensured that teaching remains a semi-profession. This tension noted by Etzioni and identified by Rinaldi adds a further dimension to our analysis of what profession and professional might mean for people working in newly devised roles with children.

Professional and professionalism

In everyday use professionalism is seen as the conduct, expertise, competence or skill that characterizes or identifies a profession or professional person and the set of values, behaviours, and relationships that underpins the trust they are given. While this professionalism sustains the recognition and status bestowed upon professions or professionals by society, it also controls them and can be imposed rather than emerging and developing from within a profession. Whitty and Wisby (2006: 44) identify the increasing control of the professions by the state, 'now a major stakeholder in defining professionalism in modern societies', and the 'professional mandate' or kind of bargain that professionals have struck with the government of the day that is granted by the state rather than assumed as an inalienable right by members of a profession. Whitty and Wisby describe this as 'steering at a distance' (2006: 46).

Both managerial professionalism and audit-based professionalism cede control to external agencies, mainly the state. Clarke and Newman (1997: 78, 80) describe a 'managerial professionalism' as, 'accountable, it has rules and outcomes and it is still continuing to be written. It is as if professionalism is being written by governments because the trust that was afforded to "gut" feeling can no longer be trusted.' Judyth Sachs (2003) characterizes managerial professionalism as 'management is the answer to everything', 'only the private sector provides the best model of practice' and where the professional must take up their designated role in 'contributing to the school's formal accountability processes' (Brennan 1996: 22). The 'audit based professional' is legitimated by the call for 'quality' (Dahlberg et al. 1999, 2007; Urban 2005). According to Dent and Whitehead (2002) the move to 'audit-based professionalism' requires that trust, credibility and respect are earned by professionals, not acquired through status, qualifications, expertise or traditional expectations. The work of an 'audit-based professional' is evaluated when it is measured through outcomes achieved against performance indicators and objective external criteria (Furlong 2003). This works as a mechanism to hold professionals in agencies and organizations involved in the education and care of children to account by measuring progress and performance and enforcing a regulatory framework for all work with them. Woods and Jeffrey (2002: 105) describe the effect of audit-based professionalism on teachers as: 'From a notion of the "good teacher" based on personal qualities, the emphasis is now on teacher competencies, such as subject expertise, coordination, collaboration, management and supervision.'

Managerialism and audit-based professionalism sit uneasily with the professional autonomy which many studies have identified as the defining feature of being a professional, both in the mind of the incumbent and also in the mind of society (Hall 1968; Hoyle and John 1995; Freidson 2001; Dent and Whitehead 2002; Atkinson 2003; Furlong 2003). Apart from having the specialized knowledge base and ethical basis for action referred to earlier, the traditional concept of a professional is that the professional is expected, and expects, to work with autonomy and independence. Katz (1985), for instance, is one of many writers who view autonomy as an expectation of a professional. She includes autonomy in her list of eight criteria of professionalism in the field of working with young children. The idea associated with autonomy is that lengthy specialized training validates professionals to be able to use their discretion in the relevant area of expertise and to be trusted to behave altruistically in the best interests of the client and society and thus their autonomy is justified. Inevitably expectations of professional autonomy may cause conflict when professionals work in organizations that try to standardize or change their ways of working. In fact, while professionals may 'police' themselves on a day-to-day basis, the reality is they have always been broadly held to account by clients, colleagues and their professional body (Freidson 2001). Commenting on Hoyle and John's (1995) list of knowledge, responsibility and autonomy as the three traditional dimensions of professionalism, Furlong notes a dynamic of destabilization of perceptions of 'professionalism' arising from tensions and challenges. He argues that 'The questioning of one has led progressively to the questioning of the others' (2003: 16–17).

In terms of professional autonomy, then, existing models of professional and professionalization do not match current experiences. However, another way to conceptualize professional autonomy is to see it as choosing the values and principles by which decisions and actions as a professional are taken and being aware of the process of learning from experiences as well as an ability to make critical judgements (Chene 1983). An autonomous professional has the capacity, freedom, and responsibility to make choices concerning his or her own way of working. Autonomy can be seen as the ability to determine what is right and wrong for oneself rather than independence in decision-making. Among Children's Centre Leaders the phrase 'strategic non-compliance' defined by Campbell et al. (2003: 680) as 'the thoughtful and selective application of medical advice rather than blind adherence to it' is used to describe dilemmas where professional autonomy, as defined earlier, is needed and decisions are taken using their professional expertise and local insight rather than following established practice guidelines or external directives.

The development of autonomy through learning is a theme of Mezirow's (2000) transformative learning. Mezirow argues that learning that facilitates greater awareness of the influences on one's own thinking by developing the capacity to reflect critically on the lenses we use to filter, engage, and interpret the world, encourages autonomous thinking. According to Mezirow, becoming more autonomous is an aim and outcome of transformative learning. He suggests that transformations occur in four possible ways: by elaborating existing frames of reference; learning new frames of reference; transforming points of view and transforming habits of the mind. Thus autonomy, for Mezirow, is being able to be self-directed and more emancipated from the influence of one's assumptions, beliefs and cultural context because one is more aware of them. However, this book argues that narrating one's own professional values and practices to oneself and others facilitates professional autonomy and interprofessional working and constructs one's professional identity or interprofessional identity.

The new interprofessionals?

In recognition of this mismatch and the tensions and conflicts arising from it, there have been a number of attempts to define what kind of 'profession', 'professional' and professionalism fits with current work with children and their families that is 'specific to times and contexts' (McCulloch et al. 2000: 6). Oberhuemer (2005), for instance, proposes a 'democratic professional' for those working in the field of early childhood education and care. Oberhuemer characterizes the democratic professional as a reflective practitioner who deals with complex situations and relationships and who recognizes and acknowledges adults and children alike as social agents who are 'participating in constructing and influencing their own lives' and who forges 'partic-ipatory relationships and alliances and foregrounds collaborative, cooperative action between professional colleagues and other stakeholders . . . engaging and networking with the local community.' (2005: 13). Democratic professionals portray and commu-nicate their work openly and have an inclusive attitude to entry into their profession. They are participative in their approach to others and strive to engage and empower clients, community and colleagues (Preston 1996) rather than comply with the rules that govern the discourse – in this case the discourse of professionalism and the 'closed shop' protectionism of the traditional construct of professional. A democratic professional recognizes and resists the 'regimes of truth' and power 'inscribed' in everyday reasoning (Foucault 1980). He or she opens up opportunities for debates, encourages others to ask questions rather than accept received traditions of thought and encourages critical thinking in their area of work.

The democratic professional has some similarities with Hoyle's (1980) concept of extended professionality in which professional work is placed in a wider context, is collaborative and also explores the theory of practice and engages in professional development. Evans argues that this type of position is more fundamental than a mere variety of the more traditional professional. Her view is that it represents 'an ideo-logically-, attitudinally-, intellectually-, and epistemologically-based stance on the part of an individual, in relation to the practice of the profession to which s/he belongs, and which influences her/his professional practice' (2002: 6–7).

There is a thread in the chapters that follow that explores the agency of profes-sionals themselves in the process of the construction of their professional identity. The authors of the chapters narrate stories of agency in their negotiation, generation and shaping of practices that matter to them and crucially how they share control over the meanings and practices of the professional community in which they are invested. They do not invoke an 'unencumbered self' one who, with adequate knowledge, is free and independent, entirely self-determining (Sandel 1984), nor a 'sovereign self', the self as independent, isolated free-agent thinking and acting independently of any and all influences (Richardson et al. 1998). Anderson's (1996) description of the 'activative' individual is closest to the meaning of professional agency threaded through these chapters. Anderson (1996: 90) defines the activative individual as 'an artful co-conspirator who materializes collective resources of action in local and partial performances within the realm of his or her own agency'. He sees agency as 'dialogic participation' (1996: 91). In his concept of agency the self is neither a unity nor a fixed entity. It comes into being in action developing ontological and personal dimensions of the construct of professionality as well as professional expertise which he sees as composed of reflective craftsmanship (relevant knowledge and skills) and mastership (qualities and dispositions) which define a profession's identity.

As an idea linked to the democratic professional, Judyth Sachs also foregrounds agency as key in professionalism. She proposes the construct of 'activist professionals' (Sachs 2001, 2003b: 181) who are moving from being 'victims of change' to being 'agents of change' (Johnson and Hallgarten 2002). Day and Sachs (2004) see opportu-nities for a practitioner in a changing role to be encouraged to find ways of repositioning his or her professional identity and professionality and believe that this can be best achieved in a collaborative culture and in the spirit of democratic professionalism.

Moss, however, goes further than Sachs and rejects the traditional construct of 'professional' entirely. He argues that it is 'bordered and exclusionary' (2006: 38) and tainted with its old values. He questions whether it can ever be cleansed of its disempowering characteristics so he proposes a new construct of 'worker as researcher' whose values are 'border crossing, uncertainty, subjectivity and inclusionary democratic practice' (2006: 38).

While Moss eschews the construct of professional entirely, Rinaldi (2005: 126) proposes the 'dialogic professional' in her search for a viable professional identity for practitioners working with children and their families. The construct of dialogic professional draws on thinking from Vygotsky (1962), Dewey (1916) and Mead (1962) that social interaction and active participation in learning and thinking are crucial. Rinaldi's much quoted depiction of the ethics of an encounter by a dialogic professional (below) proposes that active listening, responsiveness to others and respect for their autonomy are key qualities of professional behaviour and essential features of professionalism. For Rinaldi, professionalism is

> built on welcoming and hospitality of the Other – an openness to the difference of the Other, to the coming of the Other. It involves an ethical relationship of openness to the Other, trying to listen to the Other from his or her own position and experience and not treating the Other as the same. The implications are seismic for education.
>
> (2005: 15)

The open-hearted, outward-facing version of professionalism proposed by Rinaldi offers a sharp contrast to that of a professional as a member of an (exclusive) 'community within a community' engaged in self-protectionism (Goode 1957).

The dialogic professional echoes the educational and political work of Paolo Freire (2000) and offers a way to reconceptualize the professionalism of such practitioners. Rinaldi sees the dialogic professional as a new way of working with children and their families. Like Moss's 'worker as researcher', Rinaldi's (2005) 'dialogic professional' researches and co-constructs meaning, identity and values but does it always in relation to others. Rinaldi views the research element of her construct as a stance or attitude with which the professional makes sense of life and creates meanings from his or her experience. For Rinaldi's dialogic professional there are opportunities to learn in change and uncertainty:

> [Uncertainty is a] quality that you can offer, not only a limitation . . . You have to really change your being, to recognise doubt and uncertainty, to recognise your limits as a resource, as a place of encounter, as a quality. Which means that you accept that you are unfinished, in a state of permanent change, and your identity is in the dialogue
>
> (2005: 183)

Rinaldi sees the value of recognizing one's own knowledge as partial and under construction as one questions dominant discourses and power relations and argues that it needs to be part of the way that the dialogic professional makes sense or meaning from their experiences.

These reconceptualizations of 'professional' constructed by Oberhuemer (2005), Sachs (2001, 2003), Moss (2006) Rinaldi (2006) and others and the notion of an 'interprofessional' proposed earlier in this chapter have arisen because of a perception that the received construct of the traditional 'closed-shop' professional does not accord with either the subjective self-conceptualization associated with the role or professional reflexivity or working practices required by health professionals, educators, social workers and the other professionals working with children and families in current UK contexts. This is because a closed-shop approach to being a professional is at odds with the interprofessional ontology and principles of current practice.

The constructs of 'democratic professional' (Oberhuemer 2005), 'activist professional' (Sachs 2001, 2003b), 'dialogic professional' (Rinaldi 2006) 'worker as researcher' (Moss 2006) and 'interprofessional' conceptualize professionals as actively constructing their professional identity. In the following chapters authors make explicit some of the influential discourse about professionalism that surrounds professionals working in interprofessional roles such as Children's Centre Leaders and problematize behaviours, knowledge, skills and understanding linked to traditional versions of professional practice, in order to engage in that construction as well as to contribute to a vocabulary and rationale for change.

REFLEXIVITY CHECK-IN POINT

Do the following affect you personally or professionally?

- What makes you *feel* like a professional?
- Have you ever been aware of professional exclusivity (your own and that of others) getting in the way of high quality work with and for children?
- What makes you feel like an interprofessional? When and how does it occur?

References

Anderson, J.A. (1996) *Communication Theory: Epistemological Foundations*. New York: The Guilford Press.

Argyris, C. and Schön, D. (1974) *Theory in Practice: Increasing Professional Effectiveness*. San Francisco, CA: Jossey-Bass.

Atkinson, L. (2003) Trusting your own judgement (On allowing yourself to eat the pudding) in T. Atkinson and G. Claxton (eds) *The Intuitive Practitioner*. Maidenhead: Open University Press.

Atkinson, P. and Delamont, S. (1990) Professions and powerlessness. *Sociological Review*, 31: 90–110.

Becker, H.S. (1970) *Sociological Work: Method and Substance*. New Brunswick, NJ: Transaction.

Brennan, M. (1996) Multiple professionalism for Australian teachers in the information age? Paper presented at the annual meeting of the American Educational Research Association, New York, April.

Campbell, R. et al. (2003) Evaluating meta-ethnography: a synthesis of qualitative research on lay experiences of diabetes and diabetes care. *Social Science and Medicine*, 56: 671–84.

Chene, A. (1983) The concept of autonomy in adult education: a philosophical discussion. *Adult Education Quarterly* 34: 38–47.

Clarke, J. and Newman, J. (1997) *The Managerial State*. London: Sage.

Dahlberg, G., Moss, P. and Pence, A. (1999) *Beyond Quality in Early Childhood Education and Care: Postmodern Perspectives*. London: Falmer.

Day, C. and Sachs, J. (eds) (2004) *International Handbook on the Continuing Professional Development of Teachers*. Maidenhead: Open University Press.

Dent M. and Whitehead, S. (2002) *Managing Professional Identities*, London: Routledge.

Dewey, J. (1916) *Democracy and Education: An Introduction to the Philosophy of Education*. New York: Macmillan.

Dingwall, R. (1976) Accomplishing profession. *The Sociological Review* 24: 331–49.

Edelstein, L. (1943) *The Hippocratic Oath: Text, Translation, and Interpretation*. Baltimore, MD: Johns Hopkins University Press.

Eraut, M. (1994) *Developing Professional Knowledge and Competence*. London: Falmer Press.

Etzioni, A. (ed.) (1969) *The Semi-professions and Their Organization*. London: Collier-Macmillan.

Evans, L. (2002) *Reflective Practice in Educational Research*. London: Continuum.

Evetts, J. (2003) The sociological analysis of professionalism: occupational change in the modern world. *International Sociology*, 18: 395.

Flexner, A. (1915) Is social work a profession? *Research on Social Work Practice*, 11: 152–65.

Foucault, M. (1980) 'Body/Power' and 'Truth and Power', in C. Gordon (ed.) *Michel Foucault: Power/Knowledge*. London: Harvester.

Freidson, E. (1970) *Profession of Medicine: A Study of the Sociology of Applied Knowledge*. New York: Dodd, Mead.

Freidson, E. (1984) The changing nature of professional control. *Annual Review of Sociology*, 10: 1–20.

Freidson, E. (1994) *Professionalism Reborn: Theory, Prophecy and Policy*. Cambridge: Polity.

Freidson, E. (2001) *Professionalism: The Third Logic*. Cambridge: Policy Press.

Freire, P. (2000) *Pedagogy of the Oppressed*. New York: Continuum.

Furlong, J. (2003) Intuition and the crisis in teacher professionalism, in T. Atkinson and G. Claxton (eds) *The Intuitive Practitioner*. Maidenhead: Open University Press.

Geison, G.L. (ed.) (1983) *Professions and Professional Ideologies in America*. Chapel Hill, NC: University of North Carolina Press.

Goode, W.J. (1957) Community within a community: the professions author(s). *American Sociological Review*, 22: 194–200.

Hall, R.H. (1968) Professionalization and bureaucratization. *American Sociological Review*, 33(1): 92–104.

Hanlon, G. (1998) Professionalism as enterprise: service class politics and the redefinition of professionalism. *Sociology*, 32: 42–63.

Harding, G. and Taylor, K. (2002) Power, status and pharmacy. *The Pharmaceutical Journal*, 269: 440–2.

Hoyle, E. (1980) Professionalization and deprofessionalization in education, in E. Hoyle and J. Megarry (eds) *World Yearbook of Education 1980*. London: Kogan Page, pp. 42–57.

Hoyle, E. and John, P. (1995) *Professional Knowledge and Professional Practice*. London: Cassell.

Hughes, E.C. (1958) *Men and Their Work*. Glencoe, IL: The Free Press.

Johnson, M. and Hallgarten, J. (eds) (2002) *From Victims of Change to Agents of Change: The Future of the Teaching Profession*. London: Institute for Public Policy Research.

Katz, L. (1985) The nature of professions: where is early childhood education? in *Talks with Teachers of Young Children*. New Jersey: Ablex Publishing Corp.

McCulloch, G., Helsby, G. and Knight, P.T. (2000) *The Politics of Professionalism*. London: Cassell.

Mead, G.H. (1962) *Mind, Self, and Society from the Standpoint of a Social Behaviorist*. Chicago, IL: University of Chicago Press.

Mezirow, J. (2000) *Learning as Transformation: Critical Perspectives on a Theory in Progress*. San Francisco, CA: Jossey-Bass.

Millerson, G. (1964) *The Qualifying Associations: A Study in Professionalisation*. London: Routledge and Kegan Paul.

Moss, P. (2006) Structures, understandings and discourses: possibilities for re-envisioning the early childhood worker. *Contemporary Issues in Early Childhood*, 7(1): 30–41.

Oberhuemer, P. (2005) Conceptualising the early childhood pedagogue: policy approaches and issues of professionalism. *European Early Childhood Research Journal*, 13(1): 5–16.

O'Day, R. (2000) *The Professions in Early Modern England (1450–1800)*. Harlow: Pearson.

Parsons, T. (1939) The professions and social structure. *Social Forces*, 17, 4: 457–67.

Parsons, T. (1954) *Essays in Sociological Theory*. New York: The Free Press.

Parsons, T. (1968) Professions, in D. Sills (ed.) *International Encyclopedia of the Social Sciences*. New York: Macmillan Company and The Free Press, pp. 536–47.

Popkewitz, T.S. (1994) Professionalisation in teaching and teacher education: some notes on its history, ideology and potential. *Teaching and Teacher Education*, 10: 1–14.

Preston, B. (1996) Award restructuring: a catalyst in the evolution of teacher professionalism. In T. Seddon (ed.) *Pay, Professionalism and Politics*. Melbourne: ACER.

Rice, V.J. and Duncan, J.R. (2006) What does it mean to be a 'professional' . . . and what does it mean to be an ergonomics professional? Available at http://www.ergofoundation.org/FPE1_Professionalism.pdf on 23rd May 2010.

Richardson, F.C., Rogers, A., and McCarroll, J. (1998) Toward a dialogical self. *American Behavioral Scientist*, 41: 496–515.

Rinaldi, C. (2005) *In Dialogue with Reggio Emilia*. London: Routledge.

Rinaldi, C. (2006) *In Dialogue with Reggio Emilia: Listening, Researching, and Learning*. New York: Routledge.

Royal College of Physicians (RCP) (2005) *Doctors in Society: Medical Professionalism in a Changing World*. Report of a Working Party of the Royal College of Physicians of London. London: RCP.

Sachs, J. (2001) Teacher professional identity: competing discourses, competing outcomes. *Journal of Education Policy*, 16: 149–61.

Sachs, J. (2003a) Teacher professional standards: controlling or developing teaching? *Teachers and Teaching: Theory and Practice*, 9: 175–86.

Sachs, J. (2003b) *The Activist Teaching Profession*. Buckingham: Open University Press.

Sandel, M. (1984) *Liberalism and Its Critics*. New York: New York University Press.

Shaw, G.B. (1906) *The Doctor's Dilemma*. London: Penguin.

Squires, G. (2001) Management as a professional discipline. *Journal of Management Studies*, 38: 473–87.

Urban, M. (2005) Quality, autonomy and the profession, in H. Schonfeld, S. O'Brien and T. Walsh (eds) *Questions of Quality*, Dublin: Centre for Early Childhood Development and Education.

Vygotsky, L.S. (1962) *Thought and Language*. Cambridge, MA: MIT Press.

Watson, T. (2002) Professions and professionalism: should we jump off the bandwagon, better to understand where it is going? *International Studies of Management and Organization*, 322: 93–105.

Weber, M. (1904) *The Protestant Ethic and the Spirit of Capitalism*. London: Routledge.

Whitty, G. and Wisby, E. (2006) Moving beyond recent education reform and towards a democratic professionalism. *Hitotsubashi Journal of Social Studies*, 38: 43–61.

Woods, P. and Jeffrey, B. (2002) The reconstruction of teachers' identities. *British Journal of Sociology of Education*, 23: 89–106.

PART 2

Learning

4

ANNE RAWLINGS AND PATY PALIOKOSTA
Learning for interprofessionalism: pedagogy for all

Introduction

Until we begin to provide training where students, children's workforce practitioners, strategic managers, teachers, researchers, social workers, nurses and 'new' professionals in the emerging children's workforce can learn, work and draw upon a wide range of perspectives together, becoming and being an interprofessional will be difficult to achieve. These different perspectives can present many opportunities for multi-professional, multi-disciplinary approaches to be studied and used as ways forward for the development of knowledge, skills and understanding, both about childhood (birth to 19 years) and about high quality learning and teaching.

The learning and teaching should encompass continuing professional development and multi-professional, interprofessional practice to inspire, refresh and extend an expanding learning community. It should bring contemporary work with children and young people into close focus, and stimulate inspirational resonant leaders and managers of the future. Part of becoming and being an interprofessional is the notion of belonging. A sense of identity and feeling of belonging, whether it is in a family, learning community or profession can build supportive and trusting relationships which enable effective learning to take place. This includes building an environment where risks can be taken, mistakes can be made and achievements are celebrated. If this is what we try to achieve with the people we work with, there is certainly scope for this practice to be modelled in our own practice.

Holistic learning for a transformative workforce

The issue of learning to be an interprofessional for the children's workforce has become an even more pressing matter of public and governmental concern following a number of highly publicized child protection cases. The combined impetus of the *Every Child Matters Agenda* (2003a) and the Integrated Qualifications Framework (IQF), supplemented by the proposals of the *Laming Review* (Laming 2009) regarding mandatory training for children's services managers to contribute to a policy climate in which the demand for education and learning in interprofessional practice at all levels is very likely to increase. *Championing Children* (CWDC 2005) highlights seven aspects of management and/or leadership, all but one of which map directly onto either the NHS Leadership and Management Standards or the refreshed Common Core of Skills and Knowledge (refreshed CWDC 2010) for the front-line children's workforce.

This chapter will investigate ways of supporting practitioners in the children's workforce to be life-long learners rather than adhering to their known learning and experience, as this can be limiting and isolating for their personal and professional development in a rapidly changing workforce; a workforce that will work with children, young people and families in the context of a holistic and informed pedagogy. At Kingston University our years of experience of working with a variety of work-based learners indicates possible areas that need to be addressed to equip practitioners with the tools for creativity, leadership and confidence in a new transformative workforce.

REFLEXIVITY CHECK-IN POINT

Do any of the following affect you personally or professionally?

- Overcoming and dealing with fear of the unknown.
- Understanding our own and others' values and beliefs that other people may impose on roles and responsibilities.
- Feelings of bereavement for old, safe roles and responsibilities.
- Denial that leads to no action as a way of being, which can result in a limiting professional identity.
- Having to respond to the overwhelming elements of constant change.
- Limited opportunities for exposure to wider learning communities.

Policy context

When we are approaching policy, we consider looking at the notion of levels or scales. The term 'scales' (Swyngedouw 1996; Uitermark 2002, quoted in Blommaert 2006) is a metaphor of the levels in which social events and processes move and develop on a continuum of layered scales, with the strictly local (micro) and the global (macro) as its extremes and several intermediary scales (e.g. the level of the State) in between (Lefebvre 2000; Geertz 2004, cited in Blommaert 2006). There is a certain degree of conflict identified between the beliefs, intentions and orientations of policy makers and those of practitioners (Garner 2006), which creates confusion and often disengagement on behalf of the practitioners at the local level. The confusion is greater when the practitioners or professionals at the receiving end do not necessarily share the same cultures, contexts and rituals or the same perception about what constitutes their professional boundaries in working with others.

The *Every Child Matters Green Paper* (DfES 2003b: 51) refers to the need to begin 'integrating professionals through *multi-disciplinary* teams responsible for identifying children at risk, and working with the child and family to ensure services are tailored to their needs'. This led to the creation of the Integrated Qualifications Framework, which supported the vision of having 'one children's workforce' and the culture of integrated working, in which the common core of skills and knowledge was embedded. The interesting point here is that this 'new' workforce emerges from a wide range of professionals whose training and experience do not necessarily have common elements. Members of this workforce are asked to sit together in the context of 'Team Around the Child' meetings and make decisions about babies', children's and young people's lives. What practitioners were faced with were expectations that were also strengthened after the latest *Laming Review*, (Laming 2009) without a conceptual preparedness in the context of multi-agency interagency working or joined-up working.

It would be worthwhile at this point to try and approach some definitions around the different ways that multi-professionalism is referred to. According to Lloyd et al. (2001; cf. Barrow et al. 2002) interagency working involves more than one agency working together in a planned and formal way, rather than simply through informal networking either at strategic or operational level. Multi-agency working on the other hand implies more than one agency working with a client but not necessarily jointly. It may be prompted by joint planning or simply be a form of replication resulting from a lack of proper interagency co-ordination. Often the terms 'interagency' and 'multi-agency' (in its planned sense) are used interchangeably.

Lloyd et al. (2001; cf. Warmington et al. 2004) go on to define joined-up working, policy or thinking as referring to deliberately conceptualized and co-ordinated planning that takes account of multiple policies and varying agency practices. This has become a totem in current UK social policy.

The distinction between 'interprofessional education', 'interprofessional learning' and 'interprofessionality' made by the Centre for Interprofessional Practice in Education (CAIPE 1997) may be more useful for the purpose of this chapter. 'Interprofessional Education (IPE) is: occasions when two or more professions learn with, from and about each other to improve collaboration and the quality of [service]'. And, interprofessional learning is 'the process through which two or more professions learn with, from and about each other to improve collaboration and the quality of service'. Moreover interprofessionality is 'an education and practice orientation, an approach to care and education where educators and practitioners collaborate synergistically' (d'Amour and Oandasan 2005: 10).

At policy level 'joined-up' working is promoted as a 'self-evident good' but strategy and operation both remain problematic (Allen 2003; Puonti 2004, cited in Warmington 2004). There are certain complexities in relation to:

- professionalism and
- multi-professionalism.

Issues relating to professionalism

Freidson's (1994: 10) uses the following definitions:

> I use the word 'profession' to refer to an occupation that controls its own work, organized by a special set of institutions sustained in part by a particular ideology of expertise and service. I use the word 'professionalism' to refer to that ideology and special set of institutions.

This could be seen as a more 'old school interpretation' of professionalism and would certainly raise issues in relation to 'ideology', 'expertise' and 'service' by a 'special set of institutions'. How are all the above interpreted in different contexts, such as early years settings and is there such a homogeneous set of institutions? There was an attempt to address this lack of homogeneity in the introduction of the 'one children's workforce' as an effort to recognize common ideologies and skills among professionals involved with babies, children and young people.

This recognition can heighten awareness of their professionalism for a group of practitioners, such as Early Years practitioners, who do not necessarily think highly of their profession or who believe others do not hold their profession in high esteem. According to Hargreaves and Hopper (2006) practitioners have identified a correlation between high reward and respect and low external control to describe a high status profession. Early Years is characterized by low reward and respect and high external control. Practitioners who participated in their study explained that they felt undervalued by others with little recognition of their skills:

> Our people management skills, our communication skills are undervalued by people in other professions . . . we are exceptionally good leaders and managers that other professions could learn from but we always seem to be the poor relation in that regard, I think.
>
> (Hargreaves and Hopper 2006: 176)

This lack of recognition by others has created a historical undermining of the Early Years profession and has imposed barriers to effective participation of Early Years practitioners in wider decision-making. This has established a practice of exclusion of Early Years practitioners that affected their confidence as managers of change.

Issues relating to multi-professional practice

This historical exclusion has isolated practitioners who then face the fear of the unknown when expected to act in the context of multi-professional practice. As mentioned earlier in relation to professionalism, ideology, expertise and service are important themes to investigate when looking into people's responses in the context of their profession and even more so in the context of multi-agency work. This requires understanding our own and others' values and beliefs that may be imposed on roles and responsibilities. Ideology covers a set of aims that may direct goals, expectations and direction.

Ideology has an impact on the way people create and understand their own identity and there are certain dilemmas stemming from this understanding. In the context of multi-professionalism, Rose (2009) identifies tensions are created between an individual's specialist expertise and knowledge and their wider knowledge that exceeds their professional boundaries. Is carrying a mix of experience, knowledge and approaches enhancing or reducing to a professional? The type of identity created in this context often causes insecurity to professionals (Leadbetter 2006) who are unsure about the way they perceive themselves in relation to how others perceive them.

'Sharing disciplinary expertise and changing status can be threatening to professional identity, particularly when such knowledge exchange would enable another professional to undertake your own role or require you to take on another professional's role.' (Abbot et al. 2005; Robinson et al. 2005; Leadbetter 2006; Frost and Robinson 2007, cited in Rose 2009: 4). In addition to the issues arising in relation to expertise, the concept of territory and the power this can generate also presents concerns. Losing power that may have been taken for granted for a long time may cause feelings of bereavement for old and safe roles and responsibilities and/or denial that leads to inaction as a way of being. This may result in a limiting professional identity. Power is also expressed through practitioners' linguistic repertoire, which can be characterized by particular discourses relating to the specific area of practice. Discourses and terminologies used by other professionals can be alienating due to lack of understanding of particular terms relating to expertise.

Examining the topic from a different perspective, the need for a new professional role, along the lines of the 'social pedagogue' or 'animateur' found in large parts of Western Europe and Scandinavia could be envisaged. Education in this context is much more than schooling, rather it is based on a fundamentally holistic concept of children and adults wherein teachers concentrate on teaching but not in isolation. The well-being of the whole person is the focus of high status occupations that combine elements of teaching, social work, child-care and counselling (Whitney 2007). Under this umbrella, different types of social pedagogues, some behaving like conventional teachers, others more like social workers, therapists or nursery nurses, are employed in schools and other educational settings. Arguably, the UK response to this paradigm has been the advent of the 'Early Years Professional'. The recent Cambridge Primary Review (2009) also highlighted the importance of extending the Early Years values and curriculum as underpinned by the Early Years Foundation Stage (DfES 2000) to the next stages in learning and development. Ideally, commonly shared values will be enhanced by the development of and use of a shared language and understanding in relation to reconceptualizing interprofessional working.

A holistic concept in practice cannot just happen naturally. It will require interprofessional learning that could take place in many different formats and would promote collective preferences. Such interprofessional learning was considered by Gilbert (2001) as a tool that encompasses shared purposes, joint responsibility for and commitment and finding ways to explore strategies for progress.

> This perspective assumes, therefore, that individuals in interaction develop commitments and a sense of shared responsibility for the group's goals and outcomes.
>
> (Rose 2009: 2)

Collective preferences are enacted when:

- the group prefers and intends to achieve the best outcome for the group; or
- the individual acts as a part of the group to achieve this outcome.

Daryl Maisey's chapter in this book discusses that while different professions may appear to be collaboratively working on child protection issues, a closer examination suggests that boundaries and the limitations of assessment tools and communication systems make it difficult for effective interprofessional practice to take place. As Marcia Daigo Daly stated in a CWDC presentation (December 2007) 'working with children, young people and families, should not be designed around professional boundaries'.

Successful interprofessional teaching and learning can work in the landscape of multi-agency working when professional knowledge and expertise are recognized and enhanced by collaborative work on joint projects and responses to complex problems. The authors of this chapter are involved in a pilot project ensuring that Early Years work-based undergraduates at Level 6 and social care and community nurse students at Level 7 have the experience of working collaboratively on joint projects. This enables dialogue about professional standards and generates knowledge and understanding of the priorities of professions other than their own. Student evaluations indicate that this approach to teaching and learning is always valued highly by students.

One of the many learning challenges facing practitioners and students is the ever-changing complex landscape of interprofessional working. For example, a 'real-time' vignette on a safeguarding issue was written for approximately 90 students to work on together as one of the joint training sessions in the pilot project (2009). This shared learning opportunity provided insights into assumptions and preconceptions about each other's knowledge, understanding and expertise of the different professionals involved. The exposure to different underpinning values and beliefs in a shared learning context raised awareness not only of the variation but also more importantly the potential for compatibility among those professionals. Exposure to the multi-layered discourses illuminated the need for a shared, non-diagnostic language for effective communication. This does not mean that the autonomy of the professional should be diffused. However, a flexibility of attitude is encouraged as part of the integrity found in different disciplines. This can then enable reasonable adjustments to the emerging needs of young children and families in an ever changing social and political context.

REFLEXIVITY CHECK-IN POINT

Do any of the following affect you personally or professionally?
   Much discussion and interrogation took place as a result of the vignette on:

- resources, who to go to for relevant information;
- notions of 'what is a professional' as the 'Early Years Professional' was an unrecognized status by most of the group aside from those that were working towards the status;
- who was accountable for what and to whom;
- limitations of tools of assessment;
- where does the responsibility lie for action;

- too much overlap and repetition on child development assessments by Early Years practitioners and social care workers. Neither group knew what each profession did in enough detail and were shocked at how much their work overlapped;
- where the actual boundaries lie;
- who should be responsible for completing the Common Assessment Framework (CAF) and where the Lead Professional (LP) responsibilities begin and end;
- lack of 'joined-up thinking and practice'.

These discussions resonate with the results that were found in Daniels et al.'s report *Learning in and for Interagency Working* (2008) which aimed to contribute to understandings of the interprofessional learning necessary to provide joined-up responses to complex problems. The emerging picture of knowledge and understanding being developed in the pilot sessions described earlier is important in re-conceptualizing and understanding interprofessional practice. However, these sessions only happen once a year for each group. What has emerged through discussion and consensus since the pilot project began, is that teaching and learning needs to begin with young people coming out of school with 'A' levels. Until interprofessional teaching and learning are embedded in training for all the professions at an early stage, progress will be slow. A vision for the future might be a four-year undergraduate degree, where those wishing to work with children and young people will have a common foundation year where they experience 'taster' sessions of different professions as well as develop a strong network of people who aspire to work together to improve the lives of children. They will develop a deep knowledge and understanding of each other's core values and expertise. The value of the above is confirmed by the *Learning in and for Interagency Working* report (Daniels et al. 2008) where participants of the study recognized that articulating the particularities of their own expertise and values in order to negotiate practices with other professionals was a basis for questioning them. Enhanced forms of professional practice arose from questioning how values-driven practices might be reconfigured in relation to other professionals. This can lead to enhanced ability to recognize and value professional identity, develop a generic relational language, higher order empathetic thinking and communication systems that promote a positive organizational climate, where informed decisions can be made for the best outcome (see Box 4.1). Figure 4.1 shows aspects of holistic learning.

Box 4.1 The 'FAIR Framework' for looking at the core values for interprofessional working

---

Fair: Regarding the welfare of all people as equally important and only treating people differently from each other if they have different needs.

Autonomy: Respecting the informed decisions of everyone, including the children and young people, about how they live and how others treat them.

Integrity: Integrating our actions with our values and stated objectives and doing our
utmost to achieve what we say we will do.

Results: By 'seeking the best results' we are aiming to minimize harm, and to be as
beneficial as possible, to everyone affected by our policies and actions.

Source: The authors of this chapter are grateful to R. Rowson for allowing them to use the FAIR
Framework developed in his book (Rowson 2006).

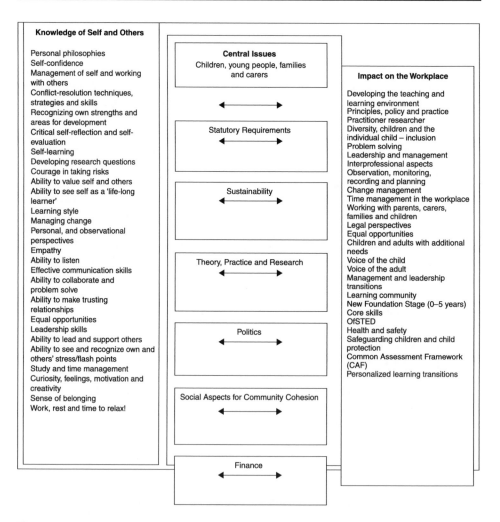

Figure 4.1 Aspects of holistic learning for a transformative workforce

Table 4.1 represents a small survey that was completed through Survey Monkey, an
on-line piece of software that is useful for gathering information quickly and effectively. The information is anonymous. The survey was available for three weeks. A link
and explanatory email was posted to local children centres, private, voluntary, state

Table 4.1 The occurrence of shared learning opportunities among different professional and identity trends

Type	Number of responses	Main role	Number having had interprofessional learning opportunities			Context in which they had them	Of those feeling that the way they work with others improved after that?			Of those stating they wanted more learning opportunities		
			Number	% Type	% All		Number	% Type	% All	Number	% Type	% All
Children's Centres	2	EY	2	100.00	3.77	CC 2	0	0.00	0.00	0	0.00	0.00
Independent	5	EY	4	80.00	7.55	LA 2 HE 1 Health care 1	3	60.00	5.66	3	75.00	5.66
Private Voluntary	9	EY 8 0–10 1	7	77.78	13.21	HE 2 LA 2 CC 1 Workplace 2	5	55.56	9.43	7	100.00	13.21
State	35	EY 8 Nursing 5 Primary 12 Secondary 6 Social Work 3 Health Visiting 1	24	68.57	45.28	CC 2 HE 10 LA 4 Workplace 7 DNA 1	19	54.29	35.85	24	100.00	45.28
Third Sector	2	Primary 1 Nursing 1	2	100.00	3.77	Workplace 1 LA 1	0	0.00	0.00	0	0.00	0.00
Total Responses	53											

and third sector settings where KU students are on current interprofessional courses. The aim was to identify the occurrence of shared learning opportunities among different professional and identify trends in relation to the context these opportunities were found. The practitioners were also given the opportunity to express a preference for further interprofessional learning.

It was evident that the majority of students embraced the opportunities they had in sharing and gaining knowledge from other professionals in the context of joint training. The instances of opportunities for shared learning in HE was significantly higher for practitioners who were in the state sector and their feedback was also very positive in relation to effects on practice. The responses of all groups are presented here. The question was 'What was the positive impact on your role?' and the following answer were reported.

- I was able to gain an insight into how their role was beneficial to the care that was being delivered.
- Being more professional.
- Encouraging the children to further develop and enhance skills and areas of development EYFS (2008).
- Working in partnership with parents/carers.
- Communication skills have strengthened.
- More confident working around colleagues, parents/carers/visitors.
- More knowledge about SEN children and needs needing to be met, etc.
- Planning for the class as well as planning for individual children has become more effective.
- More knowledge; understanding child development from another perspective; being able to put into practice in a more practical way; being more aware of early intervention for special needs.
- To be more positive in my role as a practitioner.
- Gaining an insight into the role they (nurses) play in terms of patient care, and seeing how both our roles combine to provide a continuity of care.
- Broaden my knowledge.
- Sharing knowledge.
- Working with many other professionals who share and have other areas of early years expertise. Training together with these professionals.
- It was part of CAF training and helped me to understand the various services available for families and how I can direct them to these. It also helped me to build links/contacts to help particular families with issues such as housing, benefits and law, custody etc. I really felt I could help or at least refer them on whereas previously I did not know where to go.
- Yes. I feel I have a better understanding of other professional roles and responsibilities as a result of shared learning and this helps to build links and in practice leading to a better service.

- The experience helped me to understand the work of other professionals, and gave me an insight into the challenges they faced in their work which I was not previously aware of.

- I completed a Teacher Link project where I worked in a school with a special unit for a week. This was a fantastic experience, working with children with diverse learning difficulties and a variety of practitioners: workplace, speech and language therapists.

- It is interesting to see what goes on but as I work with under-3s much is difficult to translate. I have a background in different agencies so am aware of many of the issues different professionals may face.

- I have gained an insight on how the other disciplines work and being able to apply my theory and knowledge.

- To explore others' experiences and ideas, to reflect upon and possible implement within my practice.

- It gave me a greater understanding of the differing roles.

- The children centre, although for the same age group, is aimed more at the nurturing side than the educational side that I come from working in a state-run nursery.

- Working together with other Early Years practitioners on the Foundation Degree enabled me to gain knowledge of other settings and ways of working. Also, sustained shared thinking broadened my knowledge base, reflective and evaluation skills. These have contributed to and, at times, changed the way I work with children, parents/carers and colleagues within my setting.

- I would like to build stronger links with the local schools to understand more about how teachers and key staff work, for example, the SENCo.

- Stage 1 and 2 helped me to advise parents as they often ask me questions about their children's future schooling. Also a broader understanding of tax credits and other financial support to families would be beneficial.

- As a student social worker I expect to continue to work and train within a multi-professional agency especially as I plan to work within a mental health team.

- Paramedics, social workers, physiotherapists, dieticians, play specialists and midwives.

- Social workers.

- Case Officers see the other side of the statementing process; observing 'panel' decisions; working with members from the LA – I am interested in some of the schemes in Surrey, such as 'the include me' project.

- Health.

- Social workers, paediatric health professionals.

- GPs, midwives.

- Multi-agencies and having a greater understanding of their roles to include the impact they have on the children's learning outcomes and vice versa.

- I would like opportunities to go out and see other practices to share best practice.

- Primary teachers, other early years workers who follow a specific philosophy, such as Montessori and Steiner, healthcare professionals (although I am originally a nurse, I enjoyed learning about occupational and speech therapists' work).

- It is important for everyone doing the social work degree to have experience of working with other disciplines. I am lucky to be based in such a multi-disciplinary team. However, others on the course are not. Also as social workers we have to liaise with lots of professionals to gather information.

- I currently work in a forensic community health setting which poses dilemmas for social workers who sometimes have a different perspective from their medical colleagues on the treatment and intervention of mental health disorders. Even within the placement setting, training seems not to be interprofessional, with all courses aimed at either/or rather than around good practice. I would like training in a shared environment with any other health professionals and with those in the education field so that there is a greater understanding or roles, responsibilities and of our shared interest in clients.

Comments made by the respondents in the above survey indicate that many are already working with other disciplines and agencies. Looking back and reminding ourselves of the definitions used to think about learning to become and being interprofessional, the respondents are mainly using 'occasions when two or more professions learn with, from and about each other to improve collaboration and the quality of [service]', rather than using a 'process' for learning. The comment made by the social work student exemplifies this aspect:

> It is important for everyone doing the social work degree to have experience of working with other disciplines, I am lucky to be based in such a multi-disciplinary team. However, others on the course are not. Also as social workers we have to liaise with lots of professionals to gather information.

It is essential to support learners to understand that a new discourse needs to be developed whereby the specifics of shared information are held by key members and joint decisions are made. The question for all who work with children, young people and their families is 'how can we work towards a shared identity in an increasingly complex interprofessional landscape, while at the same time taking into account the views and needs of stakeholders and users?' Interprofessional ethics and confidentiality become increasingly challenging in this environment.

Many universities have developed courses for interprofessional groups of students. However, most are within different disciplines, for example, nurses working with radiographers or teachers working with Special Needs schools. Few courses are delivered by cross-faculty teams to a group of students from different disciplines. According to Gilbert (2000: 224) 'One key problem identified is that of finding and co-ordinating time in professional curricula across disciplines.' Barr (2002) also suggests that interprofessional courses require small group experiences which are expensive and labour-intensive. It is our experience that members of staff need to have a strong commitment to interprofessional course work within and outside their own discipline as it is the interlinking where learning takes place. The Joint Education

Team (JET) conducted systematic reviews of interprofessional evaluations which indicate that interprofessional education and learning is only truly effective if it is through work-based learning. This type of interprofessional learning should be ongoing and part of a lifelong learning experience to be found in the context of communities of learning, whether it is in settings, LAs, clusters, schools or higher education colleges and universities.

REFLEXIVITY CHECK-IN POINT

Do any of the following affect you personally or professionally?
JET (2002) also found that programmes of professional learning should:

- have learning objectives that are valued by, and are clear to participants;
- be flexible enough to target generic content;
- be relevant to all participant professions;
- allow students to investigate discipline-specific issues and needs;
- allow specific project planning to be jointly negotiated by students;
- be accorded equal status with other course requirements through timetabling and assessment;
- give students adequate opportunity to gain feedback and to critically reflect on their interprofessional experiences;
- have content that explicitly studies the dynamics of interprofessional collaboration and teamwork.

Of the many complex learning issues arising around interprofessional practice which can sometimes produce fear, anger, confidence, happiness and success, it is crucial that we use the energy from these feelings to respond positively. Practitioners working with children, families and young people need resilience, good humour and ability to problem solve both in practice and learning to find positive ways to move forward in an ever-changing landscape, and as Rowson (2006) states, with fairness, autonomy, integrity and with the best results for children, young people and their families and carers, as this lies at the heart of decision-making. We leave you with this in mind just as the coalition government is making key decisions about Sure Start, CWDC and those that provide training and accreditation for its learners.

References

Abbot, D., Watson, D. and Townsley, R. (2005) The proof of the pudding: what difference does multiagency working make to families with disabled children with complex health care needs? *Child and Family Social Work*, 10: 229–38.

Allen, C. (2003) Desperately seeking fusion: on 'joined up thinking', 'holistic practice' and the new economy of welfare professional power. *British Journal of Sociology*, 54: 287–306.

Barrow, G. et al. (2002) *Multi-Agency Practice: Resources for Developing Provision in Schools and Other Organisations.* Morden: Dreyfus Training and Development.

Blommaert, J. (2006) Sociolinguistic scales. *BAAL Linguistic Ethnography Forum.* Unpublished paper.

CAIPE (Centre for Advancement and Interprofessional Education) (1997) Reference required.)

Cameron, C. and Petrie, P. (2009) 'Importing Social Pedagogy?', *Social Pedagogy in Europe Today* (ed.) G. Kornbeck, Europäischer Hochsdaulverlag, Bremen.

CWDC (2005) *Championing Children.* London: CWDC

d'Amour, D. and Oandasan, I. (2005) Interprofessionality as the field of interprofessional practice and interprofessional education: an emerging concept. *Journal of Interprofessional Care,* 19: 8–20.

Daniels, H., Gallagher, T. and Kilpatrick, R. (2008) *Learning in and for Interagency Working: Full Research Report ESRC End of Award Report,* RES-139-25-0100-A. Swindon: ESRC.

DfCSF (2010) *Common Core of Skills and Knowledge.* London: DfCSF.

DfES (2003a) *Every Child Matters Agenda.* London: DfES.

DfES (2003b) *Every Child Matters Green Paper.* London: DfES.

DFES (2000) Reference required.

Frost, N. and Robinson, M. (2007) Joining up children's services: safeguarding children in multidisciplinary teams. *Child Abuse Review,* 16: 184–99.

Garner, P. (2006) If it's not broken? A critical review of recent developments in behaviour management in England. Paper presented at the European Conference on Educational Research, Geneva.

Gilbert, M. (2001) Collective preferences, obligations, and rational choice. *Economics and Philosophy,* 17: 109–19.

Gramsci, A. (1971) *Selections from the Prison Notebooks of Antonio Gramsci* (ed. Q. Hoare and G.N. Smith) London: Lawrence & Wishart.

Hargreaves, L. and Hopper, B. (2006) Early Years, low status? Early Years teachers' perceptions of their occupational status. *Early Years,* 26: 171–86.

Joint Education Team (JET) (2002) *Learning and Teaching Support Network, Health Sciences and Practice from the Interprofessional Joint Education Team.* London: CAIPE.

Laming, L. (2009) *The Lord Laming Review: The Protection of Children in England – A Progress Report.* London: DCSF.

Leadbetter, J. (2006) Investigating and conceptualising the notion of consultation to facilitate multiagency work. *Educational Psychology in Practice,* 22(1): 19–31.

Lloyd, G., Stead, J. and Kendrick, A. (2001) *Hanging on in There: A Study of Interagency Work to Prevent School Exclusion.* London: National Children's Bureau/Joseph Rowntree Foundation.

Puonti, A. (2004) Learning to work together: collaboration between authorities in economic-crime investigation. PhD thesis, University of Helsinki.

Robinson, M., Anning, A. and Frost, N. (2005) 'When is a teacher, not a teacher?': knowledge creation and the professional identity of teachers within multi-agency teams. *Studies in Continuing Education,* 27/2: 175–91.

Rose, J. (2009) Dilemmas of inter-professional collaboration: can they be resolved? *Children & Society,* 25: 151–63.

Rowson, R. (2006) *Working Ethics: How to Be Fair in a Culturally Complex World.* London: Jessica Kingsley.

Warmington, P. (2004) Conceptualising professional learning for multi-agency working and user engagement. Paper presented to the British Education Research Association Annual Conference, UMIST, Manchester, 15–18 September.

Whitney, B. (2007) *Social Inclusion in Schools: Improving Outcomes, Raising Standards*. London: Routledge.

Further reading

Brown, S.D., Daniels, H., Edwards, A., Leadbetter, J., Martin, D., Middleton, D., Warmington, P., Apostolov, A. and Popova, A. (2009) Imaginary epistemic objects in integrated children's services. *Society and Business Review*, 4(1): 58–68.

Gasper M. (2010) *Multi-agency Working in the Early Years*. London: Sage.

Warmington, P., Daniels, H., Edwards, A., Brown, S.D., Leadbetter, J., Martin, D. and Middleton, D. (2005) *Interagency Collaboration: A Review of the Literature*. Bath: Learning in and for Interagency Working. Available at: www.education.bham.ac.uk/research/projects1/liw/publications.

5

UTE WARD

Mentoring interprofessionally: a concept of practice for peer mentoring in children's centres

Introduction

The last 20 years have seen considerable changes for staff members working with young children and their families in Early Years settings, health services, and social care. With the development of integrated children's services, multi-agency working, joint commissioning and co-location are expected everywhere; and each staff member working with young children has to embrace these concepts and adapt their practice accordingly. This is very demanding for individual workers as their responsibilities are changing and new professional roles emerge; and the expectations are high:

> [The new professionals] will need to be aware of the lessons learnt in the past but be open to change and willing to innovate as well. They will have to be able to work with colleagues from other professions and prepared to approach issues in an open-minded and developmental way. They will have to be comfortable with initial uncertainty and constant adjustment. They will have to be aware of their own and the wider picture. They will need to be well supported, mentored and have good opportunities for ongoing training and development.
>
> (Gasper 2010: 112)

This chapter will consider some barriers to effective multi-agency cooperation and explore how mentoring can improve cross-disciplinary working and contribute to professional development. We will explore how peer mentoring in particular can contribute to the development of and offer support to new professionals to help them meet these high expectations. Through comparing three established mentoring schemes we will gain an understanding of which elements support interprofessional working and develop a framework for a peer mentoring scheme in children's centres which supports the professional development of both mentee and mentor.

Multi-agency working: barriers and facilitating factors

Interprofessional, multi-agency and integrated working can take many forms. It some-times focuses on child protection but is also a key element of most other children's services; it reaches into adult services as well to offer holistic support for individual children, young people and their families. In spite of a strong commitment from profes-sionals and organizations to cooperate, we still hear about children and families who have not received the coordinated, joined-up support they need and on reflection we realize how complex and complicated the effective work across professional and organizational boundaries is. Increasing workloads, and limited resources are widespread problems but there are far more fundamental barriers to effective multi-agency working. Atkinson et al. (2005) identify the lack of knowledge and understanding of other professionals' roles as one of the barriers to multi-agency working; this can be made worse by disagree-ments over real or perceived overlaps in areas of responsibility. Even if professionals are clear about roles and responsibilities, the cultures in their organizations or teams can vary, leading to differences in practice. Atkinson and colleagues suggest a number of ways to overcome these barriers, for example, offering training to enhance the know-ledge and understanding of other agencies; creating opportunities for regular dialogue; and open lines of communication between agencies and professionals.

In a mixed group of professionals, teamwork is enhanced when they perceive each other as having equal status. Molyneux (2001) also found that it takes a particular type of person to engage in effective multi-disciplinary work – adaptable, flexible, open, and willing to share with others. In addition she highlights the need for staff members to feel confident in their own professional roles:

> [Laidler] wrote about the concept which she described as 'professional adulthood'. In her view, staff from different disciplines need to feel sufficiently confident in their own roles and in their own professional identity, in order to feel safe enough to share and defer their professional autonomy to work effectively together.
>
> (Molyneux 2001: 33)

If professional adulthood is required to give staff members the confidence to work effectively with other agencies, then it seems paramount that we establish good struc-tures for the development and learning of new professionals throughout children's services and especially for interprofessionals whose roles straddle different disciplines.

Peer mentoring

Although much has been written about mentoring, there is no unambiguous, generally accepted definition of the term and different authors highlight different aspects of the mentoring process. At the same time 'mentoring' and 'coaching' are sometimes treated as synonymous, sometimes as fundamentally different. For some authors mentoring is focused on the achievement of long-term goals rather than more immediate perform-ance targets (Downey 2003). In the context of newly qualified teachers the mentoring relationship is based on a considerable difference in the mentor's and mentee's experi-ence, knowledge and skills (Wilkin 1992). Furlong and Maynard (1995) emphasize that the mentoring of teachers is strongly influenced by our understanding of the nature of teaching itself, which in turn is linked to the level of development and expertise of the mentee. To move towards a concept of mentoring for professional development in children's services Eric Parsloe's (1992: 31) definition of mentoring may provide a helpful starting point as it encompasses developing both professionally and personally: 'To help and support people to manage their own learning in order to maximise their potential, develop their skills, improve their performance, and become the person they want to be.' This suggests that mentoring is not directed by the mentor who decides what and how the learner learns. Here the mentee directs the development of his own learning, while the mentor supports and facilitates this. What the mentee wants to learn can vary greatly; it could be a practical skill or the mentee may want to explore why he finds meetings with colleagues in a partner organization very stressful.

Clutterbuck and Megginson (2005) offer a more detailed approach and describe mentoring and coaching as activities taking place in a developmental space with different dimensions (see Figure 5.1):

> *Doing* is about achieving change in skills or performance; *becoming* about changing one's ambitions, perspectives and sense of identity.
> *Extrinsic and intrinsic feedback* relate to who observes, analyses, interprets and owns an experience.
> *Future, present and past* relate to the chronology of change.
> (Clutterbuck and Megginson 2005: 6–7)

The aspect of 'becoming' in this model seems to resonate with Molyneux's concept of gaining professional adulthood (see above). Both are concerned with the

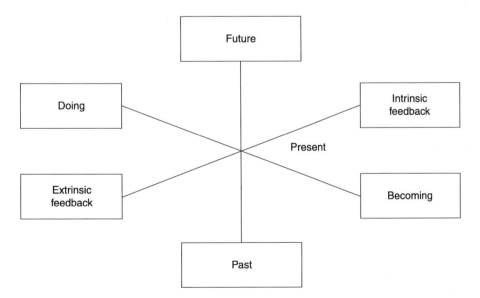

Figure 5.1 Dimensions of development space
Source: Clutterbuck and Megginson (2005).

development of a sense of identity, be it as a person or as a professional. We will come back to this and to Clutterbuck and Megginson's dimensions of developmental space later as they will help us to see the differences between mentoring schemes and gain an understanding of where to place a mentoring scheme for effective interprofessional working. However, before moving on, it is important to consider who could act as mentor, that is to say, support the learning of others.

In many children's centre teams it is the centre manager who fulfils this supportive role. In the context of mentoring to enhance interprofessional practice and to support multi-agency working, this arrangement may have some limitations. Although many managers have worked in different agencies and roles and are interprofessionals themselves, they are limited by their own professional heritage and experience. They can help the mentee to learn in general, to increase her knowledge and understanding of some different skills and roles, and to develop her professional identity (see above). However, managers may not be up to date with the practice in relevant partner organizations or have an in-depth understanding of all the agencies working in their area and their inherent professional cultures. Engaging mentors from other organizations therefore seems beneficial; it increases the range of knowledge and understanding available to mentees while enhancing open communication between professionals from different agencies and enables the shared exploration of different working practices. This dialogue can facilitate better working relationships and more effective multi-agency cooperation while also building a sense of professional identity.

The argument for colleagues or peers to mentor each other is further strengthened when considering the power differential between manager and worker and the impact this could have on the relationship. We explored earlier that multi-agency teams work best when members see each other as having equal status. This is mirrored in mentoring as Clutterbuck (2004) found that insight and trust are heightened when the partners in the relationship are of equal status. The support from a peer can also offer challenge from somebody who understands the work context and the mentee may be less concerned about being seen as lacking competence or struggling with the stresses of work. A peer mentor from a different organization or discipline can offer a new perspective on the issues and challenges in the mentee's work and stimulate discussion, learning and joint enquiry.

REFLEXIVITY CHECK-IN POINT

Does the following affect you personally or professionally?

Mentoring

Formal mentoring or coaching schemes are not yet very common in children's services but you often find colleagues mentor each other informally, for example, when supporting the induction process for a new staff member or when discussing how to extend a play activity to meet the needs of a particular child. How and when do you support the learning and development of your colleagues?

In addition to considering the benefits of mentoring for the individual and for the development of interprofessional and multi-agency working it is also important to consider whether there are benefits for the wider organization. We have already mentioned improvements in communication and a better understanding of roles and responsibilities; these support the individual as much as they improve the overall effectiveness of an organization. Mentoring can also increase staff retention, encourage the ethos of a learning culture, support the development of key competencies, consolidate organizational knowledge, and contribute to a healthier, more fulfilled and more productive workforce (Foster-Turner 2006). In times of change mentoring can help to retain focus, to develop new teams, and to adapt to new work priorities. Although the commitment of time and resources seems considerable, the potential benefits for both individuals and organizations are substantial.

We will now explore different peer mentoring schemes and reflect on their position within Clutterbuck and Megginson's (2005) dimensions of developmental space and what type of learning they support. We will look at whether the learning of the professionals from different backgrounds is mutual, and how relevant the schemes are to interprofessional development. This will lead to the development for a framework for peer mentoring in children's centres.

Case study 1: peer coaching at Blaise Primary School, Bristol

Blaise Primary School's coaching scheme developed out of their work within an education action zone. Peer coaching, which is used alongside specialist and expert coaching, is placed outside line management and performance management arrangements but seen as a considerable contributor to continuing professional development within the school:

> Peer coaching has been designed to be used to share practice between the staff. The school believes it is a powerful means of overcoming the isolation of teachers in their classrooms and of modelling for the pupils the principles of reciprocity, resourcefulness and resilience.
>
> The school keeps coaching observations quite separate from its monitoring and performance management systems. The purpose of any observation has to be made absolutely clear. For monitoring purposes, there is an observation form, but peer coaching is regarded as an equal, non-judgmental partnership with no status issues involved. Staff select their own focus for development.
>
> Peer coaching is also used as a means of embedding specialist knowledge and consolidating it in practice . . .
>
> The coaching cycle which they used involved:
>
> - choosing a focus;
> - identifying an approach to address it;
> - observing a lesson;
> - discussing what was seen; and
> - deciding on the next steps.

(Blaise Primary School 2005)

Although Blaise Primary School uses the term 'coaching' to describe their peer support scheme, which has a strong emphasis on skills development, it corresponds to some extent to Parsloe's (1995) definition of mentoring as teachers' learning is largely self-directed and the scheme helps them to enhance their skills and improve their performance. The scheme is firmly based in the education sector and focuses on the development of teachers only, which means it does not have a multi-professional aspect. However, some aspects of the scheme like reciprocity, mutuality and trusting, and non-judgemental relationships support good interprofessional working as they are based on mentor and mentee having equal status (see Molyneux 2001). The scheme also embraces many of the features Knowles (1970) outlined for effective adult learning, for example, self-directedness, immediate relevance of the learning, opportunities to apply new insights into practice, trust between teacher/mentor and learner/mentee, learning collaboratively rather than in competition with colleagues, and the recognition of the experience the learner brings to the learning situation. In addition to placing the mentoring relationship outside the school's accountability framework, the collaborative nature of the Blaise Primary School Scheme makes it non-judgemental and enables participants to express themselves freely and to explore those aspects of their work they are particularly interested in. The mutuality of the relationship and the shared enquiry approach make it difficult to place this on Clutterbuck and Megginson's (2005) extrinsic/intrinsic feedback dimension as it allows for both and benefits from either at different times and to varying degrees.

A comparable peer-mentoring scheme in a children's centre context which includes a cycle of observations and feedback would help colleagues increase their practical skills and their professional knowledge and understanding in addition to enabling shared professional enquiry as mentor and mentee work in the same environment. This is particularly useful when new staff members join a team or when an experienced staff member takes on new responsibilities. However, the strong skills focus does not give much scope for the discussion and exploration of underlying assumptions which would enhance the understanding of different professional cultures and practices. Neither is the development of the person considered in this mentoring relationship, for example, by exploring attitudes to pupils and young children, acknowledging anxieties, or discussing internal barriers to changes in working practice.

With reference to Clutterbuck and Megginson (2005), there is a greater emphasis on 'doing' than on 'becoming'. Although this approach could support greater understanding of roles and responsibilities and help to increase communication and dialogue, particularly if professionals from different agencies are invited to join, it may remain focused on practices, procedures and behaviours, rather than explore the underlying different professional cultures and assumptions. It seems based in the present, concerned with current practice rather than shaping and building the future.

Case study 2: NHS North West Mentoring Scheme

The NHS North West Mentoring Scheme was set up in 2004 by a group of strategic health authorities to support the development of leadership capacity with a view to enhancing innovation and integration of health services. It advocates peer mentoring across professional and organizational boundaries and welcomes the participation of members of the voluntary sector:

Mentors provide support in a variety of ways:

- They can help you to appreciate the value of your work.
- They can provide a critical element, to suggest other directions/widen your horizons/narrow you down to action.
- They can help you clarify, make checks and get things off your mind.
- They can enhance your capacity to make sense of and apply learning within the organisational context.
- They can enhance your ability to source new ideas and practices from outside the organisation and integrate them into it.
- They can offer the opportunity of network development across a broader spectrum than provided by your normal environment.

(North West Mentoring Scheme 2004, mentee information)

The scheme is voluntary, and mentees choose their mentors from those available within the scheme. The mentoring relationship is not part of the accountability structure, and ideally mentee and mentor come from different organizational and professional backgrounds. The goal setting for the mentoring relationship rests with the mentee although it is expected that they correlate to personal development plans and National Health Service strategies. Frequency and duration of mentoring sessions are arranged at mutual convenience.

The NHS North West Mentoring Scheme emphasizes discussion and learning across different professional and organizational boundaries which help staff members to broaden their knowledge and understanding of different work practices and to examine critically their own practice and its underlying assumptions. This will make multi-agency working, either in the health service or in a children's centre context, more effective as it explores and reduces the differences in the conceptualization of practice which act as barriers to collaboration (Easen et al. 2000). The dialogue at the centre of this mentoring scheme also supports the development of self-awareness and reflexivity, both of which can increase a sense of professional identity.

As mentor and mentee are not directly working together and as there is no element of observation and feedback, this scheme does not predominantly support the development of practical skills. Its strong focus on reflection and understanding of practice supports staff members' cognitive development by exploring the principles and values of their work, and by gaining new perspectives which can lead to improvements in practice and better outcomes. At the same time underlying assumptions are addressed with the potential to affect changes in attitudes and behaviour. There is also provision for the mentoring relationship to offer the mentee the space to acknowledge and reflect on the challenging nature of their work. This scheme is therefore much more engaged in the 'becoming' end of the doing/becoming dimension. It supports staff members to address issues in their current practice but also aims to build leadership capacity and to enhance the ability to change and innovate; it occupies a position between present and future in the developmental space.

Both mentee and mentor are seen as learners in this relationship. Although their development takes place in different areas (the mentee's beliefs and practice, the mentor's ability to support learning), there is scope for both professionals to learn about each other's practice, professional culture, and work-related challenges. The scheme sees the mentee setting the goals for the relationship and owning much of the learning experience through reflections on her/his own practice. However, there is also an expectation that the contents of the mentoring discussions links with personal development plans and overall organizational strategies in spite of placing the mentoring relationship outside the lines of accountability. This can limit the extent to which the mentee owns the process and directs his or her own learning. In the light of these contrary features it is difficult to place the relationship on the extrinsic/intrinsic feedback dimension. (It is important to note that the personalities of the mentor and mentee and how they arrange their relationship could allow for greater mentee-directed learning than may appear possible at first sight.)

As the scheme advocates reflective relationships where mentor and mentee are not working together on a daily basis, this could be an effective arrangement to support interprofessional learning in children's centres. The scheme is not dependent on observations, which gives greater flexibility in setting mentoring meetings, and should make it possible to bring staff members from various organizations together, for example, parent support advisers working in schools, Early Years staff from pre-schools and health visitors. Involving professionals from different agencies is particularly helpful for children's centres with small staff teams, who do not have a large skills mix or a number of different professional heritages among their staff members.

Case study 3: National Professional Qualification in Integrated Centre Leadership Mentoring Scheme

The National Professional Qualification in Integrated Centre Leadership (NPQICL) is a postgraduate qualification for children's centre managers. During the one-year course participants have access to three mentoring sessions (a total of seven hours). Mentors have experience of multi-agency working and many are or have been children's centre managers themselves. The relationship between mentor and mentee is one of peers based on equality, and on value and mutual respect regardless of roles, power or responsibility. It is outside line-management arrangements and separate from the course assessment processes. Mentoring encourages reflection and offers support towards goals the mentee identifies for her/himself in the work place and during the course. The scheme favours a stretching and non-directive approach to the mentoring relationship as described by Clutterbuck.

(National College for School Leadership 1999)

Mentoring support and reinforcement of NPQICL methodology (through reflection, dialogue, containment and challenge) encourages:

- deeper understanding of the complexity of multi-agency working
- application of the vision, values and principles of leadership

- exploration of participants' work practices and needs
- self-assessment of participants' effectiveness in the leadership role
- confidence-building activities
- clarification of goals and action-planning
- greater work–life balance
- authenticity through self-awareness and self-knowledge
- recognition of their own and others' reactions and responses in a range of situations
- integration of theory and practice
- opportunities to consider their leadership influence on the outcomes for children and families
- recreating such supportive and containing spaces for staff and families to reflect on their circumstances and needs.

(National College for School Leadership 1999: 3)

The National Professional Qualification in Integrated Centre Leadership mentoring scheme does not stress cross-professional aspects but children's centre managers work interprofessionally and are from a range of different backgrounds. Many mentors also work in children's services which means there is a mix of professional heritages and therefore some opportunity within the mentoring relationship to learn about different professional practices. In view of the fact that mentee and mentor do not work in the same area (organizationally or geographically), this scheme is less likely to encourage dialogue and communication between different professions in a particular community. To maximize the benefit of peer mentoring in a children's centre it seems desirable to pair mentors and mentees who work in the same community and whose teams or agencies have some contact with each other in addition to the mentoring relationship.

Both mentor and mentee are seen as learners in this relationship and can gain new insights during the discussion of practice or the exploration of dilemmas in leadership work. The mentee's learning is, however, focused on his own practice and self-awareness, while the mentor's learning also explores skills and attitudes regarding supporting the learning of others. In contrast to the two previous schemes, here the mentee cannot select his/her mentor; mentors are allocated by the course provider. This takes an element of choice away from the mentee; however, there is no consistent research evidence to indicate how mentor and mentee should be matched for the most effective mentoring relationships. Hale (2000) raises the following considerations when matching mentors and mentees:

- To support the development of the relationship between mentor and mentee, there should be some match in their value and belief system.
- The development needs of the mentee should be matched with the strengths of the mentor.
- A close match in learning styles and social type may lead to a comfortable relationship but may not offer much challenge or learning; while too much contrast in learning styles may lead to frustration and irreconcilable differences.

Gender and age are also factors to consider, as are status and position in the organizational hierarchy (Hale 2000). Even after careful consideration of needs and skills, personality type and learning style, mentor and mentee may still not be able to develop an effective learning relationship. Mentoring schemes should therefore have clearly defined processes to set targets, review progress and close relationships so that mismatches do not lead to a complete withdrawal from the mentoring process but to the selection of a more suitable partner.

Although the mentee does not choose his or her own mentor in this scheme, the relationship is owned by the mentee who decides which topics should be discussed. The mentor's role is to facilitate the mentee's analysis of and reflection on his/her own experiences. As this scheme does not involve workplace-based observations and as the relationship is mentee-directed, the mentoring here is firmly associated with intrinsic feedback. It aims to enhance and deepen the mentee's understanding of leadership issues, including underlying assumptions and principles, and his or her capacity to act as a leader. In addition, it encourages mentees to examine themselves. The reflections on the self, the mentee's reaction to events, his/her perceptions of others, and the resulting impact on decision-making form a central part of the mentoring sessions. In this scheme the mentoring relationship is therefore more concerned with 'becoming' than with 'doing'. At the same time it supports the development of the mentee's professional identity which in turn will enable him/her to operate more effectively in multi-agency contexts. Although current skills as a leader are important (present), the emphasis is on supporting the capacity to change and to shape the future.

The NPQICL mentoring scheme does not predominantly support interprofessional working but encourages the exploration of more fundamental features which contribute to the growth of professional maturity, and enhance leadership characteristics and behaviours. With its strong emphasis on increased self-awareness and reflective practice it can support the development of the new professionals needed in children's services and many of the scheme's aspects would be useful in a peer mentoring scheme for professional development in children's centres.

REFLEXIVITY CHECK-IN POINT

Does the following affect you personally or professionally?

Doing or becoming?

Consider your own developmental needs and those of your colleagues. Would a mentoring scheme for your team need to focus on gaining new skills, deepening understanding of other professional cultures, or helping individuals to gain greater self-awareness and confidence?

Peer mentoring in children's centres

Our reflections on the three different peer mentoring schemes show that none of the schemes is perfectly suited to peer mentoring for interprofessional development in children's centres but each one offers some beneficial features. Blaise Primary School's (Case study 1) commitment to developing skills and to collective enquiry is useful as it can support new staff members in children's centres to learn local ways of working and enable existing staff members to improve their practice in an environment of collaboration. The NHS North West Mentoring Scheme (Case study 2) offers a reflective approach that encourages the examination of hidden assumptions and the exploration of different practices by bringing together professionals from a variety of backgrounds and organizations. It enables staff members to analyse their own practice and to learn from others to find effective ways of working in their particular context. Along with practical skills and intellectual examination, a successful peer mentoring scheme in children's centres will also have to address the self and the affective domain, which are features of the NPQICL scheme (Case study 3). A strong emphasis on the development of self-knowledge and self-awareness helps mentees to explore their values and principles and encourages reflection on the impact these have on work practices; in addition, it allows for the acknowledgement and discussion of emotional responses to the challenging work with children and their families. John (2006) highlights the need to support workers in integrated children's services to encourage the discouraged, exploring the importance of confident and empowered leaders to foster equally confident and empowered staff members who in turn can help families to become confident and change their own and their children's lives.

In the light of the above reflections, and drawing on the *National Framework for Mentoring and Coaching* (CUREE), we can sketch the following concept for peer mentoring in children's centres to support interprofessional development and to enhance multi-disciplinary working.

A framework for peer mentoring

Peer mentoring for professional development in children's centres is a structured, formal process between two learners to enable them to share skills and knowledge from their respective professional backgrounds, explore the underlying assumptions in their practices, and support each other in their different roles of working with young children and their families.

Why?

The aim of the peer mentoring scheme is to enhance the understanding between different professions, explore a variety of work practices and find those which best meet the needs of children and their families in the children's centre. It supports the professional development of individuals while also contributing to the performance of the children's centre as a whole.

Who?

Mentor and mentee are to come from different professional backgrounds or disciplines. In children's centre teams with a good skills-mix mentor and mentee may be colleagues; in smaller teams with fewer professionals the mentee accesses a mentor from a different children's centre or a partner organization. In either case the mentoring relationship should be separate from line-management or performance management arrangements. Mentoring is available to staff members at any time during their employment and in any role within the children's centre, although the focus for the mentoring sessions may vary depending on whether the mentee is new to her post or wants the mentor to help her overcome a particular difficulty in her work. Mentors require a basic understanding of mentoring and an interest in developing others as well as learning themselves. Many of the necessary skills like active listening and supporting others to reflect on their actions are core skills for most professionals in children's services but some additional training and ongoing support for the mentors are required.

What?

At the start of their mentoring relationship mentor and mentee decide the focus for their relationship and which features and activities will be suitable and practical to meet the learning needs of the mentee.

The mentoring relationship includes all or some of the following activities:

- the mentor observes the mentee and gives constructive feedback;
- the mentee observes the mentor to see professional skills in practice;
- the mentor role models to make professional knowledge explicit;
- both mentor and mentee question assumptions implicit in each other's practice;
- the mentor supports the mentee to try new skills and different approaches to his/ her work;
- mentor and mentee discuss the challenges of working with young children and their families and develop strategies to reduce stress factors;
- the mentor supports the mentee to explore anxieties and concerns about their work and find ways to overcome them;
- the mentor initiates activities to develop the confidence and self-esteem of the mentee;
- the mentor initiates discussions to enhance the self-awareness and self-knowledge of the mentee.

Where?

Observations have to take place in either the mentor's or the mentee's workplace. For mentoring meetings any quiet and comfortable environment is suitable but mentor and mentee may prefer to meet away from their workplaces to ensure they are undisturbed and their discussions are confidential.

This framework for peer mentoring allows for skills development as much as the exploration of implicit professional cultures and personal attitudes and beliefs. It addresses the whole spectrum of becoming and doing in Clutterbuck and Megginson's (2005) developmental space as both are required to help new children's services professionals from different backgrounds to work together effectively. They have to understand each other's practice cultures and be able to draw on a range of different skills in their new roles. At the same time this framework for peer mentoring enables professionals to enter into an in-depth dialogue about their work and develop open communication between different disciplines. This will support their growing understanding of new professional roles in children's centres and help them shape new interprofessional identities.

References

Atkinson, M., Doherty, P. and Kinder, K. (2005) Multi-agency working; models, challenges and key factors for success. *Journal of Early Childhood Research*, 3: 7–17.

Blaise Primary School (2005) Peer coaching: getting started [Online]. Available at: www.curee-paccts.com/resources/publications/mentoring-coaching-case-studies

Centre for the Use of Research and Evidence in Education (CUREE) (nd) *Mentoring and Coaching CPD Capacity Building Project: National Framework for Mentoring and Coaching*. Available at: www.curee-paccts.com/mentoring-and-coaching/national-framework-and-resources.

Clutterbuck, D. (2004) *Everyone Needs a Mentor*. London: Institute of Personnel and Development.

Clutterbuck, D. and Megginson, D. (2005) *Techniques for Coaching and Mentoring*. Oxford: Butterworth-Heinemann/Elsevier.

Downey, M. (2003) *Effective Coaching: Lessons from the Coach's Coach*. London: Cengage Learning.

Easen, P., Atkins, M. and Dyson, A. (2000) Inter-professional collaboration and conceptualisations of practice. *Children & Society*, 14: 355–67.

Foster-Turner, J. (2006) *Coaching and Mentoring in Health and Social Care*. Abingdon: Radcliffe.

Furlong, J. and Maynard, T. (1995) *Mentoring Student Teachers*. London: Routledge.

Gasper, M. (2010) *Multi-agency Working in the Early Years: Challenges and Opportunities*. London: Sage.

Hale, R. (2000) To match or mis-match? The dynamics of mentoring as a route to personal and organizational learning. *Career Development International*, 5: 223–34.

John, K. (2006) Encouraging the discouraged to encourage the discouraged to encourage the discouraged. In P. Prina, A. Millar, C. Shelley and K. John (eds) *Adlerian Society (UK) and the Institute for Individual Psychology Year Book: A Collection of Topical Essays*. Chippenham: Antony Rowe.

Kelly, M., Beck, T. and Thomas, J. (1992) Mentoring as a staff development activity. In M. Wilkin (ed.) *Mentoring in Schools*. London: Routledge.

Knowles, M.S. (1970) *The Modern Practice of Adult Education: From Pedagogy to Andragogy*. Cambridge: Cambridge Book Company.

Molyneaux, J. (2001) Interprofessional teamworking: what makes teams work well? *Journal of Interprofessional Care*, 15: 29–35.

National College for School Leadership (1999) *National Professional Qualification in Integrated Centre Leadership: Facilitators' Manual*. Nottingham: National College for School Leadership.

North West Mentoring Scheme (2004) Mentee information [Online]. Available at: www. nwmentoring.nhs.uk/mentee/mentee.cfm.

Parsloe, E. (1992) *Coaching, Mentoring and Assessing: A Practical Guide to Developing Competence*. London: Kogan Page.

Wilkin, M. (1992) *Mentoring in Schools*. London: Kogan Page.

Further resources

www.coachingnetwork.org.uk   This is the website of the Coaching and Mentoring Network; it offers news, a range of different resources, and a discussion forum.

6

SUE WEBSTER AND ANNIE CLOUSTON

Interprofessional learning and support: a case study of the Children's Centre Leaders' Network 2008–10

Introduction

The complexity and vastness of the Sure Start Children's Centres project, as well as the speed with which it has developed, have produced an emerging profession reeling with the enormity of their task. The newness, the changing nature of expectations from national and local government and local communities, the uncertainty about funding and the pressures on the rest of children's services can be overwhelming. The Children's Centres Leaders Network (CCLN) was set up in recognition that the leaders of this 'flagship initiative of the Welfare State' (Dawn Primarolo, Minister for Children) needed a forum for sensemaking, influencing, being heard, supporting each other and developing.

This chapter will set the development of the CCLN in context and discuss the literature relevant to interprofessional leadership work in children's services as well as exploring styles of leadership development congruent with an enabling pedagogy for the early years. The concluding sections are concerned with what we have found out so far about the nature of children's centre leadership through CCLN; how well it can meet the needs of leaders working in an interprofessional context; and make some suggestions about how networking can be developed with children's centre leaders to promote peer learning and offer support that will 'encourage the discouraged' to have courage (John 2007).

Context

The New Labour government when elected in 1997 made the redressing of childhood disadvantage and inequality a priority. Early Excellence Centres (Labour Party 1997) and Sure Start Local Programmes (DfEE 1998) were the beginning of an ambitious programme with the ultimate aim of eradicating child poverty by 2020:

To work with parents-to-be, parents and children to promote the physical, intellectual and social development of babies and young children – particularly those who are disadvantaged – so that they can flourish at home and when they get to school, and thereby break the cycle of disadvantage for the current generation of young children.

(DfES 2001)

Children's centres established integrated service provision for under-5s and their families on a national basis for the first time (Chandler 2007). By March 2010 the Labour government had achieved its ambition of total coverage of England with 3500 children's centres each serving local communities (though it had failed in its initial objective of halving child poverty by 2010). Children's centres were to provide a 'core offer' of play and learning for children under 5, health programmes for expectant mothers and fathers and children and families, family support, and adult learning opportunities including help to return to, or find, work.

The magnitude and complexity of the core offer demanded that those responsible for developing children's centres – whatever their individual professional roots – required significant skills in leading in an interprofessional, multi-agency environment. To support the building of those leadership skills a new qualification was co-constructed, developed and piloted with leaders of integrated centres by the Pen Green Research, Development and Training Base. The resulting programme, now in its third revision, awards the National Professional Qualification in Integrated Centre Leadership (NPQICL) to its participants, when they demonstrate that they can achieve the national standards (DCSF 2007) that are expected of children's centre leaders, and write two assignments at Masters level.

The graduates of the programme, now 1807 in total (National College 2010), have no professional body that represents them as a distinct group with unique cross-disciplinary leadership responsibilities, nor a national Continuing Professional Development (CPD) programme. Neither is there a recognized national route for those working towards NPQICL. It is in this context that the need for an organization to address these issues developed.

The Children's Centre Leaders Network (CCLN) began in Autumn 2008 and was sponsored by the Department for Children, Schools and Families (DCSF), now replaced by the Department for Education (DfE). We coordinated the CCLN from August 2008 to July 2010. As members of the pilot NPQICL cohort, members of the Pen Green Research team that produced an impact study of NPQICL in the first two years of its national roll-out, and subsequently members of the regional delivery teams of NPQICL, we felt well placed to perform this role.

Our aim was to create professional networking events that were interactive, democratic, meaningful, relevant and owned by the leaders in each region. Consultation at our first round of regional events told us that leaders wanted to:

- engage in dialogue about leading and developing children's centres;
- discover more about practice in other local authorities;
- communicate directly with policy-makers;

- be in a safe environment with mutual support and be able to openly discuss challenges.

Unsurprisingly, as the funders, the Department for Children, Schools and Families (DCSF) also had expectations. They wanted:

- a direct line of communication between government and the field;
- opportunities to consult and check out ideas before committing funding;
- a chance to influence practice by offering expert speakers and bespoke training.

The CCLN has brought together leaders from many professional backgrounds, and with varied agency and life experience, to work in an interprofessional forum to have conversations about the job they do:

> If conversation is the natural way that humans think together, what gets lost when we stop talking to each other? . . . We stop acting intelligently. We give up the capacity to think about what's going on. We don't act to change anything. We become passive and allow others to tell us what to do.
>
> (Wheatley 2002: 26)

From the beginning a practitioner research approach to the coordination role was adopted. We gathered a variety of data to help us plan activities based on what the leaders told us about their observations, experiences and current leadership challenges. Because of the rapid growth and development of children's centres since 1998 there is much yet to be learned and understood about the nature of leadership tasks and responsibilities in children's centres. Do all leaders understand their task? Grint (2010) raises four basic leadership questions that apply to the leadership in children's centres:

- Is leadership defined as a *position*? Is the fact that they have *the job* that makes them a leader?
- Is leadership defined as a *person*? Is it *who the person is* that makes them a leader?
- Is leadership about *what is achieved*? Do *good results define good leaders*?
- Is leadership a *process*? Is it *how a leader does things* that makes them a good leader?

Our aim was to plan CCLN events as a forum for the development of a new interprofessional knowledge that supported leaders to interrogate these and other basic questions.

Interprofessionalism and networking

The thrust towards more integrated services at all levels of organization – which requires people from different professional disciplines and career histories to work together – was given a boost by the *Laming Report* (Laming 2003). His inquiry into the death of Victoria Climbié revealed, like too many before it, significant gaps in agency collaboration to protect children at risk. Lord Laming's recommendations about joined-up provision were formalized in government policy in *Every Child Matters: Change for Children* (DfES 2004). Joining-up was attempted at the policy-making level, at least in relation to Social Care and Education, when the Department for Children, Schools and Families was formed in 2007.

At the level of practice, *Every Child Matters* appears to summarize the role of children's centre leader (CCL) as the creator of an interprofessional system, as one who: 'is responsible for bringing practitioners from a range of different backgrounds together to achieve results for children and young people that could not have been achieved by any one of the agencies acting alone' (DfES 2004: 3).

The newness of the integrated children's centres concept means that the published literature about what leadership looks like from within is scant. However, researching interprofessionalism as part of this experience is happening. All NPQICL participants are required to write their second, of two, assignments about practitioner research they have undertaken on leading multi-disciplinary work in their centres. Applying existing bodies of knowledge to their present and emerging dilemmas, knotty problems and often scarcely recognized in the moment successes, has given rise to new theorizing to enlighten, vitalize and embolden practice.

Within children's centres interprofessionalism is more visible in relation to outreach and family support services and stay and play. Our own research has shown that the pattern of engagement with other services notably Health, Social Care and Jobcentre Plus, varies hugely between areas, local authorities, and children's centres (and planning for our events targeted relationships with these agencies). Leading in such a varied terrain is often lonely, complicated and it is easy to lose your way, as one leader put it: 'It is like spaghetti junction rather than one road, isn't it? So the skill is getting the right people around you' (Children's centre leader cited by Clouston 2007). Is 'getting the right people around you' the definition of what interprofessionalism means in integrated children's centres? There is more to it than that, for the job involves keeping people with you, working towards agreed goals, mediating the collisions as well as the gaps in services and above all 'providing an environment that values and celebrates the diversity of different professionals' (Anning et al. 2006: 105).

Since working smarter has become synonymous often with working in partnership across professional, institutional and disciplinary boundaries, more attention has been devoted to which factors promote successful collaborations rather than the outcomes for children and families. In relation to what works for children and families, are the benefits of working in multi-disciplinary teams, interprofessionally, proven? The evidence within the literature is far from resoundingly positive in terms of benefits to children and families. Siraj-Blatchford and Siraj-Blatchford (2009: 10) in their comprehensive study of the effectiveness of integrating early services note that:

> Very little hard evidence is currently available on the impact that inter-agency working is having on children's outcomes, despite extensive empirical work in a range of settings. The bulk of the research so far carried out has focused attention more on the organisational difficulties of achieving inter-agency collaboration than on any benefits accrued.

Anning et al. (2006) in their study, based on the MATch (Multi-Agency Teamwork in Services for Children) project, explored the daily realities of delivering services to children and families through multi-agency teams. They acknowledge the 'tenuous research evidence of "what works"' but that the 'rollercoaster' for more integration – and by inference interprofessional working – continued unabated. This and other studies confirm Siraj-Blatchford's contention that the focus of research has hitherto been barriers and facilitators rather than whether interprofessional working and multi-agency teams do benefit children and families (Hudson 1999; Easen 2000; Freeman et al. 2000; Molyneux 2001; Edwards 2004; Sloper 2004; Atkinson et al. 2005; Morrow et al. 2005). However, a frequent finding of this research is that proactive leadership, shared vision, agreed procedures, and continuous professional development across agency boundaries are significant facilitators of successful joined-up working.

If there are benefits for families, can networking aimed at increasing the facilitators and overcoming the barriers have a positive impact on interprofessional practice? Can CCLs be helped to increase their professional leverage and status to fulfil their demanding role by CCLN activities?

Leadership skills and new identities

Does working interprofessionally demand a different leadership style or disposition? There are a number of key works which address the need for a different kind of leadership within the complex, multi-layered environment of integrated systems. New terminology has developed to more accurately describe the nature of the task. Fullan (2004), writing about systems leaders from an educational perspective, Engestrom (2004), an activity theorist, and Frost (2001), from the perspective of lifelong learning, make similar points: the speed of change and new technological and organizational challenges demand that leadership is no longer about just being an expert in your field.

Fullan (2004: 18–19) sees successful leaders as systems thinkers in action, and cites eight elements of sustainability which leaders must enact to be systems leaders in action. One element is lateral capacity building through networks:

> People learn best from peers (fellow travellers who are further down the road) if there is sufficient opportunity for on-going purposeful exchange; the system is designed to foster, develop, and disseminate innovative practices that work – discover 'solutions that lie outside the current way of operating'; leadership is developed and mobilised in many quarters; and motivation and ownership at the local level are deepened, a key ingredient for sustainability and effort of engagement.

Engestrom (2004: 149) proposes that expertise is redefined to meet the 'pervasive challenge of radical, discontinuous change'. He has devised the term *negotiated knotworking* to describe a new way of conceptualizing 'expert work'. A CCL may be part of negotiated knotworking, for example, when coordinating a Common Assessment Framework (CAF), with a family. Various professionals may be involved to different degrees in temporary constellations:

> Knotworking situations are fragile because they rely on fast accomplishment of inter-subjective understanding, distributed control and coordinated action . . . the combinations of people and tasks change constantly. This highlights the importance of communicative and meta-communicative actions and tools for successful knotworking.
>
> (Engestrom 2004: 153)

We would argue that the methods and techniques practised and encouraged during network meetings enhance such communicative and meta-communicative skills for all those who participate.

At other times, CCLs will be bringing together more stable and defined teams of people, in what Wenger (1998) terms 'communities of practice'. Within these communities of practice new identities are forged that are a product of the needs of the task which brings them together, the knowledge, skills and experience each professional brings and the depth or strength of an individual's engagement. Multi-agency teams led by CCLs can be viewed as communities of practice. Learning is an essential component of a community of practice and being effective 'is a matter of sustaining mutual engagement in pursuing an enterprise together to share some significant learning' (Wenger 1998: 86).

Frost (2004: 48) sees effective leadership as an essential and challenging element in working interprofessionally, it requires 'individuals who can work in the new ever-changing world of joined-up working that involves networking and boundary crossing'. He and others (Skelcher et al. 2004) use the term boundary-spanner to encapsulate this ability, central to the performance of children's centre leadership. Easen et al. (2000) in their research on interprofessional collaboration at a community level identify another role relevant to CCLs – as reticulists, who are specialists in inter-organizational politics who cultivate networks of relationships and provide access to information. The founder of the Bromley-by-Bow Centre, Andrew Mawson uses the term 'social entrepreneur' to describe himself – a person who makes things happen in the way that they work with others. Professor Ferre Laevers, the distinguished writer and innovator in the field of Early Years pedagogy, identified CCLs as social entrepreneurs in his speech at the awards ceremony of the Eastern Leadership Centre's NPQICL graduates on 21 October 2010.

The CCLN events

It is important to acknowledge that children's centre leaders are not an homogeneous group. They come from a range of professional heritages, have been tasked with developing children's centres from a core offer rather than a set of principles and values. The initial key vision was to address child poverty but along the way they have also incorporated a range of local and community visions too. Therefore the nature and focus of work are varied and it is only when CCLs have engaged in meaningful discussions that this has become evident.

Furthermore with three waves of development there is a wide range of experience to be accommodated within CCLN events. The rapid growth of the sector has created a demand for leaders and CCLN planning needed to consider the range of experience the leaders brought to the events. Here Bloom's (1997) stages of leadership development influenced programme planning:

- *Beginning*, where a leader may need support from peers with opportunities to safely share experiences and discuss their role. Leaders may be unconsciously competent and feel as though they are in survival mode.
- *Competent*, where leaders are described as moving from 'struggling to juggling' often have a heavy workload and a complex organization. Networking offers them an opportunity to consider a range of solutions to the challenges they face.
- *Master*, where leaders experienced as 'agents of change' can act as mentors and role models. At this stage of development they may be research active and be motivated to create new knowledge in the field.

We drew on large group learning approaches like Open Space Technology (Owen 2008) and World Café (Brown and Isaacs 2005). They were chosen because they are flexible approaches that allow leaders to raise their own discussion topics within a general theme for each day. Themes included: 'Making your voice heard', 'Multi-agency working', 'Achieving better outcomes in partnership with health', 'Unleashing the power of collaborative thinking on the leadership task', 'Safeguarding', and 'Measuring outcomes'. We were keen to facilitate rather than attempt to impart or influence our own perspectives.

In an attempt to create a two-way dialogue between policy and practice all sessions included opportunities for a policy update from the DCSF and message walls, for example, a message to the minister, which were popular. All materials and ideas were synthesized into national and individual regional event reports which are posted on the website.

As facilitators, we cultivated the idea that each event brought together a unique learning community. We emphasized the luxury, in terms of professional development, of having the opportunity to have the collective experience of 50 to 100 leaders together in one room. In order to create a safe environment we drew on the wisdom of Wheatley (2002: 29) to influence our group working contract:

- We acknowledge one another as equal.
- We try to stay curious about each other.
- We recognize that we need each other's help to become better listeners.
- We slow down so we have time to think and reflect.
- We remember that conversation is the natural way that humans think together.
- We expect it to be messy at times.

This philosophy was enthusiastically received and many leaders took away copies to share in their work.

The primary task for leaders of children's centres in England is to create services that address some of the most complex enduring social problems in society. The application of Grint's (2010) ideas about 'tame' and 'wicked' problems (Ritell and Webber 1973, cited in Grint 2010) are worthy of consideration in the context of networking for CCLs. Tame problems have logical solutions using clear practice guidelines or protocols; the type of problems leaders in all organizations would be faced with on a regular basis. However, the nature of the task for a CCL is to find local and national solutions to the broad social issues in society. These are 'wicked' problems, both complex and complicated, social problems with no clear solution. These are the problems that require the deeper interrogation that a network can offer; leaders asking the right questions to develop collective intelligence (Levi 1994).

Most approaches to 'wicked' problems need to be collectively rather than individually led. Grint (2010) argues that the key to finding solutions is having leaders with the ability to ask the right questions. Applying this idea to the context of children's centre leadership means leaders having the 'art of engaging the community to face up to the complex and collective problems within it' (Grint 2010: 18). Children's centres need to contribute to leadership in a community that is both enquiring and creative, influencing innovative approaches rather than perpetuating past strategies and mistakes.

The CCLN provides a valuable opportunity to support leaders to share and develop ideas that focus on wicked problems. We developed an egalitarian social approach to provide opportunities in a safe environment where leaders who face similar social disadvantage in their communities can explore hypothetical and real situations and solutions. CCLs can find allies with similar challenges or find informal mentors to challenge their practice. West-Burnham (2005) informs us that to promote the deep-level learning needed by the twenty-first-century leader a forum is required for leaders which enables them to move out of their comfort zone.

A network offers the opportunity to focus on the 'wicked' problems we have been tasked to 'solve' that have no elegant solutions (Grint 2010). When leaders have come together at the network events, 'clumsy' solutions have emerged. There may be no evidence that they will work but they are a result of combining the experience and knowledge in the room. Many of the management challenges for CCLs are tame, regular day-to-day management issues, where there is evidence-based practice or well-used protocols to adopt. The clumsy solutions to wicked problems developed through networking are an essential part of the journey towards an elegant solution (Grint 2010).

Collective enquiry that is solution-focused also supports the development of collective strength. CCLs are part of hierarchies where they experience power from above. Their roles also require them to sensitively exert power over others, their teams, partners and local communities. They have been encouraged to develop normative power relationships based on shared values and the development of social capital (Etzioni 1964). One of the challenges of the egalitarian approach occurs when leaders work with partner agencies and communities and there is a clash of perspectives. CCLs need strategies to overcome the pessimism of fatalists and cynics who may feel there is nothing that can be done. These strategies include flattening the hierarchies, distributing control and inspiring individuals to engage in collective action (Etzioni 1964).

Surowiecki's (2004) idea that many leaders in dialogue are smarter than a few experts influenced the content and activities of the network events. We actively promoted the idea of the 'wisdom of crowds'. Rather than relying on speakers where leaders passively listen to 'experts', we actively encouraged those who are most experienced and knowledgeable to raise questions and find solutions, that is, those currently engaged in the process of leading children's centres.

Research

The data we have gained from the leaders in the Network has been gathered from a variety of sources, and key findings from each source will be included. It was collected from six rounds of regional meetings, covering all nine government regions in the country. All CCLs on Together for Children's database of children's centres were invited, although this was not a guarantee that all CCLs were given the opportunity to attend.

Sources of data

Sources of data were:

- focus group activities at Network meetings;
- telephone interviews conducted after the first round of events in Autumn 2008;
- an independent evaluation;
- evaluations of each event;
- messages to the Minister for Children via graffiti wall, focused discussion, Q&A sessions with DCSF representatives;
- reports from small group activities over all six rounds of events;
- questionnaires completed by CCLs attending the last three events.

During 2009–10 we decided that as we had unique access to a great proportion of the CCL workforce, we would do some research on them in relation to three main areas:

1   gender, professional backgrounds, how many had achieved the NPQICL, and their areas of particular interest;
2   their job title and the number of centres for which they had leadership responsibilities;
3   their preferences for CCLN meetings in terms of content, frequency and sitings of meeting.

These three areas were covered by a questionnaire completed by 735 CCLs over three events. A fourth area was covered by a second questionnaire that was completed by 310 leaders at the Autumn 2009 round of events only. This gave us data about the size of the leadership task for CCLs in terms of the number of people in their teams and about the areas of leadership where they felt they were doing well, and where they felt they needed help.

Findings

Like the children's workforce in general, CCLs are overwhelmingly female. Nationally, 4.6 per cent of questionnaire respondents were male, with the highest percentage regionally being in West Midlands (7 per cent) and the lowest being in London (1.5 per cent).

Just how interprofessional is the CCLN? We had been curious to know whether there had been a change in the professional mix of CCLs as greater numbers of children's centres have become operational. Previous data about the professional backgrounds of children's centre and Sure Start programme leaders was limited to earlier impact research conducted during the roll-out of NPQICL in 2005–2007. Table 6.1 shows that specialists in Early Years and education remain the largest proportion of the CCL workforce, if those who attended the network meetings are typical of the workforce as a whole.

The largest professional group attending the Network have been those with a background in Early Years, mainly from a nursery nursing background (44 per cent). If representative, this percentage represents a significant shift from the data collected from the NPQICL cohort of 2005, where the largest proportion of leaders were from teaching backgrounds. The category 'other' has also grown, but there are fewer social workers and health professionals. There were some interesting regional differences in the proportion of CCLs from different professional backgrounds, with the North-West and Yorkshire and Humber, for example, having more than 50 per cent of the leaders from Early Years backgrounds, and the South-West and North-East having 35 per cent and 34 per cent respectively. The North-East had a much greater percentage than other regions of Community Development Workers (34 per cent) than the national average of 10 per cent (Clouston and Webster 2010).

More attendees had gained or were actually on the NPQICL (60 per cent) than attendees who had not. Again there were regional differences, ranging from 68 per cent in the South-West to 40 per cent in the South-East. It would be interesting to know whether having completed the NPQICL makes CCLs more likely to attend the Network where the event format replicated much of the style and ethos of the NPQICL programme.

Table 6.2 shows the areas of children's centre work which CCLs selected as of particular interest, and which they would like to develop through the Network. It shows that family support was named nearly twice as many times as the second most often named – interprofessional working and continuous professional development. When taken in conjunction with the distribution of professional heritages, this arguably shows an overwhelming interest in extending knowledge and skills beyond

Table 6.1 Professional backgrounds of 2005 NPQICL graduates and CCLN members. 2009–10

Professional Backgrounds	Early Years/ Nursery Nursing (%)	Teaching (%)	Social Work (%)	Community Development (%)	Health (%)	Business/ Admin (%)	Other/not known (%)	
2005 Cohort NPQICL	91 (26)	104 (29)	62 (18)	45 (13)	43 (12)		9 (3)	Total 354
2009–10 CCLN	326 (44)	130 (18)	83 (11)	74 (10)	59 (8)	26 (4)	38 (5)	Total 727

Table 6.2 Members' most frequently cited areas of particular interest

What area of CC work are you particularly interested in?	Total
Family support/safeguarding/parenting/outreach/early intervention	275
Interprofessional working/CPD	142
Evidencing outcomes/monitoring/SEF	105
Engaging hard to access groups/minorities	103
Leadership/governance	81
Involving/developing parents	63
Early Years/education/childcare	56
Community development/cohesion	45
Performance management/quality/Inspection	35
Strategic planning/policy-making	27
Fathers	19
Mental health and addictions	17
Child poverty/narrowing the gap	15
Additional needs	15

narrow professional boundaries and seeing the Network as one forum in which this could happen.

Job title and role

There was huge variety in the job titles that members held. There were over 50 variants, but the most popular were 'children's centre manager' and 'children's centre coordinator'. The job titles tended to reflect local organizational issues: whether a centre leader coordinated services rather than the people who delivered them; what phase of children's centre they were running; the stance of their lead agencies (local authorities, for example, being more likely to have coordinators than voluntary sector); and whether the centre was located in a school where the headteacher was regarded as the head of centre. Needless to say, pay and conditions are as varied as the job titles, and are the cause of some not unreasonable resentment, as evidenced by the number of times this was raised as an issue at Network meetings.

The average number of centres managed by each attendee was 1.74, with some attendees managing as many as eight children's centres.

Meetings

Most CCLs wanted the pattern of meetings to be more frequent than they were, that is, quarterly, held regionally, and an annual national conference. A significant minority wanted meetings to be based more locally and this was largely because of restrictive travel budgets. Many respondents had experience of local meetings for leaders, but often these were operationally focused rather than developmental. There was a strongly held view that the cross-fertilization of ideas, the lifeblood of the Network, needed to happen within a larger context.

CCLs' areas of confidence in their leadership

The final data from 310 completed questionnaires that is relevant to this chapter shows that while many leaders feel that they do multi-agency working well, coded as 'relationships' in figures 6.1 and 6.2, many (though fewer) also feel this is where they need help. The same can be said of the children's centre work which by its nature most demands interprofessional work, such as reaching groups with the highest needs, coded as 'community development'. An explanation of the coding of these categories is available on the website report (Clouston and Webster 2010).

Figure 6.1 shows the areas where leaders felt they were performing well, while Figure 6.2 shows that the area where CCLs feel they most need help is in data collection and evaluation. Additional comments signified difficulties with particular agencies, Health being named most frequently. The beauty of the Network is that some leaders have excellent strategies with those same partner agencies to get much-needed data, and these strategies are shared and inspire others to try something different, as exemplified by one CCL: 'I like to know what's going on and what others are thinking ... I look outside the box and get ideas from hearing others share their experiences' (CCL, Autumn 2009).

Finding that interprofessional relationships with Health are the most vital to the children's centre project of early intervention, but at the same time often the most frustrating, events in Summer 2009 were aimed at promoting those interprofessional

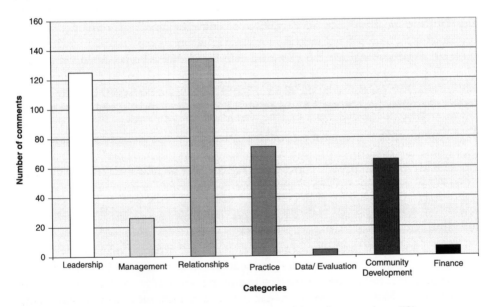

Figure 6.1 Responses to the question 'What are the things that you do well?'

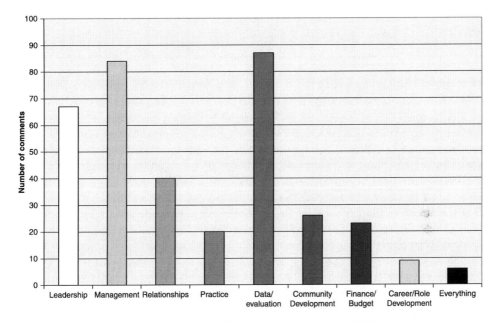

Figure 6.2 Responses to the question 'What do you need help with?'

relationships. Each CCL was encouraged to invite their lead health professional to attend the network meeting with them. These events were attended by 491 leaders, 132 of whom brought a colleague from Health. A participant commented: 'Really important to bring other CC partner colleagues to these meetings, it gives another perspective.' After a similarly organized day in the Spring 2010 events programme when social work colleagues were invited, one participant said:

> a very informative day . . . the relationship between children's centres and social care safeguarding teams is a big concern – some misunderstandings about roles and thresholds.
>
> (CCL, Spring 2010)

The finding that so many CCLs were most troubled by data collection and evaluation led to the Network addressing this directly in Summer 2010 with a programme designed to increase leaders' confidence in this area. Working in partnership with C4EO (Centre for Excellence in Outcomes) we provided an introduction to *Results Based Accountability* (Friedman 2005), as one method to systematically plan, deliver and measure outcomes in collaboration with partners in children's services. A CCL said in her evaluation of this event:

> I really hope the Network stays – it is a vital professional development mechanism for centre leaders. A good overview of the principles of accountability, it has got me started to think differently about how I set things up, often rush into things but need to be more reflective.

Discussion

During 2008–10 the CCLN was an organization that never really reached a consensus about its purpose. There were different and therefore confused expectations, and while the members gave their views about its purpose, the agenda was not set by them. In practice the Network performed two very significant functions. It was a forum in which 'to engage with others in our professional community in the exploration of its accumulated knowledge' (Whitaker 2006) and also one in which the new professionals, CCLs, could debate, affirm and fight for their values: 'It's an important time to link with others, out of our area. We need to get together, we could really have a strong voice' (CCL, Summer 2010). As the pressure mounts to shift the whole CC project to a different philosophical footing, this becomes an even more vital function.

The membership expressed a majority preference for consolidating their ownership of the Network for CCLs before admitting others. This has had the effect of limiting its interprofessional impact, for it excludes strategists from the local authorities and Health, for example, who are part of the learning and values framework required to make CCs work. As one participant said: 'More networking would be great. To have local authority leads present would be great – we would get to the people who can make the changes.'

The tension between some CCLs and their local authority leads has historical roots in the frustration of many experienced Sure Start Local Programme Managers and CCLs. Some feel they have been insufficiently engaged by local authorities in planning for the expansion of children's centre services.

The Network has been dependent on central government funding and therefore always subject to their control. The lack of engagement or support from some local authorities – perhaps as a direct result of this – has also meant that some CCLs struggled to get permission to attend Network meetings. This has made stark another disparity between the members: the extent to which they are able to act autonomously in their own CPD.

In what ways can these issues be addressed organizationally and philosophically? From a policy perspective the Network needs to be free of external control. As we say in NPQICL, there is a need to 'trust the process' (Marshall 1994) and enable CCLs to run their own Network and to agree its purposes and terms of reference.

Few of those leaders whom Bloom (1997) would identify as 'master leaders', such as those who had been in the pilot and the 2006 and 2007 cohorts of NPQICL, attended the Network on a regular basis. These are the people with the confidence and experience who can stick their heads up above the parapet and lead a bottom-up organization. The Children's Centre Leader Reference Group consisted of some of these leaders and the organizational and functional separation of the Reference Group from CCLN depleted the Network's strength. In order to be sustainable there is a necessity to move towards a democratically based Network. However, for this to happen it will be necessary, in Grint's words, to rethink our approach and recognize that 'hierarchists also have a part to play: collaborative leadership still requires someone or somebody to take a lead' (2010: 32).

Organizationally and philosophically the logical basis for the Network is within the regional NPQICL communities. They have fostered a research and learning culture and provided leadership mentoring support. There are existing strong relationships built over five years and an ethos of interprofessional collaboration. Those essential elements of Wenger's (1998) communities of practice – joint enterprise, mutual engagement and shared repertoire – are present. Also present are the conditions for Bettner and Lew's (1989) crucial Cs for containment and support. Bettner and Lew explain that people have four basic needs, the Crucial Cs, four cornerstones of well-being; to connect, to feel capable, to count and to have courage.

In Figure 6.3 we have attempted to conflate these two concepts as a rationale to support our logic. The three elements of the community of practice can provide the support structure for CCLs to have courage, take risks in their practice and their learning, and survive.

The NPQICL regional communities have inter-regional links through the National College, which also hosts the NPQICL online learning community. Cross-boundary mentoring can be brokered where a CCL's need for confidentiality requires it. Successful events in one region could also transfer or be exchanged with their facilitators to others, or be used as the basis for national conferences.

These proposals will require a significant organizational shift, some start-up funding and a willingness by leaders to contribute financially and with their leadership skills to the Network. It may be possible to find independent sponsors to contribute. Some CCLs have undertaken ground-breaking systems leader training

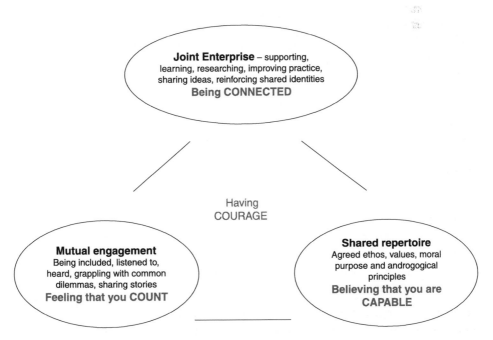

Figure 6.3 The elements of Wenger's community of practice linked with Bettner and Lew's Crucial Cs

at the National College, and their knowledge and skills as coaches and mentors to other leaders should be harnessed. There are many CCLs who have yet to commit to the Network, and their reservations may have been organizational or philosophical in nature, so a more democratically based Network may generate more participation.

The Network has been a great supporter of CPD and this should be a vital part of its future; with members formulating pre-NPQICL courses, supporting practitioner research, encouraging further study to complete Masters courses, forming partnerships with the university sector, and organizing and facilitating Action Learning Sets (Revans 1980). Online learning can be expanded with online debates, hot seats, conferencing and used for dissemination of good practice and research.

The Network should model good practice in learning and development so that this can be disseminated by leaders to their colleagues, teams and ultimately to the children and families they serve. A successful Network must keep in mind the interests of the end user and commit to 'the whole domain of social responsibility for children, their well-being, learning and competence' (Moss and Petrie 2002: 138). In so doing we must ensure that interprofessional work is not used to increase professional power at the expense of progress in the development of services whose primary focus is to meet the needs of children and families.

Conclusion

CCLN has been an important instrument for interprofessional learning in bringing together, in particularly challenging times, a widely disparate group of people to engage in reflection and dialogue about what matters to them. It has also, we would argue, been instrumental in promoting and consolidating a new professional identity for its members. Being connected – as one of the crucial Cs that promote well-being – through a shared identity will strengthen and support CCLs to do their job and to hold onto their values when times are tough.

> Individuals can still link hands and enact democracy. They can still establish their own dominion and supremacy by rejecting the givenness of the mechanical and impersonal. Working together, reflecting together, forging community together, individuals may at last surpass what is intolerable: they may yet transform their world.
>
> (Greene, cited in Boot et al. 1994: 184)

References

Anning, A., Cottrell, D., Frost, N., Green, J. and Robinson, M. (2006) *Developing Multiprofessional Teamwork for Integrated Children's Services*. Maidenhead: Open University Press.

Atkinson, M., Doherty, P. and Kinder, K. (2005) Multi-agency working: models, challenges and key factors for success. *Journal of Early Childhood Research*, 3: 7–17.

Bettner, B.L. and Lew, A. (1989) *Raising Kids Who Can*. Newton, MA: Connexions Press.

Bloom, P.J. (1997) Navigating the rapids: directors reflect on their careers and professional development. *Young Children*, November: 32–8.

Brown, J. and Isaacs, D. (2005) *The World Café: Shaping Our Futures through Conversations that Matter*. San Francisco: Berrett-Koehler Publishers, Inc.

Chandler, T. (2007) *An Analysis of the Impact of the NPQICL Programme on the Practice of Participants from Teaching and Nursery Nurse Origins*. Corby: Pen Green.

Clouston, A. (2007) *An Analysis of the Impact of NPQICL on Graduates with a Background in Social Work*. Corby: Pen Green.

Clouston, A. and Webster, S. (2010) Report to CCLN members concerning data gathered through questionnaires during CCLN regional events in Autumn 2009 and Spring and Summer 2010. Available at: www.childrens-centres.org/CCLN/CCLNSupportDocuments.

Department for Children, Schools and Families (DCSF) (2007) *National Standards for Leaders of Sure Start Children's Centres*. Nottingham: DCSF.

Department for Education and Employment (DfEE) (1998) *Meeting the Childcare Challenge*. London: DfEE.

Department for Education and Skills (DfES) (2001) *Public Service Agreement for 2001–2004*. London: HMSO.

Department for Education and Skills (DfES) (2004) *Every Child Matters: Change for Children*. London: HMSO.

Edwards, A. (2004) The new multi-agency working: collaborating to prevent the social exclusion of children and families. *Journal of Integrated Care*, 12: 3–9.

Engestrom, Y. (2004) The new generation of expertise, in H. Rainbird, A. Fuller and A. Munro (eds) *Workplace Learning in Context*. London: Routledge.

Etzioni, A. (1964) *Modern Organisations*. London: Prentice Hall.

Freeman, M., Miller, C. and Ross, N. (2000) The impact of individual philosophies of teamwork on multi-professional practice and the implications for education. *Journal of Interprofessional Care*, 14: 237–47.

Friedman, M. (2005) *Trying Hard Is Not Good Enough*. Victoria, BC: Trafford.

Frost, N. (2001) Professionalism, change and the politics of lifelong learning. *Studies in Continuing Education*, 23: 5–17.

Frost, N. (2005) *Professionalism, Partnership and Joined-up Thinking: A Research Review of Frontline Working with Children and Families*. Totnes: Blacklers.

Fullan, M. (2004) *System Thinkers in Action*. Nottingham: DfES.

Grint, K. (2010) *Leadership: A Short Introduction*. Oxford: Oxford University Press.

Hudson, R. (1999) Primary health care and social care: working across professional boundaries. *Managing Community Care*, 7: 15–22.

John, K. (2007) Sustaining the leaders of children's centres: the role of leadership mentoring. *European Early Childhood Research Association Monograph*, September.

John, K. (2008) Sustaining the leaders of children's centres: the role of leadership mentoring. *European Early Childhood Education Research Journal, Special Issue: Leadership & Management*, 16(1): 53–66.

Labour Party (1997) *Labour Party Paper: Early Excellence, a Head Start for Every Child*. London: The Labour Party.

Laming, Lord (2003) *The Victoria Climbié Inquiry Report*. London: The Stationery Office.

Levi, D. (1994) *Collective Intelligence: Mankind's Emerging World in Cyberspace*. London: Perseus.

Marshall, J. (1994) Re-visioning organisations by developing female values, in J. Boot, J. Lawrence and J. Morris (eds) *Managing the Unknown by Creating New Futures*. London: McGraw-Hill.

Mawson, A. (2008) *The Social Entrepreneur: Making Communities Work*. London: Atlantic Books.

Molyneux, J. (2001) Interprofessional teamworking: what makes teams work well? *Journal of Interprofessional Care*, 15: 29–35.

Morrow, G., Malin, N. and Jennings, T. (2005) Interprofessional teamworking for child and family referral in a Sure Start local programme. *Journal of Interprofessional Care*, 19: 93–101.

Moss, P. and Petrie, P. (2002) *From Children's Services to Children's Spaces*. London: Routledge Falmer.

Owen, H. (2008) *Open Space Technology: A User's Guide*. 2nd edn. San Francisco: Berrett-Koehler Publishers, Inc.

Revans, R. (1980) *Action Learning: New Techniques for Action Learning*. London: Blond and Briggs.

Siraj-Blatchford, I. and Siraj-Blatchford, J. (2009) *Improving Development Outcomes for Children Through Effective Practice in Integrating Early Years Services*. London: Centre for Excellence in Children and Young People's Services.

Skelcher, D., Mather, N. and Smith, M. (2004) *Effective Partnership and Good Governance: Lessons from Policy and Practice*. Birmingham: INLOGOV.

Sloper, P. (2004) Facilitators and barriers for coordinated multi-agency services. *Child: Health, Care and Development*, 30: 571–80.

Surowiecki, J. (2004) *The Wisdom of Crowds*. London: Abacus.

Wenger, E. (1998) *Communities of Practice*. Cambridge: Cambridge University Press.

West-Burnham, J. (2005) *Learning to Lead*. Nottingham: NCSL.

Wheatley, M. (2002) *Turning to One Another*. San Francisco, CA: Berrett-Koelher.

Whitaker, P. (2006) *Developing Academic Capability*. Corby: Pen Green.

PART 3
Working

7

DARYL MAISEY
Safeguarding, change and transitions

Introduction

Safeguarding, change and transitions are three words that conjure a range of complex and multi-faceted issues in interprofessional working. This chapter explores legislation and policy that impact on front-line practitioners who are involved with safeguarding and child protection practices across the children's workforce. It examines the current context of safeguarding practice and identifies some of the challenges and dilemmas facing professionals in light of the requirements to achieve effective inter-agency working to support children and their families particularly during periods of transition. Themes of co-location, joint training, efficiency of resources, the development of effective interprofessional communication skills and the establishment of appropriate strategic planning to lead and support practitioners are explored and identified as ways that may improve current practice.

Undoubtedly working in a multi-professional field is complex in terms of roles, responsibilities and relationships. Most professionals have their own sense of belonging to discrete disciplines within the children and young people's workforce. The requirements of qualifications, training and practice serve to strengthen this identity. In addition each discipline such as health, education and social services has their own professional expectations to deliver effective systems to meet the needs of all children. In the light of the strength of this identity, it can be uncomfortable and challenging for practitioners to examine their roles in relation to other professionals and to identify opportunities for collaborative working practices or change that may improve outcomes for children and their families. This can be uniquely exacerbated in the area of 'safeguarding' children where emotive situations can impact significantly upon rational decision-making and the risks involved can counter reasonable judgement. The roles and responsibilities of those involved in safeguarding children are further compounded by recent changes in the structures and systems within disciplines although the basic duties remain the same – to protect children from harm and ensure that they have a safe and healthy environment in which to learn and develop.

Definitions

The term 'safeguarding' is often used in conjunction with 'child protection'. Although both terms are interrelated, they are distinct in their common definitions and capture different elements of the work involved in keeping children safe and healthy. *Safeguarding* is predominantly concerned with preventing and protecting children through careful planning and early intervention whereas *child protection* tends to relate to active strategies that are implemented to protect children who are, or who could be, in immediate danger of suffering abuse. The emphasis within each profession is to be active in promoting and engaging in effective safeguarding procedures and processes in order to reduce the incidents of child protection reactive strategies. It would be unlikely that many professionals working with children and young people would disagree with these expectations, although in reality there can be confusion between roles and responsibilities both intraprofessionally and interprofessionally when identifying and managing safeguarding issues.

Safeguarding and child protection in context

In terms of legislation what is understood by 'safeguarding' is relatively new. It would appear that the first recorded reference to safeguarding children was mentioned in the Home Office Report 1960–1970 on a page discussing private fostering (Singleton 2010, unpublished lecture). In the 1960s, American literature explored the possibility that children were being harmed intentionally and the phrase 'battered baby' was coined and in the mid-1970s the first child protection register was established as a requirement for local authorities to improve communication between agencies following the tragic death of 7-year-old Maria Colwell (Lindon 2008). Since then there have been several key pieces of legislation and major policy initiatives and inquiries specifically related to improving safeguarding and child protection policy and practice (Kirton 2009). For example, the Laming Report (Laming 2003) was the result of a public inquiry into the death of Victoria Climbié. This identified several key factors that if attended to might have prevented the tragic outcome: the failure of communication between professionals, inadequate support systems and ineffective intervention strategies. Most significantly, the subsequent Children Act (2004) and the Safeguarding Vulnerable Groups Act (2006) placed a duty on professional bodies to make arrangements to safeguard and promote the health and well-being of all children. Guidance such as *What to Do If You're Worried a Child Is Being Abused* (DCSF 2006a) aided clarification of procedures and was made available to all practitioners working across different agencies in the children's workforce. In summary, local government had the responsibility to ensure multi-professional collaboration and the national government now had the right to intervene if those services were not effectively safeguarding children and young people within the local authorities.

From legislation and guidance documentation, it is evident that there is an expectation that all practitioners working with children and young people are responsible for understanding the implications of safeguarding by having an awareness of policy and practice, being able to recognize signs of harm, understanding the importance of information sharing and knowing how and when to act (CWDC 2010). However, knowledge of legal and procedural frameworks is very different to the application of that knowledge and the resultant implications of such actions. The onus appears to be on individuals within each discipline to interpret current guidelines and this, it could be argued, is open to misunderstanding and potentially ineffective or inappropriate action being taken. Understanding the implications of safeguarding is therefore complex and challenging. However, clarification of legal requirements, systems and procedures and discussion of key terms, issues and dilemmas facing frontline practitioners and stakeholders can only serve to highlight the need for effective collaboration between professionals from different disciplines and ultimately minimize risk to children.

Practitioners working with children

When examining the field of safeguarding it seems appropriate to initially consider the very people who have chosen to work with children and young people whether in an employed or voluntary capacity – the practitioners. Regardless of the discipline pre-recruitment checks on the suitability of practitioners applying to work with children and young people should be completed. The old 'List 99' established in 1926 was the first register of *teachers* considered 'not suitable' to practise. Interestingly the emphasis then was not on protecting children as victims but on what was considered 'inappropriate behaviour' for the teaching profession. The currently used enhanced Criminal Records Bureau (CRB) check provides information to prospective employers of any previous convictions relating to children. However, the CRB check is updated every three years and therefore the information provided on individuals working with children ceases to be current on the date of publishing until further renewal.

Currently the Independent Safeguarding Authority (ISA), a non-departmental body sponsored by the Home Office, maintains the two 'Children's and Vulnerable Adults' lists from information collated from local authorities, police and employers. These lists contain the names of individuals deemed to pose a risk of harm to children and any organization that knowingly employs someone on this list would be in breach of the law. The legal requirement is that an employee (paid or voluntary) who is dismissed or has left as a result of harming a child must be reported to the ISA who considers each case and makes a decision in light of collective evidence whether the person could or should be prevented from working with children again. This process is not infallible and the following case studies highlight how difficult judgements can be when considering the evidence against employees in the children's workforce.

Case study 1

A 23-year-old newly qualified male teacher who works with 4–5-year-olds goes out one evening to celebrate a friend's birthday. He has several alcoholic drinks and decides to leave the car and walk home. Still some distance from his house he is 'caught short' and nips into a front garden to relieve himself. The elderly owner of the garden sees him from her window and calls the police. The young man is arrested for 'indecent exposure' and the elderly lady presses charges. The young man admits the charge, although he claims that he was not aware that he was in view of somebody else. He is now subject to being reported to the ISA. He could potentially lose his job and be prevented from working with children again as a registered sex offender.

Case study 2

A group of seven 13-year-old school children, both boys and girls, report to their headteacher that a man has been indecently exposing himself regularly to them from his bedroom window opposite the school when they leave at the end of the school day. The headteacher witnesses the middle-aged man naked in front of the window smiling at the children and appearing to 'rub' himself as the children pass by his house. She immediately reports this to the police. The man is arrested but claims that his work shifts, as a children's nurse, means that he is home mid-afternoon when he takes his shower and that he was unaware that the children could see into his room. In fact he expresses concern that he is the victim of the children's intrusive behaviour. The police consider that there is not enough evidence to proceed to a conviction (Singleton 2010).

At present the ISA would consider all relevant information and make a decision as to whether these persons would present an immediate or potential risk to children and therefore be included on the barred lists. Following a review of the Vetting and Barring Scheme published in February 2011, the Coalition Government has recommended the merger of the CRB and the ISA to establish a new body responsible for checking the suitability of those working with children. Whichever body is given ultimate responsibility, the above examples illustrate how the decision-making process is complex and challenging and relies upon the expertise of individuals to make the right informed choices not only to safeguard children now and in the future but also to safeguard the interests of practitioners who can also be vulnerable to serious allegations and accusations of malpractice. The need for appropriate policy and procedure, including clear lines of accountability, is therefore essential.

Safeguarding policy in practice and evaluative reviews

In terms of overseeing the effectiveness of safeguarding policy in practice between organizations, eight inspectorates are jointly involved in reviewing the arrangements every three years. These currently include the Commission for Social Care Inspection, the Office for Standards in Education (Ofsted), the Healthcare Commission, Her Majesty's Crown Prosecution Service Inspectorate, Her Majesty's Inspectorate of Constabulary, Her Majesty's Inspectorate of Probation, Her Majesty's Inspectorate of Prisons and Her Majesty's Inspectorate of Court Administration. The most recent *Safeguarding Children's Review* were published in 2008 and 2011 and, subject to government changes, the next Report is due in 2011. The purpose of the review is to identify the effectiveness of safeguarding policy and procedures including the intervention of different agencies in all aspects of child protection.

Key issues raised as a result of the 2008 review highlighted ongoing challenges that face practitioners in the children's workforce as the report clearly states:

> Most children feel safe, and are safe, in their homes and communities. However, there are still serious concerns that some children are not well served and these children need particular attention to ensure that they are properly safeguarded.
>
> (Ofsted 2008: 2)

One aspect of safeguarding practice mentioned as effectively enabling collaborative working across disciplines is the establishment (from 2006) of the Local Safeguarding Children Boards (LSCBs). These are the statutory bodies that take a leadership role in specifying how relevant agencies, professionals and organizations should work together to promote the health and well-being of every child. It is currently the responsibility of the Local Authority to establish an LSCB within Children's Trust governance (which is accountable for the planning and commissioning of children's services within the wider remit of the Local Authority), and to ensure that the board has experienced and senior representatives from different agencies across the private, voluntary, maintained and independent sectors. The 2008 review indicates that the LSCBs are beginning to address planning for the wider implications of safeguarding as well as establishing systems to manage child protection issues effectively. This is corroborated by research into the effectiveness of LSCBs which has highlighted aspects of positive practice such as recognizing that safeguarding is a shared responsibility between different agencies and that effective communication channels are vital in ensuring the success of procedures. However, the research also identified that there was little accountability and 'links and mechanisms, to ensure the effective dissemination of information to inform operational practice, were relatively weak' (France et al. 2010: 2). While the establishment of the LSCBs would appear to be a positive move forward in prevention, there is currently little evidence to 'measure' the effectiveness of the LSCB's impact on safeguarding in general as board members are subject to their own profession's or service's accountability. In addition, the requirement of an annual report by the LSCB (DCSF 2010a) into the effectiveness of safeguarding within individual Local Authorities is self-regulating and may be more appropriately undertaken by an independent review. This may ensure the identification of effective practices and areas for development that could be shared locally and nationally thus demonstrating transparency and improvement plans of policy in practice across agencies.

Interestingly, in 2009 the Care Quality Commission (CQC), an independent regulator of health and social care services in England, reviewed arrangements in the National Health Service (NHS) for safeguarding children. While finding positive indicators such as the establishment of systems to manage safeguarding issues, the report also highlighted concerns including inadequate training of staff, confusion in the clarification of roles and the lack of effective monitoring of commissioned services. It would appear, in the light of these conclusions, that safeguarding 'systems' have been introduced within organizations with the need for further monitoring to ensure they are effective in the short and long term.

As with other agencies the police also play a vital role in safeguarding and child protection. While all officers are responsible for ensuring the protection and welfare of children under criminal law, each police force also has established child abuse investigation units (CAIUs) whose predominant role is to lead any criminal investigation involving allegations or evidence of harm against a child. Targeted professional development involving designated officers and some joint training with social care practitioners serve to illustrate a willingness to embrace the need for collaboration with other agencies in order to carry out duties for effective safeguarding practice. In 2008 a review undertaken by Her Majesty's Inspectorate of Constabulary entitled *Protecting Vulnerable People*, reported key aspects of effective practice and highlighted several interesting points that would impact significantly on effective safeguarding policy in practice. Key issues raised included the need for a consistency of approach in terms of the structures and systems in place; the need for continued appropriate and approved training for strategic roles as well as front-line officers; and the recognition of effective information sharing across agencies to aid investigations. In addition the report emphasized 'the need to develop multi-agency strategies to define common objectives and priorities for targeted partnership action' (HMIC 2008: 46).

Lessons learnt

It would appear that across the agencies involved in safeguarding children, patterns are emerging that indicate common threads of concern and highlight issues that need addressing. Considering these it remains intriguing that *Working Together to Safeguard Children* (DCSF 2009) sets out the aspirations of effective interprofessional practice and yet the evaluative reviews and government policy in relation to safeguarding are still undertaken in different departments. Any improvements may then be developed and implemented through *intraprofessional* practice. As the *Working Together* document is the key statutory guidance used by all safeguarding professionals, it may be the precursor to viewing safeguarding practice holistically across different disciplines and therefore promoting true *interprofessional* practice. As identified in the evaluative reports, there would appear to be common challenges and dilemmas facing each agency. Reviews from across the children's workforce in terms of safeguarding practice consistently make reference to the importance of having shared strategic objectives, a parity of approach between and within disciplines and the need for appropriate training for all practitioners. It may be beneficial for strategic managers and key professionals to collaborate on the most efficient and effective ways to develop a more cohesive and standardized response to improvements.

The emphasis on ensuring that effective safeguarding procedures are adhered to across different disciplines is not in doubt and even one death or serious injury to a child that could have been prevented is not acceptable. It is encouraging that agencies across the children's workforce are actively demonstrating commitment to safeguarding children's welfare. For example, in the educational system Ofsted is responsible for inspecting a school's overall performance. At present, if a school is judged to be 'poor' in safeguarding, this overrides any rating in the other areas of practice even if these are judged to be 'good' by the inspectors. The essential element of this work must be to learn from inspection outcomes and to recognize effective practice as well as identifying areas for improvement. Examining systems and procedures across the children's workforce it is clear that practitioners need encouraging to engage in critical reflection to ensure that lessons are learnt and improvements are implemented but not in isolation. Front-line practitioners across agencies need the mechanisms by which they can inform strategic managers of challenges and dilemmas and offer ways to influence the process of reform.

Serious Case Reviews (SCRs) are an example of where professional practice across different disciplines is scrutinized. They involve detailed inquiries into the events and systems surrounding a child who has been the victim of serious injury or death. The review process became mandatory in April 2008. The primary purpose of the reviews is to establish the facts surrounding the case and to identify any issues that may need

addressing locally or nationally to ensure effective safeguarding measures are implemented (Sinclair and Bullock 2002). However, Serious Case Reviews are considered by
some as controversial as published results may be open to misinterpretation (Munro
2005). Recent SCRs have identified the failings of individuals involved with the child
with little reference to the broader context and some may argue that this is inappropriate and creates a climate of mistrust between professionals, agencies and within
disciplines as 'hindsight can create a misleading sense that events could have been fore-
seen and prevented' (Kirton 2009: 80). Police, health visitors, social workers and other
practitioners involved with child protection cases make judgements in emotionally
demanding circumstances, attempting to make sure of the right conclusions. Criticism
of the SCRs identify that an emphasis on procedure is counterproductive to ensuring
that professional judgement is valued (Ayre 2001). In the future it may be that generic
recommendations may be made as a result of SCRs and local partnership case
studies will be the measure in pinpointing professional shortcomings. Certainly the
most recent report into child protection has identified a shift in practice towards a
system-driven process rather than supporting professionals in front-line practice:

> A dominant theme in the criticisms of current practice is the skew in priorities
> that has developed between the demands of the management and inspection
> processes and professionals' ability to exercise their professional judgment and
> act in the best interests of the child. This has led to an over-standardised system
> that cannot respond adequately to the varied range of children's needs.
>
> (Munro 2010: 5)

Professionals involved in safeguarding children should be held responsible and
accountable for their actions. However, this needs to be within an ethos of support and
cooperation between agencies with an enhanced consistency of approach and clear
identification and parity of systems available. The Common Assessment Framework
(CAF) is an example of where effective collaboration between disciplines could be
utilized to protect the welfare of children and potentially safeguard them from harm.
The statutory framework was introduced in 2006 as the procedure by which any
agency with a concern about a child that might need additional services to meet their
needs can instigate a process of assessment. However, initial evidence suggested that
there were difficulties for professionals recognizing its purpose alongside their 'own'
established systems of assessment. In addition, concerns expressed by practitioners
that initiating a CAF may make them vulnerable and open to possible criticism from
other professionals with opposing or different views, may be hindering the effective
utilization of this method of assessment.

Further guidance published by the Department for Children, Schools and Families,
the *National Quality Framework for the Common Assessment Framework Process* (2010),
attempted to clarify the use of this assessment tool and at present the system continues
to be refined alongside the Integrated Children's System (ICS), which is computer
software to record, collate and analyse information for agencies electronically (DCSF
2010). Interestingly it has been noted that in order for these systems to be effective, the
strategies that need to be implemented include establishing key personnel from different
agencies to 'steer' their development, identifying appropriate joint training opportunities

and establishing an agreed strategy to facilitate the sharing of information electronically (DCSF 2008a).

The recurrent themes of training, effective communication and clarification of strategic objectives have been recognized in departmental reviews concerning safeguarding from across the children's workforce. Common challenges require collaborative problem solving and it is suggested that difficulties in safeguarding policy implementation cannot be successfully addressed without a shift in thinking about interprofessional practice. There is an increase in referrals and full care order applications; for example, in 2009–10 demand increased by 34 per cent in comparison to preceding years and this has caused deep concern in partnership agencies. Currently up to 40,000 children are the subject of child protection plans and the impact of this work on front-line professionals is critical (DCSF 2010, online data). In the current economic climate it is judged to be enormously difficult to pool financial resources across agencies and therefore the overarching indication is that practitioners across disciplines are expected to do more, do it better but for less. This is compounded by the fact that when there is professional shortcoming the focus will undoubtedly be on where it goes wrong and who is responsible. While it is essential that professionals should be held accountable, there is little consideration given to workload and contextual issues for safeguarding practitioners; issues that need addressing before safeguarding children will truly become effective.

One recommendation for working effectively across disciplines is the notion of *co-location*. Enabling professionals to share practice examples, concerns, and effective strategies to manage safeguarding issues on an informal daily basis may result in a better knowledge and understanding of each other's roles and be the foundation for enhanced professional relationships and mutual trust. Having key professionals present at the initial referral stage would undoubtedly enable expertise to be shared and informed decisions made. However, there are complex challenges to be overcome in order for co-location to work effectively. For example, one of the major stumbling blocks of effective interprofessional working is the use of a common and shared language.

Case study 3

In 2006 it became apparent when planning the content for taught modules at Kingston University on the subject of 'critical issues in education' that we should address what is meant by 'working with other professionals' as this was a key recommendation of legislation. Being co-located on the same site, colleagues from the School of Health and Social Care Sciences and the School of Education came together and planned to deliver joint training to students from three different courses. The students were all work-based learners and as such were employed across a range of services in the children's workforce. These included practising social workers, managers and owners of children's centres or Early Years settings and teaching assistants or learning support assistants predominantly employed in schools. The session was delivered with all the students together arranged in small groups, each containing a practitioner from different disciplines. The format was the unravelling of a case study involving complex issues in relation to a potential safeguarding and/or child protection matter. The students were asked to debate and identify appropriate intervention strategies at different points of the 'scenario'.

It became apparent early into the session that there were not only strong differences of opinion but confusion over the language and common acronyms used in the discussions. For example, the Social Work students assumed HV meant 'home visits' whereas to the Early Years students it was reference to the 'health visitor'. The ensuing discussions resulted in some confusion and the identification of role 'overlap', particularly when discussing the need for assessment evidence. The education practitioners were unaware of the statutory requirements imposed upon the social workers and the social workers were unaware of the extensive information collated about young children and their families by those employed in educational establishments that could be shared to support their recommendations. Overwhelmingly the students' feedback requested more opportunities to explore each other's roles and to experience further training together.

Research for the Department of Children, Schools and Families and the Department of Health examining the effectiveness of interprofessional training reported that

> the opportunity to learn together to work together was very highly valued by participants, even more so at the end of the course than at the beginning. By the end of the course there were very substantial improvements in their self-reported understanding of the roles of different professionals who engage in work to safeguard children and in their confidence and comfort in working with these colleagues.
>
> (Carpenter et al. 2010: 166)

The students recognized the need for further examination of the safeguarding procedures as a result of information gleaned during their discussions with other professionals. The outcome of this work was the precursor to the establishment of the 'Institute of Child Centred Interprofessional Practice' which initiated a suite of programmes to train professionals from different disciplines together. This work continues to grow and its effectiveness and impact on practice are being monitored closely.

Ultimately *training professionals together* and the *co-location* of multi-professional teams may be considered to be appropriate ways forward in order for different disciplines to address safeguarding and child protection issues more effectively and efficiently. This is particularly important when considering the implications of *transition* and *change* on safeguarding and child protection systems, procedures and practice.

Issues and dilemmas in transition

Transition practices vary considerably between disciplines and the term itself is undeniably difficult to formalize in the context of interprofessional practice. Undoubtedly the word itself suggests a *change* in circumstances but the impact of this is dependent upon the nature of the transition itself. Fabian and Dunlop (2002: 3) state that transition is 'the process of change that is experienced when children (and their families) move from one setting to another'. While this suggests that transition is primarily concerned with a physical movement from one place to another, transition practices may involve impact on other aspects of the health and well-being of children and their families. It is likely that professionals from across the children's workforce would agree that all children undergo periods of transition that may impact significantly upon their cognitive, emotional and/or physical well-being at some point during their lives.

Transition and change are inevitable. In terms of safeguarding and child protection this may mean a child moving from an unsafe situation to a place of safety. For others it might entail a change in family circumstances that results in child and adult support services implementing strategies to prevent the child becoming at risk of harm. Whatever the situation, 'it is vital that transition is regarded, by everyone involved, as a process and not an event' (Beckett 2008:20). In addition, the impact of transition on a child or young person should not be underestimated by all those involved. Lam and Pollard (2006) consider the process of transition as 'states' described as *pre-liminal, liminal* and *post-liminal*. They consider that each of these states requires differing amounts of time invested depending upon the child, environment and issues involved in order for the transition to be effective. Undoubtedly having a shared understanding of *transition* has important and far-reaching implications for professionals in terms of time, resources and utilizing experience to meet the needs of the child and family during periods of change, uncertainty and adjustment.

Undergoing any change in personal circumstances is challenging for individuals. Predominantly adults may have the ability to rationalize the need for change and be able to foresee any difficulties that they may encounter. On occasion they may identify the support needed to facilitate positive outcomes and engage the support of appropriate services. However, children, particularly the very young, have little or no experience in managing change and consequently have few strategies to draw upon when coping with transition in practice: 'Transition is stressful for children, just as it is for adults, and the resulting stress can have a far-reaching impact on children's emotional well-being and academic achievements' (O'Conner 2007: 1). Vulnerable children and young people are subject to experience anxiety in varying degrees during periods of transition and this can manifest itself in many different ways through behaviour, emotions and actions. Therefore, working collaboratively with agencies, settings, parents and other professionals across the children's workforce is essential. This importance is further highlighted when supporting children with additional needs as these 'children and young people with disabilities or special educational needs may need additional support to manage transitions' (DCSF 2005: 17). It is the duty of all those involved with the child and their family to ensure that they 'provide integrated, high quality, holistic support focused on the needs of the child ... based on shared perspectives ... understanding and agreement' (DfES 2001: 135).

Every child's and family's needs through transition will be unique. Therefore it becomes apparent that in order to fulfil effective practice requirements the professionals involved, across different agencies, need a very sound understanding of the child's stage of development as this is crucial in preparing the child and family for any transition. If professionals are not able to identify the child's physical, emotional and cognitive ability, planning for any transition may be problematic, poorly resourced, inadequately tailored to the needs of the child and subsequently may result in long-term difficulties. Transition is unpredictable and does not follow a clear set plan with a known or anticipated outcome and, as such, agencies need to be flexible in their approach to arrangements (Dee 2006). Expertise from health, social care, police and educational practitioners can facilitate the identification of the child's specific needs and strategies to support the child through transition can then be focused on what is needed at different stages of the process, thus minimizing stress and risk to the child.

One of the most challenging aspects of safeguarding and child protection prac-tice, particularly through transition, is the involvement of parents. By definition parents have legislative rights as to how they bring up their children and there is enormous flexibility in acceptable thresholds which includes cultural and religious diversity. Most professionals actively engage in developing positive partnerships with parents and predominantly this is considered essential in developing an ethos of mutual trust and respect. Some legislative documentation clearly outlines this as a requirement for effective practice across disciplines such as the Early Years Foundation Stage (DCSF 2008b). Depending upon the situation and the role of the parent in regards to any safeguarding issue, transition is supported when professionals work in partnership with parents. This enables all those involved to have a clear understanding of the transition process and is crucial to its short- and long-term success.

A transition occurs when a child or young person's circumstances are changed from or within their 'typical' environment. This could be a change in living conditions, contact between carers and physical movement between settings and service providers (Brooker 2008). Bronfenbrenner's (1979) ecological theory of human development outlines the relevance, importance and impact of the child's environment and practi-tioners across the children's workforce should not underestimate its significance and influence on a child's well-being. Any change in a child's environment requires a period of careful consideration and planning examined from different perspectives. Practitioners should explore the *needs of the child* and the *needs of the parents* as well as the requirements of policy that could translate as the *needs of the professionals*.

An area of key importance in any transition process is the need for *effective communication* between all involved. Planning prior to a transition, support through a transition period and continued monitoring after the transition, are only as effective as the knowledge and understanding of the professionals, agencies, carers and chil-dren involved. A simplistic model for practitioners in the children's workforce to remember is 'everyone knows'. This is particularly important in relation to the involve-ment of the children themselves. The United Nations Convention on the Rights of the Child (1989) presents a global consensus about the rights of children and the import-ance of hearing the children's voice in decisions that concern them. Together with the UK legislation of the Children's Act 1989 and 2004 there is a legal framework for listening to children's views, concerns and feelings (Lancaster 2007). By consulting with children where appropriate during times of transition, practitioners can ensure that children play an active part in the process. Research has found that when chil-dren have had their views and needs listened to, 'young children can experience increased self-esteem and social competency' (Clark et al. 2003: 9).

Effective transition is an increasing issue for all agencies particularly involved with safeguarding and child protection. The number of children and young people with complex health needs is increasing, with more than 6000 children in England dependent upon assistive technology (DoH 2004). In addition there is an increase in the number of children with statements of Special Educational Needs and there are the complexities of supporting children and families with diverse cultural and religious beliefs (DCSF 2007).

One of the most contentious issues relating to effective communication in safe-guarding and child protection cases is the difficulty of sharing information between the professionals and agencies involved. In order to fully support effective transitions it is crucial that services have a consistent approach to the advice and support they offer and a coherent and transparent approach to the procedural frameworks. The sharing of information may be the means by which early and effective intervention can be deployed. However, the sharing of information between professionals and across disciplines is challenging for many reasons. The effective exchange of data can be made extremely difficult by families that drift between local authorities or when co-location of multi-professional teams is not feasible. In addition it could be argued that there is genuine misunderstanding of *data protection* and what this means in terms of *data sharing*. Some organizational cultures have embedded views against sharing what is considered confidential information between the service user and the profession, for example, the medical field. One of the first centrally accessed data bases of information held on children in England, 'ContactPoint', was closed by the government in August 2010 as it was deemed ineffective and unsuitable in supporting the most vulnerable children. What is undeniably agreed, and reflected in evaluative reviews across workforce practice, is that effective information sharing is essential for safeguarding children and young people.

However, there is inconsistency between agencies as to what and how information should be shared (to LSCBs or direct to practitioners in other agencies) as well as concerns over legalities of access to confidential data. Despite attempts at clarification (DCSF 2008a) clear guidance and joint training are required to ascertain a commonly held understanding intraprofessionally as well as interprofessionally. All stakeholders including strategic managers, front-line practitioners and service users need to have a shared knowledge and understanding to enable information to be transferred appropriately and sensitively. This may be achievable if strategic professionals from across the agencies could agree a multi-professional protocol.

The way forward

In terms of effectively safeguarding and supporting children through transitions, one of the key issues to be addressed is a requirement for *interprofessional learning*. Currently initial training for safeguarding is completed predominantly in separate disciplines which may result in inconsistencies of approach and a lack of understanding as to how professionals can support each other. There is evidence of ongoing joint training in safeguarding, once professionals have qualified within their own disciplines, but the content and delivery are very much dependent upon each local authority and local training provider (HMIC 2008). Practitioners involved with safeguarding and transition practices need a greater understanding of the thresholds across agencies. Inappropriate training may result in risk-adverse practice or, alternatively, a raised awareness of risk that may lead to higher levels of inappropriate referrals. As Anning et al. (2006: 78) state: 'The shift towards joined up thinking and working has highlighted the importance of knowledge distributed across groups of people through both formal and informal mechanisms.' A coordinated approach to learning for trainees across the children's workforce would significantly assist successful interprofessional practice and ultimately enable more effective safeguarding of all children.

Practitioners need to engage in active communication intraprofessionally and interprofessionally in order for effective practice in safeguarding and transitions to be established and maintained. Appreciative dialogue can encourage ongoing conversations, a building of professional trust and a common shared language. In addition, practitioners need to be able to listen carefully. Children, young people, parents and carers need to be heard. Other practitioners and professionals need to be listened to and their thoughts, feelings and opinions valued. It is easy to focus on policy and procedure at the expense of making informed decisions that specifically focus on the needs of individuals. As Clark (2010: 101) states: 'Meaningful participation requires a genuine collaborative relationship which respects other parties as equal partners.' Essentially listening needs to be a two-way process. Front-line professionals need to be able to communicate effectively with service users and feel able to influence strategic objectives in the short and long term.

In addition, practitioners involved in highly emotive situations need to be working within a supportive ethos across agencies. In the current economic climate increased demands and resource issues are common challenges facing practitioners across the children's workforce. It is essential that all practitioners are supported and workloads are reasonable to enable effective practice in safeguarding, child protection and transition. Ultimately efficiency cannot be achieved without the cooperation and collaboration between different agencies. Strategic managers need to ensure that they do not polarize quality practice and quality systems as each relies heavily upon the other.

The purpose of inspection is improvement (HM Government 2006). Agencies need to learn from evaluative safeguarding reviews but not at the expense of adjusting internal intra-disciplinary mechanisms without reflecting upon the wider implications. To enable and maintain quality front-line safeguarding support for children and their families, professionals from across the workforce need to understand when and why there is policy and/or procedural change. Stress related to transition is not just experienced by service users but by service providers as well. Strategic planning could take account of commonly identified issues arising from reviews within different agencies. Establishing shared objectives in safeguarding may then result in an efficiency saving through shared problem solving, for example, joint training or joint commissioning of services. It is important to ensure that any improvement is accompanied by a clarification of shared expectations across the workforce and that effective and consistent quality assurance procedures are systematically adhered to and monitored independently to ensure transparency across and between different agencies.

Conclusion

Practitioners from across the children's workforce are encouraged to reflect upon and analyse their own professional practice with a view to identifying what is effective and recognizing areas for development. While couched in personal development, in terms of safeguarding, change and transition, this practice has far-reaching implications for the success or otherwise of effective interprofessional practice. It is challenging for individuals to adopt a broader perspective of practice but it may be essential in order to build strong partnerships and mutual trust between agencies. Professionals need to know and understand themselves to recognize when they need support from other agencies. Identifying professional limitations and recognizing professional boundaries may begin to create a foundation of a truly integrated working culture for safeguarding children and young people.

Interestingly, the establishment of the Integrated Qualifications Framework (IQF) (Children's Workforce Network 2008) has highlighted the need for qualifications that reflect a shared vision and shared values across the children's workforce. Professionals involved in safeguarding children and young people recognize the need for further engagement in finding creative solutions to the issues and dilemmas facing front-line practitioners every day. Interprofessional practice in safeguarding is not just about having input from different agencies to try and address an issue as it has arisen, through a multi-agency review meeting. It is about working at the very foundations of practice; identifying a shared vision and strategic objectives across the children's workforce; sharing initial learning and ongoing training in safeguarding, thus enabling a consistency of approach; co-locating teams of professionals to promote a shared understanding, common language and ethos of support and trust; implementing lessons learnt across agencies and addressing common themes holistically. In simple terms all practitioners, professionals and agencies need to recognize and understand that safeguarding any child cannot be achieved in isolation. At the time of writing impending changes in safeguarding and child protection legislation, systems and procedures may provide the opportunity for practitioners from across the children's workforce to engage in innovative ways to protect children and enable them to cope with change and transition to reach their potential in a healthy and safe environment.

REFLEXIVITY CHECK-IN POINT

Do any of the following affect you personally or professionally?

Taking into account the issues discussed in this chapter, consider the following questions:

- Whose responsibility is it to ensure that all practitioners in the children's workforce are considered 'suitable' to work with children and how can this be monitored?
- How can practitioners ensure that they have the knowledge and understanding of appropriate safeguarding and child protection policies within and across each discipline? How might parity and consistency of approach be achieved and effectively monitored?
- In each local authority who are the representatives on the LSCBs? Are practitioners aware of decisions made by them? How is this information shared with, and what are the implications for, front-line practice?
- How can different agencies support professional learning? How can they create a supportive working ethos, as opposed to a 'blame' culture, when challenging safeguarding or child protection situations arise and professional shortcomings are identified? How can professionals learn from evaluative reviews and inspections and maintain the focus on protecting children rather than on amending 'systems'?

References

Anning, A., Cottrell, D., Frost, N., Green, J. and Robinson, M. (2006) *Developing Multiprofessional Teamwork for Integrated Children's Services*. Maidenhead: Open University Press.

Ayre, P. (2001) Child protection and the media: lessons from the last three decades. *British Journal of Social Work*, 31: 887–901.

Beckett, L. (2008) All change. *Nursery World*, 19 June.

Bronfenbrenner, U. (1979) *The Ecology of Human Development*. Cambridge, MA: Harvard University Press.

Brooker, L. (2008) *Supporting Transitions in the Early Years*. Maidenhead: Open University Press.

Carpenter, J., Hackett, S., Patsios, D. and Szilassy, E. (2010) *Outcomes of Interagency Training to Safeguard Children: Final Report to the Department for Children, Schools and Families and the Department of Health*. Bristol: DCSF.

Children's Workforce Development Council (CWDC) (2010) *The Common Core of Skills and Knowledge: At the Heart of What You Do*. Leeds: CWDC Publications.

Children's Workforce Network (2008) *Integrated Qualifications Framework*. London: CWDC Publications.

Clark, A., McQuail, S. and Moss, P. (2003) *Exploring the Field of Listening to and Consulting with Young Children*. Nottingham: DfES Publications.

Clark, R. (2010) *Childhood in Society*. Exeter: Learning Matters.

Dee, L. (2006) *Improving Transition Planning for Young People with Special Educational Needs*. Maidenhead: Open University Press.

Department for Children, Schools and Families (DCSF) (2006a) *What to Do If You're Worried a Child Is Being Abused*. Nottingham: DCSF Publications.

Department for Children, Schools and Families (DCSF) (2006b) *Common Assessment Framework*. London: DCSF.

Department for Children, Schools and Families (DCSF) (2007) *A Transition Guide for All Services: Key Information for Professionals About the Transition Process for Disabled Young People*. Nottingham: DCSF Publications.

Department for Children, Schools and Families (DCSF) (2008a) *Information Sharing: Guidance for Practitioners and Managers*. Online publication available at: www.dcsf.gov.uk/ecm/informationsharing.

Department for Children, Schools and Families (DCSF) (2008b) *Practice Guidance for the Early Years Foundation Stage*. Nottingham: DCSF Publications.

Department for Children, Schools and Families (DCSF) (2009) *Working Together to Safeguard Children: A Guide to Inter-agency Working to Safeguard and Promote the Welfare of Children*. Nottingham: DCSF Publications.

Department for Children, Schools and Families (DCSF) (2010) *National Quality Framework for the Common Assessment Framework Process*. London: DCSF.

Department for Education (2010) *Referrals, Assessments and Children Who Were the Subject of a Child Protection Plan (2009–10 Children in Need Census, Provisional)*. Online publication, available at: www.dcsf.gov.uk/rsgateway/DB/STR/d000959/index.shtml.

Department for Education and Skills (DfES) (2001) *Special Educational Needs Code of Practice*. Nottingham: DfES Publications.

Department for Education and Skills (DfES) (2004) *Children Act*. London: HMSO.

Department for Education and Skills (DfES) (2005) *Common Core of Skills and Knowledge for the Children's Workforce*. Nottingham: DfES Publications.

Department of Health (DoH) (2004) National Service Frameworks for Children, Young People and Maternity Services, Disabled Children and Young People and Those with Complex Health Needs.

Fabian, H. and Dunlop, A.W.A (2002) *Transitions in the Early Years: Debating Continuity and Progression for Children in Early Education*. London: Routledge Falmer.

France, A., Munro, E. and Waring, A. (2010) *The Evaluation of Arrangements for Effective Operation of the New Local Safeguarding Children Boards in England*. Nottingham: DCSF Publications.

Her Majesty's Inspectorate of Constabulary (HMIC) (2008) *Protecting Vulnerable People*. London: HMSO.

HM Government (2006) *Safeguarding Vulnerable Groups Act*. London: HMSO.

Kirton, D. (2009) *Child Social Work Policy and Practice*. London: Sage.

Lam, M.S. and Pollard, A. (2006) A conceptual framework for understanding children as agents in the transition from home to kindergarten. *Early Years*, 26: 123–41.

Laming, H. (2003) *The Victoria Climbié Inquiry Report*. London: TSO.

Lancaster, P.Y. (2007) Listening to children: respecting the voice of the child. In G. Pugh and B. Duffy (eds) *Contemporary Issues in the Early Years*. London: Sage.

Lindon, J. (2008) *Safeguarding Children and Young People: Child Protection 0–18 Years*. London: Hodder Education

Munro, E. (2005) A systems approach to investigating child abuse deaths. *British Journal of Social Work*, 35: 531–46.

Munro, E. (2010) *The Munro Review of Child Protection – Part One: A Systems Analysis*. London: Department of Health.

O'Conner, A. (2007) *All About Transitions: The Early Years Foundation Stage Primary National Strategy*. Nottingham: DfES Publications.

Ofsted (2008) *Safeguarding Children: The Third Joint Chief Inspectors' Report on Arrangements to Safeguard Children*. London: TSO.

Sinclair, R. and Bullock, R. (2002) *Learning from Past Experience: A Review of Serious Case Reviews*. London: Department of Health.

Singleton, R. (2010) Safeguarding children and young children, unpublished lecture, School of Health and Social Care Sciences, Kingston University.

Further reading

Foley, P. and Leverett S. (2008) *Connecting with Children, Developing Working Relationships*. Bristol: OU Press. This book examines how practitioners from across the children's workforce can learn from the views of children and their families. It includes information on children's transitions and examines the potential for children to be involved in decision-making.

Glenny, G. and Roaf, C. (2008) *Multiprofessional Communication: Making Systems Work for Children*. Maidenhead: Open University Press. This book examines a series of case studies in multi-professional work in order to understand what is effective and why.

Lindon, J. (2008) *Safeguarding Children and Young People: Child Protection 0–18 Years*. London: Hodder Education. This book examines safeguarding issues from a practitioner's perspective and provides clear guidance for effective practice.

Munro, E. (2006) *Child Protection*. London: Sage. Munro provides a useful introduction to safeguarding children, clarifying the key terms and statutory guidance presented in this chapter.

Parton, N. (2006) *Safeguarding Childhood*. Basingstoke: Palgrave Macmillan. This book presents information on child welfare policy and examines changes in philosophy and intervention that have been informed by the cultural, economic and political context.

References

Anning, A., Cottrell, D., Frost, N., Green, J. and Robinson, M. (2006) *Developing Multiprofessional Teamwork for Integrated Children's Services*. Maidenhead: Open University Press.

Ayre, P. (2001) Child protection and the media: lessons from the last three decades. *British Journal of Social Work*, 31: 887–901.

Beckett, L. (2008) All change. *Nursery World*, 19 June.

Bronfenbrenner, U. (1979) *The Ecology of Human Development*. Cambridge, MA: Harvard University Press.

Brooker, L. (2008) *Supporting Transitions in the Early Years*. Maidenhead: Open University Press.

Carpenter, J., Hackett, S., Patsios, D. and Szilassy, E. (2010) *Outcomes of Interagency Training to Safeguard Children: Final Report to the Department for Children, Schools and Families and the Department of Health*. Bristol: DCSF.

Children's Workforce Development Council (CWDC) (2010) *The Common Core of Skills and Knowledge: At the Heart of What You Do*. Leeds: CWDC Publications.

Children's Workforce Network (2008) *Integrated Qualifications Framework*. London: CWDC Publications.

Clark, A., McQuail, S. and Moss, P. (2003) *Exploring the Field of Listening to and Consulting with Young Children*. Nottingham: DfES Publications.

Clark, R. (2010) *Childhood in Society*. Exeter: Learning Matters.

Dee, L. (2006) *Improving Transition Planning for Young People with Special Educational Needs*. Maidenhead: Open University Press.

Department for Children, Schools and Families (DCSF) (2006a) *What to Do If You're Worried a Child Is Being Abused*. Nottingham: DCSF Publications.

Department for Children, Schools and Families (DCSF) (2006b) *Common Assessment Framework*. London: DCSF.

Department for Children, Schools and Families (DCSF) (2007) *A Transition Guide for All Services: Key Information for Professionals About the Transition Process for Disabled Young People*. Nottingham: DCSF Publications.

Department for Children, Schools and Families (DCSF) (2008a) *Information Sharing: Guidance for Practitioners and Managers*. Online publication available at: www.dcsf.gov.uk/ecm/informationsharing.

Department for Children, Schools and Families (DCSF) (2008b) *Practice Guidance for the Early Years Foundation Stage*. Nottingham: DCSF Publications.

Department for Children, Schools and Families (DCSF) (2009) *Working Together to Safeguard Children: A Guide to Inter-agency Working to Safeguard and Promote the Welfare of Children*. Nottingham: DCSF Publications.

Department for Children, Schools and Families (DCSF) (2010) *National Quality Framework for the Common Assessment Framework Process*. London: DCSF.

Department for Education (2010) *Referrals, Assessments and Children Who Were the Subject of a Child Protection Plan (2009–10 Children in Need Census, Provisional)*. Online publication, available at: www.dcsf.gov.uk/rsgateway/DB/STR/d000959/index.shtml.

Department for Education and Skills (DfES) (2001) *Special Educational Needs Code of Practice*. Nottingham: DfES Publications.

Department for Education and Skills (DfES) (2004) *Children Act*. London: HMSO.

Department for Education and Skills (DfES) (2005) *Common Core of Skills and Knowledge for the Children's Workforce*. Nottingham: DfES Publications.

Department of Health (DoH) (2004) National Service Frameworks for Children, Young People and Maternity Services, Disabled Children and Young People and Those with Complex Health Needs.

8

MAUREEN LONGLEY AND SAJNI SHARMA
Listening to voices of children and families, together

Introduction

This chapter argues that working interprofessionally is an imperative if we are passionate about wanting a better future for children. If we bear in mind the core values and responsibilities that we have when working with and for children, this helps us to work effectively as interprofessionals. These values underpin our shared vision of the kind of society that we want to be part of in the future and can be used to help professionals work across boundaries and cut through the misunderstandings, distrust and resentments that can sometimes arise in multi-professional teams. The notion of forming a 'team around the child' (Siraj-Blatchford 2007) positions professionals as paying attention to the child in order to meet his or her needs. In this chapter we are going to explore the interprofessional's most crucial core value and responsibility, listening to the voices of children and ensuring that their needs drive the work we do.

A child is a person, not just an object of concern.

(Butler-Sloss 1998)

One of the key unifying values and principles of working with and for children is that we believe that children and their parents are the 'experts' on their lives and children have rights that need to be listened to, championed and protected. As interprofessionals, people working with children need to explore these values and principles because they can focus them on sustainable changes in their skills, attitudes and behaviours that can benefit children and future society as well as underpin the rationale for how they focus their time and energy. Listening to children in their work contexts and acting on what they tell them requires resilience and creativity and requires interprofessionals to challenge much of the taken-for-granted practice wisdom that exists and to be open to new ways of working and thinking about themselves as professionals. When professionals strive to understand their own personalities and behaviour, it can become a lifelong process which holds the potential for positive change. For Wheatley (2005: 129), real courage comes from the heart and 'leaders need to be willing to let their hearts open and to tell stories that open other people's hearts' so they bring 'meaning' to their work and find its relevance to the lives of those children they are seeking to support.

The aim of this chapter is to raise some of the issues and questions involved in listening to children, as the issue which is at the very heart of work in the children's services sector. In so doing the chapter contributes to an interprofessional vision of listening to children *together* to help them to create a better future for them. Wheatley (2005: 204) challenges professionals to explore their 'interconnected-ness' honestly, recognize their interdependence and highlight similarities rather than differences between professions. However, *Working Together to Safeguard Children* warns, 'Some of the worst failures of the system have occurred when professionals have lost sight of the child and concentrated instead on their relationships with adults' (DCSF 2010: 5.5) bringing us firmly back to the principle of seeing the situation from the child's perspective and listening to what he or she says, observing how they are and taking serious account of their views. Different priorities according to role, varying degrees of autonomy, different support systems such as line management and supervision, different codes of confidentiality and different types of relationship with service users can get in the way of keeping a focus on the child.

Professional interconnectedness with children is no different but it carries additional responsibilities. Children need parents and professionals to provide the nurturing, safe environment that allows them to explore and grow as they gradually take on this responsibility for themselves. If children are to be supported to develop in this way, they need to be given opportunities to practise the skills they will need to influence the world around them. This will entail adults and other children helping them to make choices, to take risks and see the consequences for their actions and behaviours. Crucially, it will enable them to see how their 'interconnectedness' with others impacts on their own lives and those of others.

Listening and the responsibilities of the interprofessional

A shift of the focus of responsibility and expertise onto the child–patient–client illus-trates a fundamental aim of interprofessionals working with children, of increased autonomy for children and their families so that they develop skills and confidence in their own abilities to manage the challenges of daily life with minimal interference from service providers. However, planning for future interventions or investing in the future is not enough. It is important to acknowledge that childhood has a 'present' dimension that cannot be retrieved and relived. Using their interconnectedness to listen to children and families, interprofessionals need to question, review and develop services they are delivering *now*.

Interprofessional interconnectedness with children, families and others can be achieved and maintained by promoting a listening organizational culture. There are many benefits and opportunities to be gained from developing a listening culture despite the challenges it brings. These are outlined in Table 8.1.

Table 8.1 The benefits/opportunities and some of the challenges of developing a listening culture in an organization working for children

Benefits/opportunities	Some of the challenges
Increases understanding of the needs of individual children and their families exploring past history as well as what is happening now	In order to create the environment that will allow trusting supportive relationships with children and parents to develop, all staff and agencies need to engage with creating a shared vision or outcome for an individual child. It is sometimes particularly challenging to balance safeguarding with giving parents responsibility for decision-making
Creates opportunities to improve understanding of family dynamics. Can empower parents to engage positively with agencies and services that can support them	Seeing beyond immediate priorities and presenting issues requires time and commitment. Sensitivity and understanding are needed to see parents as the 'experts' for their child/family
Deepens understanding of how culture, and other aspects of family life are integral to children's learning and well-being	Effective empowerment is not easy but being tokenistic is. Working within an ethos of 'appreciative enquiry' needs to be balanced with being prepared to take risks, ask questions and challenge others' perception of what 'good enough' parenting is
Enhances capacity building and social inclusion so that children grow up in a community with sound values where everyone has an opportunity to contribute to the future positively	Meeting the demand for creating opportunities for evidencing outcomes within short time scales can be in tension with engaging with the wider community and allowing time for changes to make an impact. The interprofessional needs to work locally while retaining an understanding of the national and international contexts of their own work
Children can give great insights into their lives and share information with adults with whom they have secure relationships. They are more likely to talk about child protection issues if listening is part of everyday practice	It can be a challenge to convince children that what they share will be taken seriously. A key way to do this is to ensure they are informed when their views have been taken into account and equally if they have not. This requires a review of policies and practices and may require staff development and changes to appraisal and supervision
Children's views, opinions and ideas can positively contribute to the design and delivery of services, both new and ongoing activities that impact on their well-being	Staff will need to find inventive ways to ensure children of all ages and abilities are included, i.e. adults need to be in tune with non-verbal children, using all their senses and be able to respond to them in ways that are unique to them. How children's contributions can be captured and recorded also needs to be considered. Planning, time and resources are needed
There is an opportunity to learn how to work with children more effectively and tailor provision to meet their individual needs. The benefit of this is it greatly contributes to positive outcomes for all children	It can be particularly challenging to consult or listen to children who have additional or special needs. Adults will need to be tuned into the individual child's needs using different communication methods such as expression and signing. This may raise specific training needs for both staff engaged with a particular child and across the whole setting in order to be fully inclusive

(Continued Overleaf)

Table 8.1 Continued

Benefits/opportunities	Some of the challenges
Listening to and consulting children can give them opportunities to gain new skills, e.g. using a camcorder to capture areas of interest in the garden	Finding different ways of engaging children requires planning, time and enthusiasm from everyone around them. Creating a culture where this is the 'norm' rather than a one-off event is best
Provides a clear basis for planning and delivery of services that will have greatest impact. Provides evidence and evaluation to inform decision-making and priorities	It is a challenge to developing sufficient variety of consultation methods and opportunities for children and families to be involved in on-going decision-making that take into account all levels of ability and skills
Allows intervention/resources to be focused where they will be most successful and have a more sustainable longer-term impact	Balancing competing demands, some of which may be driven by the priorities within other organizations or by funders. Being an advocate for individual children and families as well as the community in different forums
Impacts positively on the relationships between professionals and agencies, by offering shared strategies for intervention	It is a challenge to work alongside some organisations where inclusion of children's and parents' views is not the norm. A 'no-blame' culture where honest discussion and the opinion of others are valued and the voices of children and parents and also those of staff from different professional backgrounds are heard is needed
Focusing on listening to children can contribute to the creation of a supportive environment between agencies and professionals where skills, knowledge and resources are deployed for mutually beneficial outcomes	It may be difficult to give sufficient time, attention and respect to gain a greater understanding of the skills, priorities and challenges within other organizations. The aim is to create an environment where sharing responsibilities is seen as positive rather than threatening and where trust, confidentiality, shared responsibilities and blurred lines of accountability are found
Informs practice allowing us to 'check out' the relevance and effectiveness of our services, shifting resources and focus in response to changing needs	Staff may need support in their roles when change is the only constant feature so they retain their positive outlook
Children are likely to comply with 'rules' that they have helped to create and engage with activities that have been suggested by them	Active listening skills need to be applied in an atmosphere of calm so children do not feel rushed
Focusing on listening to children can motivate and give direction to training and continuous professional development	There is a need to offer support to in-house staff and from other agencies to help them to understand the benefits of inclusive reflective practice and how it can be used to everyone's advantage

The culture of listening to children

The culture of listening to young voices in Early Years services is not new and this tradition is a shared principle informing practice across the interprofessional continuum of children's services. The Childcare Act 2006 places a duty on local authorities to have regard to the views of young children in the design, development and delivery of Early Childhood Services, stressing the need to consider how children's voices can help to shape and evaluate services. Likewise, Article 12 of the UN Convention on the Rights of the Child, the Special Educational Needs Code of Practice (2001), the Education Act (2002), the Children Act (1989, 2004), the Disability Discrimination Act (2005) and the Childcare Act (2006), all assert that children regardless of their age have the right to be involved in decisions that affect them, express their views and have them taken into account.

However, placing the voice of the child as a strategic driver is still a developing area. The concept of 'children as citizens' who participate in society is still not embedded in the thinking of democracy. In a democratic society 'a citizen' is someone who is recognized as a person who is involved in the decision-making process that affects them, but children under 18 in the UK do not have a right to vote and this strongly influences their position in society; how and whether they are consulted, or involved in decision-making. The younger the children, the less likely they are going to be consulted. The United Nations Convention on the Rights of the Child (UNCRC) does not establish a minimum age for children's participation but refers to children's 'evolving capacities' to be involved in decisions that affect them, suggesting that there is no reason why listening to children cannot start with the youngest people. Practitioners working as interprofessionals need to know why this principle is so important. By listening to children their right to be listened to and for their views to be taken seriously is respected so they feel safe, secure, confident and empowered. Tolfree and Woodhead (1999: 2) state that 'listening to children is about enabling them to explore ways in which they perceive the world and communicate their ideas in a way that is meaningful to them'. As well as being an integral part of effective everyday practice and incorporated into daily routines and learning opportunities, listening to children is a way of being, a position in relation to the world that has parallels with those required in interprofessional practice. An interprofessional focuses on children's perspectives about their lives to work across professional boundaries and so ensure their views and contributions shape new developments. This has a positive impact on understanding of children's priorities, interests, and concerns and how they feel about themselves and is vital in establishing secure and respectful relationships with children. However, listening not only benefits children who are being listened to, but also develops a listening culture in which listening and dialogue can sustain the work of an interprofessional learning community.

A listening culture: listening to diversity

Historically acquired attitudes and prejudices among organizations and individuals sometimes limit opportunities to act on the opinions of children with a disability.

However, the *social model of disability* (Oliver 1990) demands that we listen to all children and perceive disability as socially constructed. It is often the social and physical barriers that society creates that are seen as disabling factors and not the individual impairment.

Practitioners and parents often comment on the challenges of listening to children with limited speech and language skills. The Disability Discrimination Legislation (DDA 1995 and SENDA 2001) places a requirement on all to listen to children who are disabled with the same obligation as children without additional needs so all children are treated fairly. Children with disabilities may be less likely to be involved in a consultation process if adults act as advocates rather than listeners. For many children, using speech may not be the best way to communicate (Chamba 1999). Spoken language is only one of the ways we express ourselves. Practitioners and parents need to consider other mediums such as body language, gestures, touch, smiling, pointing as some of the natural signs of expression and communication. Picture exchange symbol (PECS), Makaton signs, and photos are some of the ways to support children's independence in decision-making.

Children with diverse needs require practitioners to build good partnerships with parents and other professionals so that they are well informed of each child's and family's values, cultural practices and individual needs. Gillespie-Edwards (2002) states that when partnership is achieved, it leads to confidence all round: confident staff, confident parents and confident children. In particular, professionals need to reflect and work together to create a positive environment which promotes equality and challenges discrimination which is reinforced by positive images, displays, activities and training support for staff to tackle discriminatory practice to establish a shared 'creative listening environment' (Marchant and Jones 2003) for all children.

Ways of listening in Early Years

Certain professional heritages favour certain tools to listen to children. Observation is a common tool used as a starting point for listening to young children to understand their abilities, needs and interests and is a strong tradition in Early Years practice. Clarke and Moss (2001) propose the 'Mosaic Approach' as a useful method that offers ways of engaging with children. This approach uses observation, interviews, photographs, drawings and child-led tours to build a picture or map of what is important to children. Practitioners then review the data (map) and discuss this with children for additional comments. This approach has been used to ascertain children's views when redesigning and developing new areas of play, in other words, finding out what the children think of their existing environment (likes and dislikes), and to inform the design of the new provision/development. When working across professional boundaries this approach could be adapted to discover not only the views of children receiving support from interprofessional teams but also the views of the different professionals involved in their care.

Early Years practitioners also use a small group 'interview' following a 'circle time' approach (Miller 1997) when each child has the opportunity to say something if they wish. Pictures, visual means of expression such as photographs, paintings, drawings, creating models, making books can be used as expressive methods for children to communicate their views. Art allows for free expression of things that may not be so easily said in words as well as creative exploration of reasons behind behaviour, emotions or likes and dislikes. The many advantages of using art and metaphor as an approach for inquiry into practice have been championed by those such as Gauntlett (2007). Similarly, role playing and imaginative play give children (and adults when they allow themselves) the opportunity to enact life situations which they have experienced so that they can communicate their experiences and what is important to them in a spontaneous and natural way. Profile books and home–school communication books are particularly useful for exemplifying children's views in interagency settings or transitions.

Case study 1: a listening culture – listening to the very young

Small people children's centre

When it came to quiet time after lunch in the day nursery, Joe (14 months) always fell fast asleep and found it hard to wake up again. His key worker, Cherie, was concerned that he tended to sleep nearly all afternoon and wondered if she should wake him after an hour or so. Cherie decided to talk to Joe's Health Visitor, Paula, after one of the Mother and Baby sessions in the Children's Centre. Paula said that she thought that Cherie should contact Joe's parents about this because they might be finding that when Joe had slept all afternoon, he found it hard to go to sleep in the evening. Cherie decided to do as Paula suggested and emailed Joe's mother straight away, asking her to pop in for a chat before 'picking-up time' on the next day, but in the meantime she decided to let Joe sleep for as long as he wished and to do an observation of him during the following morning. The observation showed that Joe became much less active as the morning progressed. He began to suck his thumb at approximately 11.30 am and follow Cherie around and almost fell asleep eating his lunch. When Cherie met Joe's mother, Anna, and mentioned her concern, Anna explained that Joe tended to stay up each evening to see his father when he got back from work at 8.00 pm. The routine was that his father would put him to bed after spending some time with him and reading a story and Joe really enjoyed it. Anna said she was quite happy for Joe to sleep longer in the afternoon than other children so that he could cope with staying up to spend time with his father and thanked Cherie for asking her about this. Cherie and Paula agreed that Joe's needs must come first and they needed to support Joe and his family in this arrangement.

Commentary

Effective listening and communication with babies require adults to have respect based on a strong belief that babies are worth listening to. This helps to build positive enriching relationships between the adult and baby (Gillespie-Edwards 2002). Babies who are not listened to grow up with low self-esteem and can present with an anxious disposition. Roberts (2002: 42) states that 'sharing children's distress in a calm way is one of the most effective things that "important people" can do to help children grow up feeling good about themselves and others'.

When babies' stress is not responded to, it can lead to them displaying aggressive and anxious behaviour when older (Bruce 2004). Adults need to acknowledge that babies are already expert communicators and that they get their needs met by displaying a variety of skilful communication skills, in other word, smiling, crying, babbling, which demand adult response. Adults constantly 'tune in' to babies especially when attending to their needs, changing a nappy, bathing, feeding, etc. Most parents are deeply in tune with their babies and therefore practitioners need to listen to parents in order to listen to babies to discover key aspects of their needs and routines. Developing positive relationships with parents is imperative for this to happen. A way to develop and share confidence in this partnership is to empower staff with this skill to share it informally and in training sessions with other practitioners who may not be hearing the voices of babies so well.

Ways of listening in health services

There are models of listening to and including people in decision-making that are shaping new practices for other professionals such as for professionals working in Health (NHS) provision. Tattersall (2002) comments that patients should no longer be seen as passive customers receiving information about their conditions and treatments as 'education'. The aim should be that patients control their treatments. This way of working, which does require a significant cultural shift in attitudes and behaviours of health professionals, is having a sustainable impact on the management of chronic conditions that require the patients to become experts in their own right.

Ethics, consent and power

The biggest ethical challenge for researchers working with children is the disparity in power and status between adults and children (Morrow and Richards 1996) and this is even more challenging when working with very young children and those with additional needs. The same challenge applies to professionals who are seeking to find out children's views on their own lives. Tacit power dynamics between different professionals who are championing the child and family can complicate this process as different professionals may 'hear' different messages and may privilege the voice of the parent rather than the child or prioritize different aspects of a child's life. Building relationships with and working alongside parents can be difficult to balance. For interprofessionals working with children, relationships with parents are very important but while there is a primary concern for the safety, development and well-being of children, practitioners also want to understand how to empower parents to be the best they can be so they actively engage in the education and development of their children. Good communication systems beween professionals are a feature of high quality interprofessional practice that can benefit parents by decreasing the numbers of times they may have to repeat details relating to their children. Professional groups differ in how far they view parents as having useful knowledge that can contribute to decision-making. In Children's Centres questionnaires can be useful to consult parents but there are other more creative ways to engage with parents' views such as graffiti walls, mapping the local area, time lines, and photograph montages. The use of cameras, video, social networking sites may enable practitioners to reach different groups of parents.

Conclusion: a focus on interprofessionalism?

It is an interprofessional responsibility that professionals get to know each other as people. Just as children and parents are empowered when they are consulted, so are interprofessional colleagues. When someone takes an interest in them as individual people as well as their workload priorities, it paves the way to interactions in which they are able to collaborate effectively and understand other ways of working. Wheatley (2005) encourages professionals to remain curious about each other, as a way of maintaining their interconnectedness and relevance to each other rather than being in competition. The aim should be an openness and meaning in interprofessional work that will underpin listening to others as a way of practising or a way of *being* interprofessional.

Anning et al. (2006) highlight one of the positive benefits of listening to other professionals as the opportunities it creates for professional knowledge and expertise of individuals to be distributed across the team. This inclusive way of working brings benefits to decision-making by helping practitioners to be better informed. It is a model used in family group conferencing in which the family are helped to see and acknowledge the issues that concern professionals and to discuss the impact of the issues, the options and potential for change and how this might be taken forward. There are demands and contradictions embodied within this approach to working with children and families that will test not only the skills but the values and judgements of those responsible for managing this process. However, the consequences and risks of not including children, parents and other professionals in decision-making are greater if we exclude them. Common sense and experience tell us that we are more likely to achieve sustainable empowering outcomes if all those who have an investment in this process are listened to and are allowed equality of contribution.

REFLEXIVITY CHECK-IN POINT

Consider your personal or professional professional responses to the following questions:

- In your work setting how can you encourage and support children to contribute to the design, delivery and implementation of the activities and services they receive?
- In your professional practice how do you ensure that disability, language, cultural or *professional* differences are not seen as barriers to participation?
- What skills and knowledge do you need to develop that will enable you to work proactively towards an inclusive interprofessional culture?

References

Anning, A., Cottrell, D., Frost, N., Green, J. and Robinson, M. (2006) *Developing Multiprofessional Teamwork for Integrated Children's Services: Research, Policy and Practice*. Maidenhead: Open University Press.

Bruce, T. (2004) *Developing Learning in Early Childhood*. London: Paul Chapman.

Butler-Sloss, E. (1988) *Report of the Inquiry into Child Abuse in Cleveland*. London: HMSO.

Chamba, R. (1999) *On the Edge: Minority Ethnic Families Caring for a Severely Disabled Child*. Cambridge: Policy Press.

Clark, A. and Moss, P. (2001) *Listening to Young Children: The Mosaic Approach*. London/York: National Children's Bureau and Joseph Rowntree Foundation.

Department for Children, Schools and Families (DCSF) (2010) *Working Together to Safeguard Children: A Guide to Inter-agency Working to Safeguard and Promote the Welfare of Children*. Nottingham: DCSF Publications.

Gauntlett, D. (2007) *Creative Explorations*. London: Routledge.

Gillespie-Edwards, A. (2002) *Relationship and Learning: Caring for Children from Birth to Three*. London: National Children's Bureau.

Marchant, R. and Jones, M. (2003) *Getting It Right: Involving Disabled Children and Young People in Assessment, Planning and Review Process*. Brighton: Triangle.

Miller, J. (1997) *Never Too Young: How Young Children Can Take Responsibility and Make Decisions*. London: National Early Years Network/Save the Children.

Morrow, V. and Richards, M.P.M. (1996) The ethics of social research with children: an overview. *Children & Society*, 10: 90–105.

Oliver, M. (1990) *The Politics of Disablement*. Basingstoke: Macmillan.

Roberts, R. (2002) *Self Esteem and Early Learning*. London: Paul Chapman.

Tattersall, R.L. (2002) The expert patient: a new approach to chronic disease management for the twenty-first century. *Clinical Medicine*, 2(3): 227–9.

Tolfree, D. and Woodhead, M. (1999) Tapping a key resource. *Early Childhood Matters*, 91: 19–23.

Wheatley, M. J. (2005) *Finding Our Way: Leadership for an Uncertain Time*. San Francisco, CA: Berrett-Koehler.

PART 4
Leading

9

SALLY GRAHAM AND JOY JARVIS
Leadership of uncertainty

Introduction

The time we are living in has been described as 'an age of uncertainty' (Barnett 2007: 136). While it has always been impossible to predict the future, it seems that the world is becoming more uncertain and this relates both to the bigger picture of issues with climate, natural resources and economies and more local factors such as roles, working practices and questions about where authority lies in a particular context. Our focus in this chapter is on leadership but who are the leaders today, when individuals can use the internet to raise issues, challenge accepted practice, bring people together to act and bring about change? Additionally, those designated as leaders are being challenged by media and individuals and groups as never before.

Uncertainty is an aspect of current Early Years practice, with multi-disciplinary working, new services and changing relationships with children, families and colleagues. Rapid change, uncertainty about the future and new role expectations can lead to insecurity and lack of clarity about how to move forward. Where there are no clear examples to follow, limited ideas of what new services and ways of working may need to look like, and in a context where rapid change is normal, it can be difficult to know how to act. We are moving into 'new spaces' in terms of ways of working as professionals with each other and with clients, and as Barnett (2007: 157) warns us, new spaces are 'spaces of uncertainty, anxiety and risk; and voyaging into such space requires courage . . . and a preparedness . . . to enter otherness; new understandings; new positions in the world'.

In this chapter we will argue that Early Years practitioners are well placed, by the nature of our knowledge and skills, to operate successfully in contexts of uncertainty. Our practice requires us to look at the world as if through others' eyes – how else would we be able to respond to the idiosyncratic communication of very young children, for example? How could we interpret their actions and respond appropriately to their initiations? We will argue that this ability, and other features embedded in

Early Years practice, enable us to rise to the challenge of an uncertain context. For all of us in Early Years settings it as an opportunity for developing new practices that are both responsive to changing situations yet deeply rooted in what is essential for high quality working.

Three stories

We will explore what 'leadership of uncertainty' might look like by focusing on three people working in a fictional Early Childhood Centre that has been open for about eighteen months. Melanie has just been appointed Centre Leader, following the retirement of the person who established the Centre. Steve is entering his second year as a social worker and has been at the Centre for six months. Jan has been the secretary in the Centre since it was set up and has lived in the area all her life.

Melanie's story (Children's Centre Leader)

I have just been appointed as Centre Leader and have never been called a leader or manager before. I know the previous leader was very charismatic – a 'human dynamo' people called her. She established the mission statement, ways of working, and the procedures which I agreed at interview to follow. Also, there is the focus on standards and checklists and ensuring we are following all the regulations. Now I have been here a couple of months I find that there are things I would like to do differently but I don't feel there is any room for manoeuvre. The team here seem to follow what they have been told to do, but don't really show any initiative. I feel they expect me to make all the decisions because I am the leader, but with all the different professionals here I don't know as much as them about their specialist areas. I don't know how to lead without telling them what to do and I am not sure about how to change things.

There is still limited research about leadership of practice in Early Years contexts, although useful studies and texts in the field are emerging (Siraj-Blatchford and Manni 2007; Whalley 2008; Miller and Cable 2011). Many of our ideas about leadership relate to traditional approaches of hierarchy, control and performance management or to notions of charismatic individuals who persuade people to action by force of their personalities. Melanie feels isolated as the only leader in her setting. However, the notion of 'distributed leadership', where all members of the organization or setting are expected to contribute to its leadership, would seem appropriate in a context where individuals hold a range of expertise (Ancona et al. 2007). Whalley (2008: 98) calls for a 'leaderful team' where each person sees themselves as a leader taking responsibility for the development and ongoing direction of the setting. Arguably, the current complexity of current practices and responsibilities in Early Years settings means that sharing leadership could be considered the only practical response. Working in this way could lead to a situation where through 'collaborative efforts teams can shape common purpose, agree on performance goals, define a common working approach, develop high levels of complementary skills and hold themselves mutually accountable for results' (O'Donoghue and Clarke 2010: 62). Melanie has read about distributed leadership but is frustrated that her team members don't take initiative themselves and she doesn't, as yet, know how to move forward.

Steve's story (Children's Centre social worker)

I have been working at this centre for about six months and I am not sure if a change of leader will make a difference or not. I like working with the families and children but I feel that the Centre has a very 'educational' view of practice and that the way we do things doesn't always relate well to my social work perspective. The teachers don't seem to understand the bigger picture sometimes and have a very narrow view of what is best for the child. Also, I feel the approach is a bit feminine, but maybe I think that because I am the only man on the staff. I don't always agree with the approaches we take so sometimes I go round them and do things a bit my own way. No one seems to notice. I just keep my head down in meetings as I find it difficult to explain why things don't seem right sometimes; it's just the way it feels. Also, I am outnumbered!

In Early Years settings people come from different professional heritages. They may have identities which have been established in their professional education and practice and they may see themselves and their work from a particular perspective. Studies of multi-professional teams have identified that the effects of these heritages need to be addressed if professionals are to work together effectively (Anning et al. 2006). Practitioners like Steve need to retain their professional knowledge and skills in order to contribute these to the work of the team, but in an integrated way, not as a source of conflict. Steve appears to be seeing himself as a social worker surrounded by those thinking differently from him. He is retaining his original professional identity. Worryingly, he is not always conforming to the identified ways of working in the Centre. Wenger (1998) has argued that a person's understanding of his or her identity informs how they act in practice. Steve sees himself as a social worker and is telling a story of practice that is divided along professional lines. White and Featherstone (2005) have argued that these stories, which build identity, can 'reinforce professional boundaries' and lead to a 'them' and 'us' perspective that does not support team working.

Steve states that he cannot articulate his problems with some of the Centre practices but it is how he 'feels'. While formal theory underlies some professional knowledge, practitioners also create their own theories based on experience. Professional decisions are made in relation to situations embedded in contexts that are unique and these decisions are likely to be made partly on informal theories that the practitioner may not be able to articulate. The idea that some knowledge underlying professional practice is tacit and may result in intuitive action is acknowledged in relation to many professions (Atkinson and Claxton 2000). Underlying assumptions about how the world is or should be are even less likely to be examined or questioned. If the knowledge and understanding that underlie much of an individual's practice are not articulated and explored with colleagues who are working together in a team, then it will be difficult for a shared understanding of practice to be developed. Melanie will need to find a way of helping Steve and the other team members to do this.

Jan's story (Children's Centre secretary)

I have lived in this town all my life and have brought up three children who have all now left home. I started working here at the Centre when it opened and I am responsible for all the administrative tasks. I have an office near the entrance which is nice in one way in that I get to see a lot of people, but it can be a problem as the young mums in particular like to talk to me and that means I get behind with my work. There has been such an increase in paperwork, even in the last few months, so I can easily get behind. I like to be efficient; I was told that was why I was appointed. I like to have everything accurate and organized so I can produce any information that we are asked for when it is needed. We usually have such short deadlines for things that if I am not on top of it, there could be a problem. I may ask the new leader for a blind for my window so that people don't know I'm here sometimes so I can get on. Some of the mums want to talk about their children's behaviour; bed-wetting and such. They know me and know I've had children of my own who've turned out fine. I tell them to talk with the practitioners as they are the professionals. I expect they do. I think there are sessions on behaviour. I don't like to talk with the practitioners about this myself as it is not my role and I don't want to interfere with their way of working. Our mission is 'Excellence in Working with and for the Community'. I think the practitioners work very hard here to do this.

Although Jan is not a designated Early Years practitioner, she is part of the staff team at the Centre. The Centre could be seen as a 'community of practice', a term Wenger (1998) uses to describe a group of individuals pursuing a joint enterprise and developing ways of working and social relationships. This practice involves distinctive procedures, rituals, language, artefacts, relationships, roles and identities that are part of reinforcing and building community and distinctiveness. The Centre staff has formed a set of 'ways we do things round here'. Jan has developed, or has been given, a particular role and she appears to see this as separate from the work with the families. It would seem important that Melanie develops a context where Jan can be more connected to the essence of the work at the Centre. The fact that she is well known and respected locally would seem to be an important asset that could contribute to the Centre's work.

A key purpose of a Children's Centre is to develop holistic services for children and families by breaking down organizational and professional barriers that can lead to fragmentation of services. However, as research in this area has shown, there are significant issues that need to be addressed if they are to be successful (Anning et al. 2006). While what is visible are features such procedures and practices, underneath are professional values, identities, power relationships and, as we noted earlier, anxiety. Although it is tempting to leave the underpinning issues unaddressed, these are what will drive practice and ultimately determine the extent to which everyone works together effectively. In order to work at this deep level, practitioners have to develop trust in each other. They have to have the confidence to recognize and articulate what they don't know as well as what they do – something that can be difficult if an individual is seen as an 'expert' in a particular area. Individuals need to acknowledge 'doubt and uncertainty, to recognise your limits as a resource, as a place of encounter, as a quality. Which means that you accept that you are unfinished, in a state of permanent change, and your identity is in the dialogue' (Rinaldi 2006: 183–4). Rinaldi's words, from the context of Reggio Emilia early childhood approaches, emphasize that we are all continually developing together and in dialogue with others we develop our individual and collective identity.

Wells (1999) identifies dialogue as shared meaning making with a focus on inquiry. Drawing on the work of Vygotsky he argues that for real learning to take place, there needs to be a co-construction of knowledge through exploratory talk. This implies the rejection of defending individual positions and requires a context of safety. There must be some form of equality in contributions, and therefore a way of establishing this is needed in a context where there may be unequal power relations. Clarke and colleagues (2001), exploring teachers' conversations, stressed the importance of safety, trust and care in the context.

Talking about a topic is not, however, necessarily simple. Pearce (1994) has noted that when we come to an interaction we bring not just our linguistic skills but also our understanding of the context, our understanding of our own and the other's roles, our history and our cultural context. Interaction is part of the way we develop our identities; Bakhtin argues that we become ourselves in dialogue (Holquist 1990). Participants in interaction, therefore, are not just exchanging linguistic meaning, they are establishing their own and each other's identities. Bohm (1996) argues that a process whereby people identify their own views, analyse them and try to 'win the game' is discussion, it is not dialogue. Dialogue, he believes, involves 'opening up judgements and assumptions' (1996: 46) by each person identifying and suspending their assumptions so that something new can form in the space between. He quotes Krishnamurti's analogy of a cup needing to be empty before anything can be put in it. True dialogue would be when we could stand back from our assumptions, identify them, see them as separate from their personal and cultural histories that made them part of us and then create something new in our understanding of the topic we are exploring. Melanie is aware that she needs to work with her colleagues in this way if she is to develop connected and effective working at the Centre, but she is not confident about how to do this in practice.

Melanie's story (Children's Centre Leader)

I am finding it quite stressful at the moment, with no time to think and work out what we really should be doing. There is so much to do that I am just grateful to get to the end of the day without anything disastrous happening. We have had a new list of procedures that we have to audit our practice against and I was going to use my first whole day in-service session with the staff team to do this. I need to show I am up to date and efficient. However, something has happened to make me change my mind about this. A friend who knows I am thinking a lot about leadership because of my new role gave me a copy of the *Resurgence* magazine she gets. It deals with environmental concerns, but this issue focused on leadership. In this magazine Satish Kuma wrote: 'True and effective leadership is more about inspiration, facilitation and right action than about outcome, achievements and unrealistic targets' (Kumar 2011: 1).

I thought about this a lot as it resonates with me but the problem is the job description is all about outcomes and we certainly have to meet targets and I think some of them are unrealistic. However, then I realized that this quote is not saying that we don't have to do these things, it is saying that they are not what leadership is about. We do need to be inspired – I would like us to have a vision of what we are doing so that we work together to do this. The 'facilitation' in the quote is about me facilitating other people to share their visions so we understand each other and can build our principles together and practices that come from this so we do the 'right action'. I like the idea of right action as it implies we have principles underpinning what we do. It is to do with what is morally right and fair and what we really want for children and families.

I am not sure how to do something about this at our away day. I would like us to go out of the Centre so we can have a space that is not influenced by our normal practice, the things we see around us and the ways we are used to working. I would like us to have an informal day where we explore ideas, perhaps using creative activities such as some of those I did on my NPQICL course. They were good for me when I was exploring my thinking with other people from different settings but I am not sure how they will work with me leading. Will people think I don't have direction? If we use creative approaches will people, especially Steve, think it's a bit emotional and girly? I would like to take the day slowly so people can get to know each other but the emphasis in practice seems to be about fast pace and getting things done and ticking things off.

One problem about planning the day is the agenda. I have looked at the agendas of in-service days at the Centre before and they were very efficiently planned in advance with a column next to each item for action to be taken. The leader seemed to know what she wanted to achieve in advance, whereas my ideas may seem vague and a bit weak. Also, before I took up this post I went on a Local Authority course on how to run meetings. The people running it explained how to 'manage' a meeting, how important it was to decide how much time to allocate to a topic and then keep to that and how to stop people from talking too much. This conflicts with what I want to do. Have I the courage to take what I think is the right action?

Melanie is beginning to articulate her ideas on leadership which move away from the idea of leader as hero towards leader as facilitator. Research in organizations suggests that leadership can be viewed 'as a set of four capabilities: *sensemaking* (understanding the context in which a company and its people operate), *relating* (building relationships within and across organisations), *visioning* (creating a compelling picture of the future), and *inventing* (developing new ways to achieve the vision)' (Ancona et al. 2007: 94). Melanie first of all wants to build relationships within her staff group and start to develop shared principles, which can lead to the development of practices aligned with these. She wants to develop shared sensemaking, whereby people in the Centre can understand how they work within the setting and how this relates to the wider community. She is looking to use the in-service day for professional development rather than for managing aspects of practice. As such she is already seeing herself as a leader of people and of learning rather than a manager of practice. In this role she is searching for a professional development approach to enable people to reflect on their practice and what underpins this. This relates to the original work by Agyris and Schön (1978) who explained 'single-loop' learning as looking at your practice in the light of whether the actions fit with your theory of how things should be done. 'Double-loop' learning, on the other hand, involves questioning and examining the assumptions underpinning the practice. This would involve exploring moral and ethical issues.

This form of professional development can be difficult to initiate. It can involve the emotional aspects of professional work which may be unacknowledged and yet often drive practice. Anning (2001) for example, records practitioners in the Early Excellence Centres she researched as talking about themselves as being 'passionate' about their jobs. Reflective practice could also be seen as relating to 'female values' in leadership. In studies of organizations the idea of expanding approaches to leadership and learning to include ways of working that have been marginalized is developing. Marshall (1994: 166) suggests that themes underlying 'male values' are 'independence, focus, control of the external world and questing outward' while those underlying 'female values' are 'interdependence, openness, cycles of change and renewal and looking inward'. While stressing that these qualities are not gender-specific, the 'male' approach has come to be dominant in ways of acting in public life. For this reason it could be labelled as being the dominant, rather than the male approach. Marshall argues that this needs balancing in order for organizations to be able to gain from both approaches. Accepting the value of intuition, tacit knowledge, personal experience and emotional engagement would allow these aspects to be acknowledged in decision-making. Extreme rationality, which may be part of the dominant approach, could mean that we are less able to respond to uncertainty, which by its nature may not be open to argument based on current information. The valuing of diversity rather than conformity can allow a wider range of perspectives and understanding to flourish which could embrace uncertainty: 'Living creatively with differences requires dedication, courage and a continual willingness to learn from discomfort' (Marshall 1994: 172). In our settings we need to create the conditions for being comfortable with discomfort in order to learn together. This relates back to the idea of trust. In order to challenge each other in a way that leads to professional growth rather than conflict, we need to trust each other. We need to be able to have uncomfortable conversations about practice knowing that we respect each other and each other's work and that we have the same vision for what we would like to achieve. Can Melanie begin to build this context of trust?

Steve's story (Children's Centre social worker)

I wasn't really looking forward to the away day as they tend to be a bit boring. We go through documents and procedures but I feel nothing really changes, although it might look as though it does. It was better this time going away to the room in a local hotel as it was more relaxing, you didn't feel so constrained about what you might say as you weren't in your own role. I felt I could be myself a bit more and perhaps say what I think. We didn't have a specific agenda which was a bit disconcerting. We usually go over the minutes of the last meeting and check we've done our actions. This was good as I couldn't remember what mine were! Melanie explained that the aim for the day was to get to understand each other better and to develop a vision for the way we want to work in the future. This seemed a bit vague and grand but I went with it as I wanted to be supportive to Melanie.

The first activity we did was that we all had to put our name badges spread out on a large piece of paper. We then had to go round everyone and find personal, not work, connections such as places we've been on holiday, food we like, hobbies, pets and on. As we found a connection with someone else we drew a line between our two name badges. The aim was to find as many connections between each other and the person who found the most in ten minutes won a prize. I clinched it by finding out that Jan and I support the same football team! It was good finding out these things as we can talk about them again and also you saw the person behind the role. Also we had a laugh, which you don't get much these days at work.

Then we were given paper and different sorts of crayons and had to draw a picture of ourselves and on sticky notes we had to write all the different areas of knowledge and skills that we brought to our work. We had to think back to our professional training as well as our different experiences and this was interesting as there were things that I can do that I had forgotten about. Then we all had to have different coloured sticky notes and go round and add to their pictures what we thought each of our colleagues brought to their work. This was good because we each discovered things we didn't know we brought to the work of the Centre. Apparently I am very good at getting fathers to open up and talk about things.

The third activity was when we put speech bubbles on a large picture of a centre. On these speech bubbles we put what we thought the children, families and other people in the community thought about the Centre. It was difficult to do this because we realized we didn't really know. Jan probably contributed most to this which surprised me as I didn't think in her role she would know much about the clients. This made us think about how we listen to people – if we do!

After lunch we were asked to create something to represent how we would see the ideal Children's Centre in ten years' time. It could be realistic or a metaphor. We could work in pairs or on our own and use a range of practical materials. Most people made a collage with materials, while I used building blocks; it was a long time since I'd got my hands on some of that! We then explained our models to each other – they were quite different in some ways but had some key words that connected them. We collected these words, and the idea is that we are going to look at these when we next work together like this and see if we can identify the principles underpinning our practice. We will then be clear what we are all working towards. We decided to focus initially on one word that kept coming up and that was 'listening'. We all put places for listening to families and children on our models and we all identified ways in which we have skills in listening to clients, including using observation schedules with children and so on. We had been surprised that we didn't really know how people saw us so we thought one thing we are going to do is to listen out for comments and collect evidence, but we also might plan a way of asking people. We will talk about this at our next staff meeting. At the end of the day I thought that this was the most I had been listened to since I started here.

The day Melanie created was a professional learning day that focused on listening to each other, exploring what people saw as good practice and beginning to ask questions about that practice in action. She is beginning to develop a 'learning community' (O'Donoghue and Clarke 2010) in the sense of the whole community learning and changing together. The ability to learn is an essential part of being able to live in uncertain times as we are continually facing new situations and creating new ways of working. Focusing on learning together can help us to develop both our principles and our practices in an open and trusting context.

Rinaldi (2006: 137) argues that 'personal and professional development and education are something we construct ourselves in relation with others, based on values that are chosen, shared and constructed together. It means living and living ourselves in a permanent state of research.' One way of moving forward together is to see the development of practice as action research. Action research is about people, often groups of people, investigating their own practice in order to improve it. It involves being able to articulate the practice, collect information from different sources about what is happening, evaluate the information and use it to implement change. This then leads to the next cycle of research where the pattern is repeated in the new context. As McNiff (2010: 22) notes in her book of guidance for action researchers: 'the action is about doing, while the research is about saying how you know what you are doing'. Following a clear set of guidelines about how to do action research gives us a clear framework for identifying and evaluating what we are doing and being part of a cycle of change and renewal. Action research will require documenting our practice which enables us to articulate it to others. This enables us to develop our professional voices and to have a sense of agency in an uncertain context.

Melanie was concerned to develop shared principles from which practice could then be derived. Early Years practitioners are well placed to work with principles as their practice is principle-led. For example, the belief underpinning practice in the Reggio Emilia approach, of the child being a competent and capable learner (Rinaldi 2006), leads to the principle of following the child's interests rather than directing the child's activities. Principles guide practice and are derived from values and beliefs. Values of respect, inclusiveness, fairness and equality come to the forefront of our minds as we work with children who are developing their way of being in the world. We are aware, as educators in the broadest sense, that everything we do will have an effect on the developing child. Van Manen (1991) argues that our values and principles, our knowledge of children in general and in particular, our understanding of the context, the past and the potential future, all lead us to act in what we see as the best way in a given 'pedagogical moment'. This pedagogical moment could be when a child shows us a picture they have created and we respond with interest, recognizing the value in the work and the effort that has gone into creating it. It could also be when we respond to a parent who shows us a video clip of how they are dealing with a 2-year-old child's tantrums and we recognize the effort and concern they are showing.

We will therefore understand the need to establish our principles of working which can guide what we do. In times of change our underpinning principles can provide the rock under the shifting sands. Our practice will change in response to new situations but having shared values and principles means that each person has a base on which to build her or his practice. This gives us confidence to act in uncertain times. It links to Barnett's (2007: 127) concept of ' "authentic uncertainty" – of being authentic amid uncertainty'.

It is interesting that 'listening' emerged as an aspect that Melanie's colleagues identified as something that is important to their practice and that this could be a focus for their investigations, which could perhaps become an action research project. Listening to children has always been an important part of Early Years practice and this concept is taken in the broadest way to include observing and following the child's lead. Work we use in our practice such as Trevarthan's (1993) observations of reciprocity between parents and babies, and Bruner's (1983) recording of sensitive adult–child interactions that scaffold children becoming learners in a cultural context, can be applied directly to dialogue development work between adults. Rinaldi (2006: 114) argues that listening means 'giving value to others; it does not matter whether you agree . . . Competent listening creates a deep opening and predisposition to change'.

Listening to people with other views, attempting to understand those views and how they came to be held has been described as 'connected knowing' (Belenky et al. 1986: 101). This is distinct from 'separate knowing' where people stand back from knowledge, see it as impersonal and talk is aimed at establishing answers through reason. With connected knowing the aim is to develop ideas through coming to understand different perspectives. The ability to do this is not gender-specific, although in cultural contexts where power and authority, and decisions about ways of thinking, acting and leading have been male, this connected knowing is often seen as a more female approach. Melanie modelled the value of listening to each other as professionals, as well as to clients, by setting up activities that involved people in listening and responding to each other in positive ways. This begins to lay the foundation of trust and shared understanding and purpose which could support more challenging conversations in the future.

Melanie showed courage in trying creative approaches in her professional development approach. As authors of this chapter we advocate this way of working, using what could be termed 'arts-based' approaches and have written about it (Jarvis and Trodd 2008). We have also worked with a range of both practitioners and researchers to understand the value of these approaches (Graham 2010). Using physical materials to model practice is a way of creating metaphors which are one way we understand the world. Metaphors allow us to explore what underpins our ideas; thinking about what it means if we represent our professional work as 'gardening', for example, can lead us to surface tacit ways of thinking. Playing with objects as representations of aspects of our work and placing them in relation to one another allows us to ask questions such as 'why do I give this aspect more prominence that the others?' or 'why have I placed a model of myself nearer to the child than to the parents?' Building and reflecting on a collage can allow an articulation of perceptions and for making new connections. As Early Years practitioners we recognize the value of play in children's learning. For adults too the opportunity to play allows exploration without constraints and enables new connections and thinking to emerge.

Imaginary case studies or stories of practice, rather than actual cases, can allow practitioners to explore different perceptions of best practice in a context where there is emotional distance between the activity and reality, so that individuals do not feel threatened and become defensive and not open to exploring. We can consider these stories in the light of whether they resonate with us or whether we experience dissonance, where we see the example as not good practice. These responses, often made initially at an emotional level, can help us to unpack our underlying assumptions. To what extent have Melanie's approaches affected her colleagues' way of working?

Jan's story (Children's Centre secretary)

I was really amazed by the away day we had. Usually I get the agenda organized, copy all the documents we need and take the minutes. This time I didn't do any of this. I joined in as one of them – or us maybe. I think people started to see me more as a person rather than just a secretary. Also, I feel we are a bit more connected with each other. Now Steve and I are usually commiserating with each other on Monday mornings as our team are not doing well in the league at the moment.

When we looked at each other's strengths I learnt so much about what the other practitioners do. I was also surprised about what they thought of me. I hadn't realized that some people saw me as a bit of a mother figure! I am older than them all and I do make the cakes for special days, but I hadn't realized that this view could be useful in working with the families who come here.

I didn't want to make a collage on my own as I was no good at creative things at school, but I worked with Melanie and we made a really good picture which had lots of my ideas in. I had thought about things that she hadn't and she found this really useful. I didn't think I could contribute to ideas for what would be done at the Centre but she really listened to me and the others thought my ideas were good.

Since we have got back I have been thinking about our focus on listening and I realized that lots of mums have been trying to talk to me but I wasn't listening to them. I don't have time and, really, I am not an expert but I thought that it would be good if we could have an informal drop-in session when the health visitor was there and parents could talk with her. It wouldn't be formal with appointments that make things seem serious but it would be an opportunity to bring things up over a cup of tea. I suggested this to Melanie and now we have a Tuesday morning session when the health visitor comes and lots of parents come. I make the cakes!

Another new initiative is that Steve decided that as the only man he should do something with fathers more. He found a fathers' network on the internet and he decided to get a group of fathers together to make some materials for our website. Some of the fathers meet to write a blog every week. We've had more men in the Centre in the past month than ever before. It wasn't in our action plan to do this but it's happened, like my drop-in session.

Melanie is developing her own leadership by facilitating the leadership of others. She is beginning to develop Whalley's (2008: 98) 'leaderful team' in the Centre. This will give her team strength in a context of uncertainty. She is also developing her leadership of community so that all those involved can be connected to the Centre and to each other through trust and mutual understanding. This will allow them to deal more effectively with discomfort and disagreement which is inevitable in complex contexts. Melanie is showing leadership of principles by exploring underlying values and principles that will drive the way of working in the Centre. Practice will need to change as new conditions emerge but if practice is developed from shared principles then new ways of working will be understood and recognized as being responsive but based on authentic principles. Melanie's team are still at an early stage in developing their principles and will need to find ways of working that will enable them to continue to do this. Her approach of identifying what practitioners think is important will need to be balanced by an investigation into what clients see as important. This will require openness to ongoing learning and a cultivation of curiosity. Leadership of learning will be essential in an uncertain context. Action research can be undertaken by using clear yet simple steps involving enquiring into our work, taking steps to improve it, evaluating what we have done and learned and then documenting this. One could argue that this is what we do in practice anyway but that we are making the process more systematic and open for discussion. The process and results could be shared on a website, a discussion session with clients and practitioners or in a professional publication so that knowledge can be shared beyond the single setting.

Leadership of uncertainty involves leadership of community, leadership of principles and leadership of learning (Figure 9.1). In new spaces it is our ability to lead our own practice, to work in collaboration with others and to imagine and create new ways of working that will enable us to be effective. In order to create responsive and developing services for children and families, each of us will need to develop our leadership strengths and be prepared to take on leadership responsibilities. Leadership of uncertainty involves all of us, not just those designated as 'leaders'. We will all need to be developing new identities as leaders.

An Early Years centre or service can show leadership of uncertainty when all involved learn together and have a leadership responsibility. Each person has an individual professional voice but this works in relation to the voices of others. Our voices do not become the same, rather they can be likened to 'the improvisation of a jazz

Figure 9.1 Leadership of uncertainty

player in an ensemble' (Barnett 2007: 56). In this context each person has responsibility for both leading and responding and for creating the way forward. A piece of jazz music can be seen as a metaphor for the leadership of uncertainty. The outcome is not defined in advance; it has the potential to become. It is realized in, and by, its quality. Each person makes an individual contribution in relation to those of others at a particular time. The work relies on improvisation based on skills and knowledge of both the subject area and human relations. At the core are shared understanding, principles and purpose. Early Years practitioners have the dispositions and potential to act in this way and to be effective leaders of uncertainty.

References

Agyris, C. and Schön, D. (1978) *Organisational Learning: A Theory of Action Perspective.* Reading, MA: Addison-Wesley.

Ancona, D., Malone, T., Orlikowski, W. and Senge, P. (2007) In praise of the incomplete leader. *Harvard Business Review*, Feb: 92–100.

Anning, A. (2001) Knowing who I am and what I know: developing new versions of professional knowledge in integrated service settings. Paper presented at the British Educational Research Association Annual Conference, Leeds, 13–15 September.

Anning, A., Cottrell, D., Frost, N., Green, J. and Robinson, M. (2006) *Developing Mulitprofesssional Teamwork for Integrated Children's Services.* Maidenhead: Open University Press.

Atkinson, T. and Claxton, G. (2000) *The Intuitive Practitioner: On the Value of Not Always Knowing What One Is Doing.* Maidenhead: Open University Press.

Barnett, R. (2007) *A Will to Learn: Being a Student in an Age of Uncertainty.* Maidenhead: Open University Press.

Belenky, M.F., Clinchy, B.M., Goldberger, N.R. and Tarule, J.M. (1986) *Women's Ways of Knowing: The Development of Self, Body and Mind.* New York: Basic Books.

Bohm, D. (1996) *On Dialogue.* London: Routledge.

Bruner, J. (1983) *Child's Talk: Learning to Use Language.* Oxford: Oxford University Press.

Clark, C. (ed.) (2001) *Talking Shop: Authentic Conversation and Teacher Learning.* New York: Teachers College Press.

Graham, S. (2010) Representing thinking in action research through alternative forms of representation. Paper presented at the Collaborative Action Research Network Conference. Cambridge, 5–7 November.

Holquist, M. (1990) *Dialogism: Bakhtin and His World.* London: Routledge.

Jarvis, J. and Trodd, L. (2008) Other ways of being, other ways of seeing: imagination as a tool for developing multiprofessional practice for children with communication needs. *Child Language, Teaching and Therapy* 24: 2: 211–27.

Kumar, S. (2011) We are all leaders. *Resurgence*, 264: 1.

Marshall, J. (1994) Re-visioning organisations by developing female values. In R. Root, J. Lawrence, and J. Morris (eds) *Managing the Unknown by Creating New Futures.* London: McGraw-Hill.

McNiff, J. (2010) *Action Research for Professional Development.* Poole: September Books.

Miller, L. and Cable, C. (eds) (2011) *Professionalization, Leadership and Management in the Early Years.* London: Sage.

O'Donoghue, T. and Clarke, S. (2010) *Leading Learning: Process, Themes and Issues in International Contexts.* London: Routledge.

Pearce, W.B. (1994) *Interpersonal Communication: Making Social Worlds.* London: HarperCollins.

Rinaldi, C. (2006) *In Dialogue with Reggio Emilia: Listening, Researching, Learning*. London: Routledge.

Siraj-Blatchford, I. and Manni, L. (2007) *Effective Leadership in the Early Years Sector: The ELEYS Study*. London: Institute of Education, University of London.

Trevarthan, C. (2004) The functions of emotions in early infant communication and development, in J. Nadel and L. Camaioni (eds) *New Perspectives in Early Communicative Development*. London: Routledge.

Van Manen, M. (1991) *The Tact of Teaching: The Meaning of Pedagogical Thoughtfulness*. London: The Althouse Press.

Whalley, M. (2008) *Leading Practice in Early Years Settings*. Exeter: Learning Matters.

Wenger, E. (1998) *Communities of Practice: Learning, Meaning and Identity*. Cambridge: Cambridge University Press.

Wells, G. (1999) *Dialogic Inquiry*. Cambridge: Cambridge University Press.

White, S. and Featherstone, B. (2005) Communicating misunderstandings: multi-agency work as social practice. *Child and Family Social Work*, 10: 207–16.

10

KAREN JOHN
Theoretical underpinnings of the NPQICL: inspiration and grounding

Introduction

A number of government, Early Years education, family support and childcare initiatives hastened the development of integrated, community-based provision for young children and families and encouraged enthusiastic and overwhelmed leaders of existing services to participate in leadership training. Many leadership development programmes focus on knowledge and technique as key to effective leadership. Such approaches are based on the belief that if we know the theories and techniques, then we will be able to apply them and achieve positive results in our places of work. In contrast, the National Professional Qualification in Integrated Centre Leadership (NPQICL) programme was designed to help participants explore *their* experiences and journeys, what it is like for *them* to be a leader, how *they* can respond best to the challenges within *their* organizations – and inspire others to join in.

Theoretical sources of the NPQICL approaches to 'learning leadership' can be traced back to the Greeks. For example, *democracy*, like most concepts and theories, has been forgotten, rediscovered and refined time and again. Such is the challenge of applying and sustaining complex ideals. Nevertheless, democracy and other key values of the programme – like equality, andragogy, humanism and humanistic and depth psychologies, feminism, cooperative inquiry and community development and action – hold enduring, intuitive appeal. When they are taken on, they inspire and ground leaders and staff to develop and sustain integrated services and working relationships that meet the complex needs of children and families.

This chapter first provides an overview of the social and political context within which integrated services for young children and families grew exponentially, the nature of those services, the development of training opportunities for the leaders and the multi-disciplinary team that designed the NPQICL programme. Subsequent sections focus on the theoretical concepts and approaches that proved so effective in inspiring and grounding leaders of the integrated, community-based centres for children and families.

The growth of integrated provision for children and families

After New Labour came to power in 1997, services for young children and their families grew markedly. Unprecedented funding explicitly acknowledged the early years as a time when social investment can have a significant impact on individual children, families and society (HM Treasury and DfES 2007). In funding Early Excellence Centres, Sure Start, Neighbourhood Nurseries, and most recently, Sure Start Children's Centres, the government sought to reduce inequalities in the quality of early education, childcare and support that both poor and better off families could expect. As with their predecessors, children's centres brought together services for children under 5 and their families in new and often radical ways, offering a range of services that integrate health, childcare, education, parent involvement, family support, and adult education and employment, and endeavouring to engage all children and families in the community – in particular the poor and most vulnerable (National Audit Office 2006).

Pen Green and the development of leadership training programmes

The development of the NPQICL represented the culmination of work undertaken over many years by Pen Green Children's Centre and Pen Green Research, Training and Development Base and Leadership Centre in Corby, Northamptonshire. Alongside developments in integrated Early Years provision, Pen Green worked with the DfES/DCSF to produce learning opportunities and experiences tailored to the needs of leaders facing the challenges of change and complexity inherent in efforts to integrate and de-stigmatize services and meet the needs of all young children and families within local communities, including the socially and economically disadvantaged. In 1998, Pen Green Research was funded by the Department for Education and Skills for a new building and to continue their work in designing, supporting and evaluating developments in integrated Early Years provision, and offering intensive work-focused training opportunities for the leaders of integrated Early Years centres.

Between 1999 and 2003, 87 Early Years centre heads and deputies completed Pen Green post-graduate leadership courses and earned a post-graduate diploma in leadership. This work-focused, experiential course evolved and formed the basis of the NPQICL. The NPQICL was piloted in 2004–05 with 41 participants and then rolled out across nine regions, with over 700 participants completing the course nationally in 2005–06 and 2006–07 (Whalley et al. 2008).

Developing NPQICL

The team that developed the NPQICL was multi-disciplinary, comprised of individuals from diverse backgrounds – all *boundary spanners*. The lead architect of the NPQICL was Margy Whalley (1994, 2000), a community educator, visionary leader and innovator, who founded the Pen Green Centre for Children and Families in 1983, after working in Brazil and Papua New Guinea, and went on to establish the Pen Green Research, Training and Development Base and Leadership Centre in 1994. She and her colleague of 20 years, former primary headteacher and influential consultant and author of educational, leadership and management texts, Patrick Whitaker (1983, 1993), together developed and honed programmes made up of individual and group experiential learning opportunities and team tasks, as well as academic studies that challenged participant-leaders to be deeply reflective and authentically themselves.

Other developers were: Sheila Thorpe OBE (Thorpe and Gasper 2003), former head of one of the earliest and most significant integrated early years and family centres, Hillfields in Coventry, and a key government advisor on developing centres of excellence, supporting leaders and the NPQICL; Colin Fletcher (1993), professor of sociology and community development and avid proponent of practitioner-led action research, and myself, academic developmental psychology researcher in psychiatry, former director of human resources and training for a national community mental health services organization and Adlerian psychotherapist, psychotherapy supervisor, trainer and organization consultant (John 2000, 2008).

From our diverse heritages and experiences, we had come to the same basic belief that developing and sustaining egalitarian and supportive environments and leadership, which promote reflectivity, open dialogue, invite challenge and also a shared vision, values and agreed standards for practice and relating, unlock the creativity of individuals and groups – children, families and communities – and maximize their potential for lifelong growth, development and resilience.

Philosophy

Implicit within the NPQICL is that by the time participants enrol in the programme, they already have acquired considerable knowledge about leadership through family life, through schooling, through education and work experiences – through observations of the world around them. They had developed their own *particular* ways of leading, based on their values and beliefs about how people need to be treated if they are to work effectively. The NPQICL programme invites participants to share their experiences, values and perspectives and to see learning leadership as a lifelong endeavour, one that requires regular and deep reflection, dialogue and cycles of evaluation and research.

Theoretical sources of NPQICL approaches to 'learning leadership' can be traced back to the Greeks. For example, *democracy*, like most concepts and theories, has been forgotten, rediscovered and refined time and again. Constructivist John Dewey (1916/1966) and social psychologist Kurt Lewin (1948) agreed that democracy must be learned anew in each generation, and that it is far more difficult to attain and to maintain than is autocracy. Such is the challenge of applying and sustaining complex ideals. Through experience, each person and generation find their own truths. It is no wonder that governments, organizations and groups are attracted to pat answers and simple solutions even though they do little more than reassure and relieve their immediate anxieties.

The NPQICL programme was designed to address the *complexity* and *turbulence* that the leaders and staff of integrated children's centres face and to be ever mindful of issues of *sustainability*. It invites participants to challenge themselves and each other, to question their own and others' practice and motivation and to support others to do the same. Rather than ask participants to compromise their values and principles, they are encouraged to ask questions that begin: 'How can we . . .?'

Theoretical underpinnings

Andragogy is an approach to learning that places the needs, feelings, thoughts and experiences of participants at the heart of any educational programme. Andragogy is based on the belief that individuals achieve a self-concept of essential self-direction when they psychologically become adults (Knowles 1970). This self-concept includes a deep need to be regarded by *others* as self-directing (Ryan 1995).

Adults tend to experience internal tension and display resentment or resistance in situations that do not allow or acknowledge their need for self-direction. Interestingly, those working in the Early Years tend to appreciate that even small children respond in much the same way. Respecting and valuing the learners and the led, and recognizing and developing their instrumental roles in learning and leading, most often head participants' lists of the principles and practices underpinning effective approaches across *pedagogy, andragogy* and *leadership*.

The andragogic model asserts that five issues be considered and addressed in formal learning. Educators need to: (1) let learners know why something is important to learn; (2) show learners how to direct themselves through information, (3) relate the topic to the learners' experiences, (4) remember that people will not learn until they are ready and motivated to learn, which requires (5) helping them overcome inhibitions, unhelpful behaviours and beliefs about learning.

Democracy and equality

For there to be *equality*, which is a necessary condition of democracy, every human being – regardless of age, gender, sexual orientation, race, ethnicity, religion, family background, social class or status – needs to be seen to have equal value, needs to be entitled to equal rights and opportunities and needs to be treated with respect. Government guidance and officials regularly refer directly or indirectly to these principles. For example, former Secretary of Health, Andy Burnham (2009) in his speech to the Unite/Community Practitioners' and Health Visitors' Association conference said: 'The Healthy Child Programme is the vision, built on a sound understanding of how we can support families and ensure the effects of deprivation and disadvantage on young lives are minimized.'

And early on in his role as Prime Minister, speaking to the Centre for Social Justice, David Cameron (2010) declared: 'For the Conservative Party I'm leading, social justice is a vital issue. The reason is simple: the degree of social injustice in our country.'

The principles of democracy and equality – that every human being feels at home on this earth – are at the heart of children's centres. Yet we grapple with how we can realize these ideals, both in light of gross material inequalities and within organizational and professional hierarchies. One of the earliest depth psychologists, Alfred Adler (1938), observed that feeling equal to others is an essential element of mental health.

In order for the principles of democracy and egalitarianism to be realized, a deeper understanding of *human psychology* is needed – one in which our innate *compensatory* striving for power and superiority is balanced by developing and expressing our innate *interest in – and need for –* others. In other words, we need to be aware of how our sense of smallness, inadequacy and vulnerability can lead to defensiveness, false bravado and useless competitive striving for power *over* others, rather than cooperating *with* others and contributing our talents to creatively solve our common problems and improve our own and others' quality of life.

At the beginning of the twentieth century, Alfred Adler (1964 [1956]) argued that equality is a prerequisite for social living, without which there can be no stability (Dreikurs 1971). Adler was concerned with equality in terms of being of equal value and equally entitled to be taken into account and respected in all relationships, private and public. Privately, between partners and between parents and children – as well as at work and in other public domains, so-called feminine values are often missing (Marshall 1994). The recent book by Wilkinson and Pickett, *The Spirit Level: Why Equality Is Better for Everyone* (2009), brings together data from several large-scale research studies on health and well-being from around the world, which show that people are much healthier and happier in countries and states with the smallest gap between rich and poor. Ideas about democracy and equality lead naturally to another main source of inspiration to the NPQICL architects: *humanism* and *humanistic psychology*.

Humanism and humanistic psychologies

An emphasis on the importance of *self-concept* and *self-actualization* provides a natural link between humanism as a philosophy and as a theory of psychology. *Humanism* as a philosophy attaches prime importance to human, rather than divine matters, and stresses the potential goodness of human beings, emphasizing common human needs and seeking rational ways of solving human problems. *Humanistic psychologies* focus on each individual's potential to be good, with the belief that mental and social problems result from deviations from a natural striving for growth and self-actualization. Humanistic therapies, most notably the *person-centred* approach developed by Carl Rogers (1961), posit that growth and self-actualization require the therapist's unconditional positive regard for the person, deep empathy and belief in the person's ability to grow and change within a therapeutic environment that provides space and time for self-reflection and growing self-awareness that lead to self-actualization.

Educationalist Jack Mezirow (1978, 1981, 1991) developed the notion of *transformational learning*, which describes a process of engaging in self-reflection and increasing self-knowledge, which, while a rational exercise in some ways, also involves a profound emotional or spiritual transformation not unlike that which occurs in successful psychotherapy. For example, the experience of undoing racist, sexist and other elitist and oppressive attitudes can be painful and emotional, as these attitudes often are developed as ways to cope with and make sense of a world in which we tend to feel small and insignificant. This type of deeply self-reflective learning requires taking risks and a willingness to be vulnerable and have one's attitudes and assumptions challenged.

The other well-known humanistic psychologist, Abraham Maslow (1954/1970), developed a *theory of human motivation* in which our many varying human needs are seen to arise hierarchically. Maslow held that in order to attend to our 'higher' needs, each of our *basic* needs must be met. The first of our basic needs is the *physiological* requirement for food and shelter; the second is the need for *safety*; the third is the need for *love, belonging and identification*; and the fourth is the need for *respect and self-esteem*. The *basic* needs are regarded as *deficiency needs*, but the crowning need is a different type, that is, the need for *growth and self-actualization*. According to Maslow's theory, the basic needs predominate when they are unsatisfied, but the higher ones predominate when the lower needs are satisfied. Maslow's hierarchy of needs offers a useful framework within which to account for *regression* in adaptation and functioning, particularly when basic needs are not being met, are threatened, or the individual believes them to be threatened.

Economist and well-being researcher, Richard Layard (2005: 227) found that 'people are deeply attached to the status quo. They hate loss of any kind, and they care less about gains than losses.' Impending change generally threatens loss and tends to evoke fear that our basic needs will not be met. This is particularly important for NPQICL participants to remember when leading change – particularly across professional boundaries and encountering defensive and less-than generative behaviour among those involved.

Depth psychologies

Humanistic psychologies grew out of depth psychologies, and while the NPQICL did not major on them, ideas offered by such theoretical formulations as *iceberg theory* and *group dynamics* are vital in helping participants to appreciate that there is more going on within and between individuals and groups or teams than can be seen and that much of human behaviour is motivated by needs, which if not met, are expressed in unhelpful, uncooperative or even dysfunctional ways (e.g. Obholzer and Roberts 1994; Huffington et al. 2004).

Experience-based, reflective learning and action research

Practitioner-led action research (Heron 1971; Schön 1983; Reason 1988; Fletcher 1993; Reason and Bradbury 2001; McNiff 2002) extends the reflective process of grappling with the experience of leading by offering a dynamic method of learning leadership through inquiry and investigation. *Action research*, also called *collaborative inquiry*, offers a powerful tool to help NPQICL participants to involve others in managing change. Participants are asked to involve their staff teams, other agencies and professionals as well as members of the communities they serve in 'spirals' of *participative enquiry* in order to study, reflect upon, lead and make progress towards shared goals. As in all reflective, experience-based learning, the process is likely to be at least as important as the outcome.

Community development and community action

The National Standards for Leaders of Children's Centres document (HM Treasury and DfES 2007: 9) states that:

Children's centres have the potential to transform the way in which families gain access to and can benefit from local services . . . raise expectations and aspirations so that families and the local community are encouraged to enjoy new opportunities for learning and better health.

Communities can only take responsibility and action when they achieve critical awareness of what affects their lives and gain the confidence to change what oppresses them. When communities are downtrodden, they are unable to credit their perceptions, experiences and skills. In my experience, the same is true for children's centre leaders and staff members.

Community development and action begin when those in power meet members of the community as equals, respecting, valuing and trusting them to identify and build on their individual and collective strengths and to exercise choice about things that really matter to them. To quote from the Pilot NPQICL Study Programme booklet, which draws on Paulo Freire (1970/1986):

[I]t is not enough that we reflect in order to know or understand, it is necessary to reflect in order to make a difference – to bring about change. Praxis is a self-directed process springing from our core professional values, demanding that we continuously consider the impact and effect of our own actions. Praxis involves honouring our experience and relating it to theory, and thinking deeply about future action. Sometimes this deepening of awareness and reflexivity will result in us feeling uncomfortable, and realising it is our *own* actions rather than the actions of others that need attention. This may be particularly difficult in our leadership roles, since we have grown up being encouraged to believe our leaders are superior, with inherently powerful capacities and qualities.

(Whalley et al. 2004: 38)

Conclusion

I have been involved in three initiatives designed to increase and improve provision for young children and their families in England: Early Excellence (1997–2006), Sure Start (1999–2006), and most recently, integrated Sure Start Children's Centres, which now have subsumed the others.

Sure Start funding, which at its peak in 2004–05 reached about 20 per cent of the population of children under 4 and their families, was increased by about 10 per cent in 2005–06. However, in *more-for-less* fashion, that funding was expected to reach over 40 per cent of children 0–5 and their families *and* to provide care before and after school for older children. Over the past five years, local authorities have been charged with 'finding' the money to cover budget shortfalls, but this has proved to be unrealistic in practice, and services have had to be cut. Ironically, with the publication of Graham Allen's commissioned independent report, *Early Intervention: The Next Steps* (2011), integrated Early Years services now are facing even more radical cuts in funding. Despite evidence that early intervention is needed to promote positive health and educational opportunities for families in the bottom 20 per cent income bracket (Feinstein et al. 2007), back is the idea of targeted services for families in the bottom

5 per cent income bracket. What continues to be ignored is the irrefutable evidence that the widening gap between rich and poor contributes more powerfully to poorer health and attainment at all ages than relative poverty (Wilkinson and Pickett 2009).

Another challenge to those who lead children's centres has been that the focus on providing family support and high quality education and care for young children shifted to accommodate the government's agenda of providing childcare places to enable more mothers to take up employment – the cornerstone of New Labour's strategy to end child poverty. This is continuing under the Conservative leadership of David Cameron, even though it has proved entirely unrealistic in communities with high rates of unemployment. Also, working parents are expected to pay for childcare, but even when Working Families Tax Credit and Child Care Allowance were available, they were not enough to cover childcare costs. Thus, issues of 'sustainability' continue to bedevil us all. Yet we need to stay put and sustain relationships if we are to make a real difference.

Under the Conservatives, the challenges for integrated children's services and their leaders are increasing. What the leaders require is the courage to stand up for their principles and the confidence to hold on to what they know to be in the best interest of children, families and the communities they serve. They will need to work across professional and organizational boundaries, gather valid evidence and thereby ensure that the services and any changes to them are locally driven and locally owned in order to develop and sustain integrated services and working relationships that meet the complex needs of children and families.

References

Adler, A. (1938) *Social Interest: A Challenge to Mankind*. London: Faber & Faber.

Adler, A. (1964 [1956]) *The Individual Psychology of Alfred Adler*.

Allen, G. (2011) *Early Intervention: The Next Steps – An Independent Report to Her Majesty's Government*. London: HM Government.

Burnham, A. (2009) Launch of Action on Health Visiting Programme. Address to Unite/Community Practitioners' and Health Visitors' Association Conference, Southport, Merceyside, 15 October.

Cameron, D. (2010) Speech, Centre for Social Justice, Kids Symposium. *Guardian*, 10 July.

Dewey, J. (1916/1966) *Democracy and Education: An Introduction to the Philosophy of Education*. New York: Free Press.

Dreikurs, R. (1971) *Social Equality: The Challenge of Today*. Chicago, IL: Adler School of Professional Psychology.

Feinstein, L., Hearn, B., Renton, Z., Abrahams, C. and MacLeod, M. (2007) *Reducing Inequalities: Realising the Talents of all*. London: National Children's Bureau.

Fletcher, C. (1993) An analysis of practitioner research. In B. Broad and C. Fletcher (eds) *Practitioner Social Work Research in Action*. London: Whiting and Birch.

Freire, P. (1970/1986) *Pedagogy of the Oppressed*. New York: Continuum.

Fullan, M. (2001) *Understanding Change: Leading in a Culture of Change*. San Francisco, CA: Jossey-Bass.

Heron, J. (1971) *Experience and Method: An Inquiry into the Concept of Experiential Research: Human Potential Research Project*. Guildford: University of Surrey.

HM Treasury and DfES (2007) *Aiming High for Children: Supporting Families*. London: HM Treasury and DfES.

Huffington, C., Armstrong, D., Halton, W., Hoyle, L. and Pooley, J. (2004) *Working Below the Surface: The Emotional Life of Contemporary Organizations*. London: Karnac.

John, K. (2000) Basic needs, conflict and dynamics in groups. *Journal of Individual Psychology*, 56: 419–34.

John, K. (2008) *Leadership Mentoring and Staff Supervision in Children's Centres*. Corby: Pen Green Research, Development & Training Base and Leadership Centre.

Knowles, M. (1970) *Modern Practice of Adult Education: Andragogy versus Pedagogy*. Englewood Cliffs, NJ: Prentice Hall.

Layard, R. (2005) *Happiness*. London: Penguin.

Lewin, K. (1948) *Resolving Social Conflicts: Selected Papers on Group Dynamics*. New York: Harper & Row.

Marshall, J. (1994) Revisioning organizations by developing female values. In J. Boot, J. Lawrence and J. Morris (eds) *Managing the Unknown by Creating New Futures*. London: McGraw-Hill.

Maslow, A. H. (1954/1970) *Motivation and Personality*. New York: Harper.

McNiff, J. (2002) *Action Research Principles and Practice*. London: Routledge.

Mezirow, J. (1978) Perspective transformation. *Adult Education Quarterly*, 28: 100–10.

Mezirow, J. (1981) A critical theory of adult learning and education. *Adult Education*, 32: 3–23.

Mezirow, J. (1991) *Transformative Dimensions of Adult Learning*. San Francisco, CA: Jossey-Bass.

National Audit Office (2006) *Sure Start Children's Centres*. London: The Stationery Office.

Obholzer, A. and Roberts, V.Z. (1994) *The Unconscious at Work: Individual and Organizational Stress in Human Services*. London: Routledge.

Reason, P. (ed.) (1988) *Human Inquiry in Action: Developments in New Paradigm Research*. London: Sage.

Reason, P. and Bradbury H. (2001) *Handbook of Action Research: Participative Inquiry and Practice*. London: Sage.

Rogers, C.R. (1961) *On Becoming a Person: A Therapist's View of Psychotherapy*. London: Allen & Unwin.

Ryan, R.M. (1995) Psychological needs and the facilitation of integrative processes. *Journal of Personality*, 63: 397–427.

Schön, D. (1983) *The Reflective Practitioner*. New York: Basic Books.

Thorpe, S. and Gasper, M. (2003) Who cares for the carers? An exploration of support provided for leaders of integrated Early Years Centres. *Leadership & Management Bursary Report, October 2003*. London: DfES.

Whalley, M. (1994) *Learning to be Strong: Setting up a Neighbourhood Service for Under 5s and Families*. London: Hodder & Stoughton.

Whalley, M. (ed.) (2000) *Involving Parents in Their Children's Learning*. London: Paul Chapman.

Whalley, M. et al. (2004) *NPQICL Study Programme*. Nottingham: NCSL.

Whalley, M. et al. (2008) Developing and sustaining leadership learning communities: implications of NPQICL rollout for public policy local praxis. *European Early Childhood Education Research Journal*, 16: 5–38.

Whitaker, P. (1983) *The Primary Head*. London: Heinemann.

Whitaker, P. (1993) *Managing Change in Schools*. Buckingham: Open University Press.

Wilkinson, R. and Pickett, K. (2009) *The Spirit Level: Why Equality Is Better for Everyone*. London: Penguin.

PART 5

The future

11

IAN DUCKMANTON

The possibilities of an imagined future: observing critical dilemmas in interprofessional and multi-agency working

Introduction

This chapter focuses on key aspects of interprofessional working by practitioners from different professional heritages working together in a Sure Start Children's Centre cluster. Appreciative Inquiry (AI) is used as a research methodology to observe and analyse positive learning outcomes experienced by practitioners from an interprofessional community of Early Years practitioners, revealing examples of how those practitioners work effectively together to improve the life chances of children and their families. This chapter aims to show the value of practitioners using their individual and collective imagination to think beyond the usual limitations of job title, organizational membership and common perceptions of roles and responsibilities to develop new knowledge. The chapter argues for the importance of revealing the positive in order to remove barriers that might restrict interprofessional working. The traditional concept and perception of a 'team' are challenged and reinterpreted to develop a new framework of understanding about interprofessional working. The chapter proposes that individuals who are passionate about a particular area of practice can be invited to step out of their professional heritage to participate in a working environment in which their experience and knowledge are acknowledged, celebrated and used to contribute to the creation of new knowledge using this framework. This new knowledge drives the community of practice towards development of innovative and visionary practice. As an example the subject of breastfeeding, which bridges the divide between many different professional heritages and practice, is used to illustrate how people with significant professional differences can create a courageous and imaginative process of working together to break through potentially immovable interagency and interprofessional obstacles.

In conclusion, this chapter advocates the need to support the further development of interprofessional communities and reflects on the importance of continued investment of time and resources in developing robust, long-lasting relationships between practitioners to enable them to deliver more effective services for children and their families and by doing so, to improve their life chances.

> Though no one can go back and make a brand new start, anyone can start from now and make a brand new ending. (Anonymous)

Interprofessional working in Early Years children's services grew through the political changes in the decade which began in 1997, during which New Labour-led government of the United Kingdom developed policies that required integration of services from different professional heritages for the purpose of achieving better outcomes (DoH 1998; DfES 2003). These policy documents focused on developing the systems and processes required to enable joint working to take place such as interagency cooperation, sharing of locations and secondment of staff to ensure shared management systems. More recent researchers (Sloper 2004; Robinson and Cottrell 2005; Hughes 2006; Watson 2006; Hyams 2006) have observed what actually happens to people from different professional heritages when they are drawn together, either by directives or by voluntarily seeking to be involved, to jointly deliver services for children and families.

This chapter foregrounds the people involved in multi-agency working, the relationships between those people and how those relationships affect the functioning of the 'teams' that are formed as a result of creating a multi-agency, interprofessional service. As a professional working in children's services, I am dissatisfied by the use of the word 'team' to describe this group of practitioners and I continue to strive to find a way of describing them that more accurately captures their true character. I believe that when these interprofessional relationships are nurtured successfully we see the groups function well and then we see the positive difference that multi-agency and interprofessional working makes to children and their families. In order to exemplify how this works two cases studies follow.

Case study 1: co-location prevents integration!

Experience shows that successful interprofessional working is not a guaranteed outcome of practical and technical processes such as co-location or interagency information sharing protocols. In 2004 a team of health practitioners and family support teams from different agencies were accommodated in a shared office in order to facilitate the integration of practice for children and families. Unexpected interprofessional and interagency conflict resulted. Practitioners from different professional heritages, with different protocols, cultures and working practices had not been properly supported and prepared for sharing the same office space as colleagues from other agencies and professional heritages. These issues led to behaviours which directly contradicted the desired concept of interprofessional integration. Practitioners would leave the room to make a telephone call if they didn't want their discussion to be heard by others and teams from each agency would convene meetings off-site to discuss agency-specific issues.

This apparent lack of trust between the different heritages led us to create a confidentiality agreement which was accepted by the different statutory, voluntary and private sector agencies involved but made absolutely no difference to the practitioners as this was attempting to make a radical and fundamental change to a deeply embedded practice culture.

Anning (2001: 2) notes that 'practitioners had little choice in being translated into multi-agency groupings and moving to shared working spaces'. On reflection we exacerbated the concerns and dilemmas our colleagues were facing because we naïvely assumed that moving everyone into the same shared working space and inviting them to work together would result in effective multi-agency working. We had not considered the importance of addressing the issues arising from creating what Wenger (1998) calls a 'community of practice'.

Our reflections helped us to realize that we gave little, if any, consideration to how it felt for practitioners to work in, what was to them, a radically different way in an environment in which their professional knowledge and practice were exposed to scrutiny, even if only casual, by practitioners from outside their profession. These teams of practitioners had not been given the opportunity to find a way of safely declaring their personal and professional knowledge or of understanding how to communicate that knowledge with colleagues from other professional heritages. Even more importantly, colleagues had not been given the opportunity to reflect on their own knowledge, or to develop their understanding of the nature and origin of that knowledge gained from years of training, evidence-based practice and participation and its reification within the relatively safe confines of their own professional heritage. It is by gaining this heightened level of understanding that practitioners develop the confidence to declare and share their knowledge with others.

The learning from this difficult period of interprofessional development was profound and far-reaching. It became very clear that trust was and still is a fundamental requirement of interprofessional working in our community of practice and that this trust grows when time is spent getting to know ourselves and each other. The geographically dispersed nature of this team led to delays in the process of getting to know each other because there were very few naturally occurring opportunities for different practitioners to interact on a personal level – commonly referred to as 'water-cooler moments' – where people chat about things other than work and get to know about each other beyond the limitations of profession or job title. It became necessary therefore to manufacture these opportunities through regular team gatherings which, although unnatural, at least offered some informal networking time alongside planned activities within those gatherings to enable colleagues to get to know each other better. The results of these activities are still emerging but there is a clear and positive improvement in relationships which directly correlates with the time spent together. The challenge, of course, is to justify spending time together just for the sake of spending time together when colleagues have busy diaries and caseload pressures which lead to a risk of such activities being seen as a waste of their time. Our dilemma then becomes different – to find a reason to be together that justifies time out from 'normal' duties but also to enable practitioners to see the benefit of simply spending time together.

Our reflections as a team and my development as a reflective leadership practitioner led us along a very different pathway as a result of these negative experiences. The work we have done to build team relationships and understandings has impacted positively on the functioning of our teams. In 2009, more than half our weekly activities were delivered jointly by practitioners from different agencies and different professions. After separating the teams and returning each agency group to their original locations, we spent energy and time on addressing feelings, emotions, anxieties and fears. We worked together to investigate motivations, values and principles and to expose what is referred to by Cooperrider et al. (2005) as the *deeper corporate spirit and soul* of the team. Since co-locating again we have created a high-functioning multi-agency team in which practitioners with radically different professional heritages, theoretical approaches and social and emotional contexts, co-operate and share information, resources and support systems.

My view is that, on the basis of these examples, if the relationships are successfully developed and nurtured slowly and carefully so that they become strong and sustainable, the technical functions necessary to support effective joint working will occur as a natural consequence. When the team members understand and trust each other they will want to share an office because, for instance, they learn that their new colleagues will maintain confidentiality. They will seek opportunities to share information and ideas and to develop their own model of working together. We can, to some extent at least, control the choice of people and influence their actions. The time factor is, however, the unknown variable as each individual in each team will need different amounts of time to build the trust and confidence in their new colleagues and in the new ways of working in which they are being invited to participate. These thoughts suggest a very simple theoretical formula:

(The right people + the right actions) × as much time as it takes = effective joint working.

(Duckmanton 2010)

Case study 2: becoming baby friendly

Breastfeeding is arguably one of the most scientifically robust, evidence-based practice issues in the Early Years interprofessional environment. The benefits of breastfeeding to the child and mother cut through any cultural, economic or interprofessional boundaries and the responsibility to promote breastfeeding as a first feeding choice falls to all the different professional heritages from midwifery to health visiting, family support to speech and language development. The benefits to both the mother and the child in terms of physical and mental health outcomes are unquestionable and evidence is emerging all the time suggesting that those benefits extend throughout life (Marild et al. 2004; Gutman et al. 2008). It is a profoundly emotive subject on which to base an interprofessional research study.

It is impossible to fully understand the influences of information gathered by the individual or provided by her family, personal preference, experience and understanding that an individual woman has gained up to the point at which the choice to breastfeed is made. Experience suggests that it is apparently easier for some women to make that choice than it is for others. One point of view of midwife colleagues who are evangelical about breastfeeding is that, with the correct support and the right information, a woman should never have to say, 'I can't'. Another point of view is that the woman who, even with the right support and information available chooses to say, 'I don't want to' or even 'I can't', should not be made to feel guilty or diminished as a mother. How then do we balance the research evidence that suggests unquestionable benefits of breastfeeding with the, often more influential, social, family and cultural pressures which can lead women to make a choice not to breastfeed? This is especially difficult when some of these deeply embedded, value-based influences form part of the value base of the very practitioners who are tasked to promote breastfeeding and who are sympathetic or empathetic to the difficulties that some women face in making such choices.

It is entirely plausible and very common for a woman who may be undecided in her feeding choice, to be intensively supported with information, advice and encouragement from health practitioners and other influencers which would ordinarily lead her to make a fully informed choice to breastfeed but for a friend, relative or in some cases another 'professional' who, even knowing about the beneficial evidence may, through an expression of their own personal values, unwittingly allow the mother to justify a different choice and therefore undermine all the support that would have enabled her to breastfeed her baby. This exemplifies how powerful the culture and ethos of the interprofessional community have to be to counteract the influences from outside of that community. The strength of the relationships between different practitioners with different professional heritages within that community is crucial to the creation of this culture and ethos.

In my setting our attempt to begin the process to achieve UNICEF's (2009) coveted 'Baby Friendly' status began in the context described above. After six years of developing a multi-agency community of practitioners from many different professional heritages we decided to take the next big step in our breastfeeding work by launching a strategy to become Baby Friendly. An invitation was sent across the whole of our practice community for colleagues interested in breastfeeding to be part of an interprofessional working group to drive the strategy. This approach meant that status, professional heritage, experience or knowledge were not a requirement to participate in the strategic development of a specific area of practice. The qualifications required were quite simply a desire to increase the number of women who choose to breastfeed and to increase the length of time they continue to do so.

This radically different approach brought together professionals of different heritage, age, experience and gender, under the auspices of staff with the training and technical knowledge to ensure compliance with the clinical or other procedures of each of the different agencies employing practitioners in the interprofessional community. This group of people gathered together because they share a belief. The majority did not have the technical knowledge or understanding to be able to evidence the origin of their belief. They had not had the opportunity to reflect on why they believed so strongly in the subject they had been brought together to promote and it was not a core requirement of their role, yet here they were. Of significant importance to the functioning of this group was the lack of hierarchy. Participation was based on interest in the practice issue and desire to improve our work on this specific strategy; leadership was based on knowledge and desire. Neither was based on status. Staff in more senior roles were being led by colleagues they would ordinarily line-manage. Traditional structures had been deconstructed to enable those best placed to lead to do so without the limitations or restrictions of line management protocol. Many of those participating in this group had experienced the difficulties referred to earlier in this chapter. One of the joys apparent to me as a practitioner researcher was the successful way that those difficulties had been put behind everyone.

The '4D Cycle' – 'Discovery', 'Dream', 'Design' and 'Destiny' – within the 'Theory of Appreciative Inquiry' (Cooperrider et al. 2005) encourages us to *enquire into the art of the possible*. By exploring the positive and successful elements of working across professional boundaries, effective interprofessional working that increases the life chances of children and their families will be enabled. 'Discovery' introduces the idea of observing and revealing what is going well in a particular system or context, in contrast to finding the problems and trying to fix them, and invites reflection on why and how those elements are working. The 'Dream' phase provides an opportunity to build on that success by imagining what else could be achieved by the team, system or context being observed. This approach removes the limitations of systems or processes and instead advocates open-mindedness and visionary thinking. 'Design' is the phase in which the detail of how the vision can be achieved is planned by combining the observed successes of 'Discovery' with the new ideas of 'Dream'. 'Destiny' is the culmination of the first three, the product of combining the success, creativity and technical implementation skills of the team which then provides a further opportunity to use AI again to evaluate the effectiveness of the new way of working.

The observed example used here is the formation and initial functioning of a breastfeeding working group, as referred to in Case Study 2, formed by representatives from each of the different professional heritages in our programme to lead the programme to achieving UNICEF's Community Baby Friendly Status (UNICEF 2008). Achievement of this means that the professional and social community in which we function will ensure that women are informed and empowered to choose breast milk as their feeding choice, and having done so they are then welcome to breastfeed wherever they go, supported by whoever they meet and celebrated for making a good choice for the future health and well-being of their children.

'Discovery'

A significant developmental shift in my personal and professional leadership practice resulted from my participating in the National Professional Qualification in Integrated Centre Leadership (NPQICL) in 2006. I have learned to focus my energies on enabling and allowing practitioners over whom I have leadership influence, both in my own team and across professional and agency boundaries, to create their own pathways for development of our services and to lead change processes. I advocate concentrating on the emotionality of leading an integrated team (Harris 2004), enabling individuals to explore how what they are doing feels to them and the people they work with and to reflect on how those feelings affect their professional interactions.

Anning (2001) cites Wenger's (1998) model of how knowledge is created in communities of practice, referring to the two complementary processes of 'participation' and 'reification'. Personal and professional heritage and experiences lead to expectations of how things should be in certain professional contexts. In the first few years of leading a children's centre programme I led in a certain way, believing that I was displaying attributes that Marshall (1994) labelled as 'male' such as 'control', 'rationality' and 'separation'. My NPQICL research project revealed that I was in fact displaying far more of the 'female' attributes (Marshall 1994) such as 'receptivity', 'intuition', 'containment' and 'attachment' than I had previously been aware.

This gave me permission to be the leader, and in fact the person, I wanted to be rather than the leader or person I thought I was expected to be.

For many of the practitioners I work with, participating – by which Wenger (1998) means being involved in the daily shared experiences of the community – in this new way of working is uncomfortable, confusing and disruptive, and has taken considerable time and reinforcement of the new way of working to be seen as normal. Even now, after several years of working together when, for example, I encourage colleagues to 'check-in' – a process of sharing our thoughts and feelings before the business of a meeting starts – there is a tangible feeling of discomfort for some, countered by the obvious satisfaction of others for whom such a process creates a feeling of being valued and contained. This reification (Wenger 1998) is represented for us by the differences in the way meetings are run, the differences in the way decisions are made through reflection and consideration rather than immediate reaction, and through the distribution of leadership responsibilities across the whole team.

Appreciative Inquiry (Cooperrider et al. 2005) permits us to use the positive aspects of the system in which we function to reveal the elements that 'give life to the system'. In my example those aspects include the way we care about each other, the way we share practice and information and the way we are interested in the people we work with and their lives outside of work. This then gives me permission to analyse my dilemma by considering the people as the solution to any challenges we face rather than as the problem.

In his reconceptualization of Vygotsky's (1978) activity theory, Engestrom (2001) offers a contextual format through which to consider the historicity of activity systems stating that 'activity systems take shape and get transformed over lengthy periods of time'. In this example, the activity system which is the multi-professional team in question has a complicated and difficult history, some of which I have alluded to earlier in this chapter, which led to emotional outbursts including crying and shouting – none of which would be behaviours normally associated with those individuals in their professional context. This historicity plays a significant role in the function of the team as those individuals who experienced those difficulties with and between each other now largely work well together. The spectre of those past episodes does still remain in the collective memory of the team and, one can assume, plays a part in the way the professional and personal interactions take place. Considering the people as the solution allows us to see that they have negotiated through those difficulties and have found new ways of working without allowing any difficulties which may still exist to disrupt the objectives of the team.

The breastfeeding working group, led by a community midwife and supported by a family support manager, drew together health visitors, midwives, family support workers, playworkers and childcare practitioners. All but one in the group had been working together for more than three years. For the one colleague, a health visitor, this was the first time they had been involved in a multi-agency-themed project. The significance of this will be discussed later.

In our check-in at the first meeting of the group a colleague stated, 'the programme is ready for this'. Once again we need to consider the historicity behind this statement in order to appreciate its value. The individual who made the statement was involved in a very difficult and challenging phase of interprofessional and multi-agency development. This involved sensitive negotiation with a long-established voluntary sector service provider to become a major partner within a children's centre including dealing with massive opposition from a powerful and determined minority of parents, parish councillors and voluntary sector representatives. Robinson and Cottrell (2005) report the experiences of five multi-agency teams delivering services to children. Their study revealed examples of professionals experiencing 'loss of their specialist identity' when working in multi-agency teams. Their observations led them to suggest that 'team members with different backgrounds, training, explanatory models . . . and language cannot be expected to work together effectively from day one' and that 'time should be set aside for team building'. Anning (2001) pre-empted this by showing that the lack of time built into contracts for workers to meet each other to plan new ways of working was a major constraint in the development of team functions. In my example the process of achieving baby friendly status will take up to seven years – far beyond our current funding period. We understand that, as a team, we may not exist for that length of time. However, knowing that we might allows us to move to the second D of the 4D Cycle.

From 'Discovery' to 'Dream'

Leadership of Children's Centres has existed as a profession in its current form for around a decade. The incumbents of this profession were employed to lead change, to challenge the norm and to develop, innovate and *imagine* new ways of working. Their remit was, and in many cases still is, to *invent* ways of achieving better outcomes for children and their families by using the resources of the community of practitioners already working with children in the areas in which we work and adding new ideas, resources, people and practice approaches to service delivery. This visionary behaviour contradicts the traditions of many of the practitioners working with children and families who rely upon evidence-based practice in order to ensure they are doing what is already proven to be effective.

Harris (2004) discusses the difficulties apparent when the emotional capacity of a group of professionals to cope with change had not been given due consideration. She goes on to suggest three emotional conditions necessary to successfully implement and sustain change:

In phase one of these conditions, 'mistrust and trust', we see how mistrust between professionals can overwhelm any positive attributes of a system and create barriers that exclude change as an option. In the development stages of my own setting such mistrust was acutely apparent in myself as much as it was in my colleagues as we struggled to change the system in which we existed to meet the needs of changed political priorities. In phase two we see how the system begins to allow itself to imagine that the power to influence change exists within it rather than being reliant upon or controlled by outside influences. Phase three relates to Harris's assertion that this transformative process of empowerment, distribution and containment enables the system to innovate: *'the growing self esteem of teachers in this phase clearly influenced the amount of risk taking the teachers were willing to undertake'*.

(2004:398)

I suggest that those teachers had begun to imagine the future they thought was right for their school and to imagine what they would do to make that future exist.

Appreciative Inquiry suggests that envisioning involves passionate thinking, creating a positive image of a desired future. Day (2004: 427) argues, passionately of course, that passion is fundamental to success in school leadership and relates many versions of how that passion manifests itself including passion for 'achievement, caring, collaboration, commitment, trust, inclusivity and courage'. The common expectation at work is that we will follow traditional behaviour patterns. Meetings will have agendas, processes will be formal and procedures will be imposed by managers in order to ensure that practice is safe. For some, the haven of tradition is reassuring and the exposure of emotions such as passion is unsettling.

Jarvis and Trodd (2008) suggest that imagination is formed in our early years. In our work with very young children we model the use of imagination as a learning tool by nurturing their ability to imagine things they have yet to experience. I observe a link between this practice and my invitation to my colleagues to imagine new ways of working in order to envision the future of our work and what we can do to achieve that imagined future. Although existing models of practice may offer an evidence base for safe working processes, it can be those very embedded practices that lead to gaps in service provision. These in turn may lead to weakened systems and processes, which prevent concerns from being shared or cause information to be withheld that may have led to better outcomes for children. The concept of imagining how things can be, even though we have no evidence of their effectiveness, is a powerful tool in our portfolio. This is particularly the case when combined with leadership that encourages and enables practitioners to take risks in a measured and controlled way with the appropriate levels of support and supervision.

We know that children who are breastfed are more likely to thrive in their future education (Fewtrell 2004), health (Howie et al. 1990; Marild et al. 2004) and relationship well-being (Gutman et al. 2008). With this as our justification for our project and a foundation from which to challenge any resistance we may encounter, we are allowing ourselves to imagine how the community in which we work will look in the future in relation to women who breastfeed their children. We imagine that women who breastfeed will be given consistent support and advice from all the different professionals with whom they interact. We imagine that wherever those women take their babies – to libraries, cafes, shops, museums, schools and the like – they will feel welcome and comfortable when breastfeeding. We imagine that those women will never be challenged for making the right choice for their children because we will have empowered them and the community in which they live, work and socialize with the new knowledge necessary to create that so far only imagined world.

From 'Dream' to 'Design'

We have looked at how Appreciative Inquiry allows us to discover the positive elements of our system and to dream of ways to use them to achieve greater and greater outcomes for children and their families. How then can we put this into practice?

To enable me to make visionary, strategic and operational plans I conceptualize an individual child with any number or combination of complex, physical, mental, developmental, environmental or sociological needs at the very centre of my personal and professional values. Imagining this unique child helps me to understand how the services an integrated multi-agency and multi-professional programme develop or commission will meet the needs of different children, whatever those needs may be and however complex those services have to be in order to meet those needs. Jarvis and Trodd (2008) state that in order to contribute to a multi-agency team, a professional needs to have a clear understanding of his or her knowledge, skills, beliefs and values. They go on to explain how this knowledge provides professionals with the ability to enable others to understand who they are. In my own experience of team building activities colleagues have often used phrases such as 'we need to understand each other's roles and responsibilities'. Such comments are usually examples of individuals expressing their need to be known by others as well as, if not more than, to know others.

According to their professional heritage, individual experience and value base, each of the members of our breastfeeding working group, although sharing a common passion for the benefits of breastfeeding and a common understanding of the objective of the group and the actions needed to achieve that objective, will be considering a particular aspect of each child's development. For example, from a professional perspective a social worker will be more interested in the mental health benefits of the close attachment relationship nurtured by breastfeeding. On the other hand, a speech and language practitioner will be more interested in how that close relationship involves the mother talking and singing to her child, leading to improved speech development in the child in later years. Engestrom (2001) asserts that an activity system is always a community of multiple points of view. In my example there are the points of view of the practitioners but, I would argue, there are also the points of view of all the service users with whom those practitioners have interacted during their journey to this particular place in their professional development. The multi-voicedness of this community is, then, more than just the voices of the people in the room.

There is also a hierarchy of voice. In certain professions the view remains that qualification, length of service and even level of salary lead to an individual having a greater say in the community than others, even though those others may have more specialist knowledge of, for example, a particular child or a particular technical concept such as lactation. Anning (2001) cites Eraut's (1999) distinction between 'codified knowledge' which is primarily evidence-based and stored in the form of books, databases and qualifications, and 'personal knowledge' based on experiences and reflections. She goes on to relate examples where this personal knowledge is given a more credible status than the codified knowledge. Where practitioners might feel disrupted and insecure about their professional status in a newly formed multi-professional context they will rely upon codified knowledge even though their personal knowledge may be more relevant. Where a practitioner may be less qualified or less well read, this has the potential to suppress their voice in the face of strongly articulated evidence. This may happen even when such evidence contradicts their personal knowledge, because it is presented by colleagues they perceive to be better qualified to express a professional opinion. In team-building exercises such issues can be declared (Robinson and Cottrell 2005) and strategies can be developed to address them. However, where those issues have been left unresolved or never identified, the hierarchy of opinion may lead to incomplete or unsatisfactory services going unchallenged. Leadbetter (2006) offers evidence showing that 'professional identity is a concern and a factor in . . . changing working practices'.

In order to create a functioning system that becomes productive and leads to the achievement of agreed outcomes we must consider the effectiveness of the team, separated from the achievement of the common goal, as an outcome in itself. In the same way as we consider the needs of a child through common or other assessment models we need to discuss and agree the team working outcomes and plan how we will achieve them. Appreciative Inquiry invites us to consider how this group of diverse individuals with vast professional difference and significant common passions can '*co-construct the future*' and create a culture in which the '*exceptional becomes everyday and ordinary*'. Hymans (2006) offers a list of key factors and skills required for multi-agency working which include: 'commitment, understanding roles and responsibilities, common aims and objectives, communication and information sharing, leadership, relevant resources, good working relationships and adequate time'.

Many of these factors are in place in the 'baby friendly group' due to the commitment given by practitioners, based on their reflective learning (Kolb 1984) from previous difficulties, to looking at how they can work better together. Such processes are rarely, if ever, perfect. Adverse forces such as limited time and resources and, more seriously, staff turnover which results in the loss of good relationships and the need to build new relationships, have a disruptive effect on the success of the systems. In this example the involvement of one new team member in a group caused the most disruption to the process. It was through this disruption and the interactions that followed that the most profound learning about how we can move our team to the next stage of development occurred.

In his fourth principle of activity theory reconceptualization Engstrom (2001) states that 'when an activity system adopts a new object from the outside it often leads to an aggravated secondary contradiction where some old element collides with the new one'. In this example the new object is a person, the old element is their epistemology and the new element is the co-constructive, inclusive, multi-voiced activity system in which they have been invited to participate. Engestrom goes on to suggest that the contradiction 'generates disturbances and conflicts' – this was manifest in a very heated, defensive exchange of justifications of actions and opinions which significantly deviated from the core purpose of the meeting – but also 'innovative attempts to change the activity'. The result of this difficult moment for the group was to re-consider the objectives of coming together, in Appreciative Inquiry terms the 'design', and to discuss and agree how they could ensure that everyone understood their role and how they can contribute to this design. On reflection we could have predicted the possibility of this disruption but, as is so often the case, this dissonance led to a powerful learning experience. The 'design' was re-visited, re-stated and became embedded in the consciousness of the system.

From 'Design' to 'Destiny'

I have considered how the positive attributes, knowledge, history and imagined future of the activity system in which I work and function as a professional and as a person can be used to further develop the practice of our multi-professional community to achieve even more positive outcomes for the children and families with whom we work. I have also considered how the people in that system work together and how their personal and professional heritage affects their relationships. Finally I have observed what happens when contradictions occur. By taking the role of participant observer (Saunders et al. 2007) I learned that an effective multi-agency team share common passions (Blackmore 2004; Day 2004; Harris 2004), expertise (Anning 2001; Eraut 2001), and confidence in their own professional practice. I learned that disruption of their professional status (Anning 2001) leads to disruptive behaviours and that these practitioners are prepared to share professional, theoretical and personal paradigms (Wenger 1998) once they have learned to know and trust each other as individuals.

In his fifth and final summarized principle of activity theory, Engestrom (2001) proclaims the possibility of even greater productivity of the system. He states that 'an expansive transformation is accomplished when the object and motive of the activity are reconceptualized to embrace a radically wider horizon of possibilities'.

Conclusion

This is one way of approaching the challenges of interprofessional development positively and constructively. Through the use of Appreciative Inquiry as a practice-based research method I have revealed the possibilities that are available if practitioners carefully build relationships and combine their skills and experiences. In doing so I have achieved two significant new understandings: first, of the reasons why difficulties occur in relationships between colleagues who, outside of the intensity of working together, are, without exception, rational, reasonable, mature people; and second, how effective interprofessional working can be developed.

Appreciative Inquiry (AI) suggests that it is 'precisely through the juxtaposition of visionary content with grounded examples of the extraordinary that AI opens the status quo to transformations in collective action'. Most of all, I have learned that to support our common desire to be a force for positive change in the way we deliver services to very young children and their families we can imagine (Jarvis and Trodd 2008) how things can be and take steps to make that imagined future a reality.

This leads us towards achieving those transformations as we build on the successes of working together across professional, agency and personal boundaries to the extent that it will be possible to imagine that no such boundaries exist.

REFLEXIVITY CHECK-IN POINT

Do any of the following questions affect you personally or professionally?

- How do we create and embed a habit of spending time together to get to know ourselves and each other well enough to develop the trust that is necessary for us to engage in more effective interprofessional working?
- How do we enable busy people to step away from their routines which are punctuated with heavy case-loads, over-flowing diaries and a culture of being too busy doing to spend any time thinking, to allow them to imagine this 'radically wider horizon of possibilities'?

References

Adler, A. (1935) The fundamental views of individual psychology. *International Journal of Individual Psychology*, 1: 5–8.

Anning, A. (2001) Knowing who I am and what I know: developing new versions of professional knowledge in integrated service settings. Paper presented to the British Educational Research Association Annual Conference, University of Leeds, 13–15 September.

Anning, A., Cottrell, D., Frost, N., Green, J. and Robinson, M. (2006) *Developing Multiprofessional Teamwork for Integrated Children's Services*. Maidenhead: Open University Press.

Blackmore, J. (2004) Leading as emotional management. Work in high risk times: the counter-intuitive impulses of performativity and passion. *School Leadership & Management*, 24(4): 439–59.

Cooperrider, D., Stavros, J. and Whitney, D. (2005) *Appreciative Inquiry Handbook*. San Francisco, CA: Berrett-Koehler.

Day, C. (2004) The passion of successful leadership. *School Leadership and Management*, 24: 425–37.

Department for Education and Skills (DfES) (2003) *Every Child Matters*. London: The Stationery Office.

Department of Health (DoH) (1998) *Partnership in Action: A Discussion Document*. London: Department of Health.

Duckmanton, I. (2010) Unpublished M.Ed thesis, University of Hertfordshire.

Engestrom, Y. (2001) Expansive learning at work: toward an activity theoretical reconceptualization. *Journal of Education and Work*, 14:1360.

Eraut, M. (1999) Nonformal knowledge in the workplace: the hidden dimension of lifelong learning. Paper presented at the First International Conference on researching work and learning, University of Leeds.

Fewtrell, M.S. (2004) The long term benefits of having been breastfed. *Current Paediatrics*, 14: 97–103.

Gutman, L.M., Brown, J. and Akerman, R. (2008) *Nurturing Parenting Capability: The Early Years*. London: Centre for Research on the Wider Benefits of Learning.

Harris, B. (2004) Leading by heart. *School Leadership and Management*, 24: 391–404.

Howie, P., Forsyth, J. and Ogston S. (1990) Protective effect of breastfeeding against infection. *British Medical Journal*, 300: 11–16.

Hughes, M. (2006) Multi-agency teams: why should working together make everything better? *Educational and Child Psychology*, 23(4): 66–7.

Hymans, M (2006) 'What needs to be put in place at operational level to enable an integrated children's service to produce desired outcomes? *Educational and Child Psychology*, 23(4).

Jarvis, J. and Trodd, L. (2008) Other ways of seeing; other ways of being: imagination as a tool for developing multi-professional practice for children with communication needs. *Child Language Teaching and Therapy*, 24: 211–27.

John, K. (2007) Sustaining the leaders of children's centres: the role of leadership mentoring. Keynote speech delivered at Pen Green, Corby, UK. Sustainable Leadership Conference, 27 January.

Kolb, D. (1984) *Experiential Learning: Experience as the Source of Learning and Development*. Englewood Cliffs, NJ: Prentice Hall.

Leadbetter, J. (2006) New ways of working and new ways of being: multi-agency working and professional identity. *Educational and Child Psychology*, 23(4): 3.

Marild, S., Hansson, S. and Jodal, U. (2004) Protective effect of breastfeeding against urinary tract infection. *Acta Paediatrica Scandinavica*, 93: 164–8.

Marshall, J. (1994) Re-visioning organisations by developing female value. In R. Boot, J. Lawrence and J. Morris (eds) *Managing the Unknown by Creating New Futures*. London: McGraw-Hill Book Company.

Robinson, M. and Cottrell, D. (2005) Health professionals in multi-disciplinary and multi-agency teams: changing professional practice. *Journal of Interprofessional Care*, 19(6): 547–60.

Saunders, M., Lewis, P. and Thornhill, A. (1997) *Research Methods for Business Students*. Harlow: Pearson.

Sloper, P. (2004) Facilitators and barriers for co-ordinated multi-agency services. *Child: Care, Health and Development*, 30: 571–80.

UNICEF (2009) Baby Friendly Initiative. Available at www.babyfriendly.org.uk.

Vygotsky, L.S. (1978) *Mind in Society: The Development of Higher Psychological Processes*. Cambridge, MA: Harvard University Press.

Watson, H. (2006) Facilitating effective working in multi-agency co-located teams. *Educational and Child Psychology*, 23(4): 9–12.

Wenger, E (1998) *Communities of Practice*. Cambridge: Cambridge University Press.

LYN TRODD AND LEO CHIVERS
Conclusion

Becoming and being professional in the twenty-first century is increasingly 'complex' (Trede 2009), 'changing' (Hargreaves 2000) mostly implicit and hidden (Fish and Coles 2005) and, crucially, *interprofessional* (Siraj-Blatchford et al. 2007).

The chapters in this book reflect our concept of interprofessionals as internally self-aware but also outward-facing. They are capable of taking a wider, holistic or more strategic view than a professional. An interprofessional looks beyond the here-and-now and extends their perspective beyond his or her traditional practice to embrace a wider social, political and professional context. These aspects have parallels with Hoyle's (1975) distinction between restricted and extended forms of professionality. Hoyle uses teachers as an example and argues that the restricted professional teacher focuses on classroom practice, bases decisions on their singular experiences and intuitions and tends not to see his or her work in relation to others or the bigger picture. He argues that, in contrast, an extended professional teacher likes to place his or her work in a wider context, to collaborate with others and to explore theory and engage in professional development. Hoyle's (1980) 'extended' professionalism and professionality require professionals to stand back from their roles and develop their critical awareness of their cultural and social situations in a similar way to calls from Foucault (1987) and Brookfield (2005).

These critical theorists argue that members of a profession need to seek to be aware of the bigger picture in relation to the profession within which they work and maintain a close focus on what they do and the means by which they seek to do it. A key part of this 'bigger picture' is the interprofessional dimension. Chapter themes that resonate with this wider context are the abilities to deal with uncertainty and to work with creativity and courage for the outcomes that children and families deserve. As discussed in the learning chapter by Rawlings and Paliokosta, work-based learning will need to be the focus of the development of these interprofessional characteristics.

This focus presents a conundrum in the way we sometimes can think about theory and practice as disparate processes. In the very act of reading this book, practitioners are isolated from the practising of their profession as reading inevitably requires time out from the workplace. However, the notion of *praxis* rooted in a Marxist call to action is useful here as the issues and themes discussed in this book should exhort readers to see their practice as inextricably linked to the formation and criticism of theory. In short, you cannot have one without the other and the most effective practitioners have a firm grasp of this: 'It must emphasised that the praxis by which consciousness is changed is not only action but action and reflection. Thus there is unity between practice and theory in which both are constructed, shaped and re-shaped in constant movement from practice to theory, then back to a new practice' (Freire 1976: 69).

Paulo Freire (1970/1986) claimed that theory needs practice as a fish needs water and his strongly emancipatory view of education was to define it as a process that is committed to creating freedoms. It is hoped that in the reading of this book professionals have reflected on their interprofessionalism and re-affirmed the reasons behind their strivings to improve the life chances of children. In locating themselves in this struggle, they will have envisioned a kind of freedom from old ways of practising to new ways of being creative.

Those working with children have a tendency to be more aware of the tensions between the concepts of being and becoming than in other areas of work. This is because we recognize that children have a right to *be* children and not be held conceptually in an ante-room for adulthood so that they must always be becoming older or bigger and better. As people working with and for children, we need to embrace the idea of living in the moment as perhaps children are more capable of doing. This will mean that we have to learn from children an existential awareness of *being* a practitioner in the moment and what this means to us and those around us.

So what could be the outcome of all this? In interprofessional working, 'outcomes' or 'impacts' are more than the sum of their parts. The processes of interacting and working together add greater value to work with and for children. Weak interprofessional work allows actual or perceived differences in status, heritage or capacity to limit or inhibit working together for an agreed aim. Useful interventions occur when professionals use 'we' and have an inclusive and flexible concept of what they mean by this. Despite the disparity of topics and approaches between the chapters collated in this book, we hope that readers do retain a sense of shared values and an enthusiasm for creative collaborations from the work.

On the question of whether we will ever arrive at a point where working interprofessionally is natural and embedded in what we do so that we achieve 'unconscious capability' (Argyris and Schön 1996) in our practice, it can be argued that the 'jury is still out'. Perhaps we will never be able to sit back knowing that the interprofessional agenda is dealt with as the needs of children will constantly change within our fluid society. An indication of this eternal flux is the shifts created by the ongoing political debate over how to break the chains of poverty (Dorling 2010).

Interprofessionals may always be viewed, like children, as being in a state of becoming. Nevertheless, the very realization of our emergent interprofessionalism heightens our sense of being able to think during actions and interactions. This awareness develops our capacity for 'reflection-in-action' (Schön 1983). Hence, attention to the theme of this book may engender new confidence for practitioners striving to work creatively for children and families.

You must be the change you want to see in the world.
(Mahatma Gandhi, Indian political and spiritual leader, 1869–1948)

References

Argyris, C. and Schön, D. (1996) *Organizational Learning II: Theory, Method and Practice.* Reading, MA: Addison Wesley.

Brookfield, S.D. (2005) *The Power of Critical Theory for Adult Learning and Teaching.* Maidenhead: Open University Press.

Dorling, D. (2010) *Injustice: Why Social Inequality Persists.* Bristol: Policy Press.

Fish, D. and Coles, C. (2005) *Medical Education: Developing a Curriculum for Practice.* Maidenhead: Open University Press.

Foucault, M. (1987) The subject and power. In H.L. Dreyfus and P. Rabinow (eds) *Michel Foucault: Beyond Structuralism and Hermeneutics.* Chicago, IL: University of Chicago Press.

Freire, P. (1970/1986) *Pedagogy of the Oppressed.* New York: Continuum.

Freire, P. (1976) *Education: The Practice of Freedom.* London: Writers and Readers Cooperative.

Hargreaves, A. (2000) Four ages of professionalism and professional learning. *Teachers and Teaching*, 6: 151–82.

Hoyle, E. (1975) Professionality, professionalism, and control in teaching. In V. Houghton et al. (eds) *Management in Education: The Management of Organisations and Individuals.* London: Ward Lock Educational Open University Press.

Hoyle, E. (1980) Professionalization and deprofessionalization in education. In E. Hoyle and J. Megarry (eds) *The Professional Development of Teachers: World Yearbook.* London: Kogan Page.

Schön, D.A. (1983) *The Reflective Practitioner: How Professionals Think in Action.* London: Temple Smith.

Siraj-Blatchford, I., Clarke, K. and Needham, M. (2007) *The Team Around the Child: Multi-agency Working in the Early Years.* Stoke-on-Trent: Trentham Books.

Trede, F. (2009) Professionalism: becoming professional in the 21st century. *Journal of Emergency Primary Health Care (JEPHC)*, 7.

Glossary

Action research or **participative inquiry** is a type of research in which the researcher works in partnership with research participants, engaging in action-reflection cycles or spirals of planning, action, observation and reflection aimed at achieving positive changes in practice and/or relationships. The term has much in common with *cooperative inquiry*, including the central role of *moral purpose* and commitment to improving the lives of those involved.

Andragogy simply refers to the art and science of helping adults learn, but in the early 1970s, it came to be seen as an alternative to pedagogy and learner-focused education for people of all ages.

Autocracy refers to a system of government, regime, country or leader with absolute power and rule.

Boundary spanner refers to an individual with knowledge of at least two different roles, disciplines and organizations who endeavours to facilitate the interaction of the different perspectives and functions in order to promote understanding, communication and cooperation.

Children and Young People Plan (CYPP) is the strategic plan for all services for children and young people in a Local Authority's area, covering services including Local Authority Services such as children's education, social services functions and youth services, and the strategic plans of local partners.

Community development/action refers to action that helps the people who live in the same community to recognize and develop their ability and potential and organize themselves to respond to their common problems and needs.

Community of practice a phrase coined to describe the process of interprofessional collaboration.

Constructivism is a theory or belief about knowledge, or *epistemology*, which holds that there is no absolute truth, and so-called 'reality' is constructed by our social, historical and individual contexts.

Cooperative inquiry also known as *collaborative inquiry*. The major idea of cooperative inquiry is to research 'with' rather than 'on' people.

Cost avoidance is action taken in the present designed to decrease costs in the future.

Democracy refers to a system of government by the whole population or all the eligible members of a state, as well as to control of an organization or group by the majority of its members and the practice or principles of social equality.

Depth psychologies refer to psychotherapies that take unconscious as well as conscious processes into account and explore the relationships between them, seeking to discover underlying motivation and increasing self-understanding and mental well-being. The earliest depth psychologies were Freud's psychoanalysis, Adler's individual psychology and Jung's analytical psychology, with many others following from these.

Discipline is a field of professional practice such as Social Work.

Early Years practitioner is a practitioner providing services to children of pre-school age including health, family support, childcare, education and allied services.

Egalitarian principles are principles that assert that all people are equal and deserve equal rights and opportunities.

Equality refers to the state of being equal, especially in status, rights, opportunities and being valued and respected equally.

Family Intervention Project (FIP) is a targeted programme of intervention working with those families with the greatest and most complex range of needs, which seeks to join up services and contacts with these families in a more effective package.

Feminism refers to a theoretical framework that stems from the belief that women have equal political, social, sexual, intellectual and economic rights to men – and that women have been and continue to be oppressed by dominant male culture and masculine perspectives.

Humanism is a philosophy that attaches prime importance to human, rather than divine matters, and stresses the value and potential goodness of human beings, emphasizing common human needs and seeking rational ways of solving human problems.

Humanistic psychologies focus on each individual's potential to be good, with the belief that mental and social problems result from deviations from a natural striving for growth and self-actualization.

Integration, integrated is a descriptor of close multi-agency or interprofessional working which improves the effectiveness, efficiency or accessibility of services which were previously delivered separately.

Interprofessionalism is the relationships and interactions between practitioners with different professional heritages working together. The nature of this process is explored in this book, to the extent that it the term is tentatively applied to an emergent 'mindset' or way of being.

Local Area Agreement (LAA) is a three-year agreement between central government and local authorities and their partners, that reflect local priorities.

Multi-agency working is the relationships and interactions between practitioners or organizational systems of more than one agency or organization involved in working together to deliver services.

Ontology is the study of 'being', in this case the exploration of practitioner and family experience, what it is like to *be* an 'interprofessional'.

Parents are those with main responsibility for the child.

Pedagogy is the method and practice of teaching a subject or theoretical concept.

Practitioners are those employed in a private, independent, state maintained or voluntary capacity who works with individual or groups of children or young people on a regular basis.

Professional is a qualified practitioner within a discipline.

Professional heritage is the professional culture to which a practitioner may most closely ally themselves.

Reflectivity refers to the quality of thinking and seriously considering and grappling with ideas and experiences. Through reflection a person constructs a personal understanding of relevant structures of meaning derived from her or his own action in the world. (See *constructivism*.)

Single delivery plan is a joint business plan between key public sector agencies in a local area, e.g. Local Authority, Primary Care Trust, Hospital Trust, the Police.

(Sure Start) Children's Centre is the service provision for children of pre-school age bringing together different agencies involved in the delivery of Early Years services by integrating teams and systems and co-locating service providers under the direction of a Children's Centre leader.

Sustainable Communities Strategy (SCC) is a set of goals and actions whereby local strategic partnerships promote residential, business, statutory and voluntary interests of an area.

Index